D0108857

Joyce Appleby on *Thomas Jefferson*
Louis Auchincloss on *Theodore Roosevelt*
Jean H. Baker on *James Buchanan*
H. W. Brands on *Woodrow Wilson*
Alan Brinkley on *John F. Kennedy*
Douglas Brinkley on *Gerald R. Ford*
Josiah Bunting III on *Ulysses S. Grant*
James MacGregor Burns and Susan Dunn on *George Washington*
Charles W. Calhoun on *Benjamin Harrison*
Gail Collins on *William Henry Harrison*
Robert Dallek on *Harry S. Truman*
John W. Dean on *Warren G. Harding*
John Patrick Diggins on *John Adams*
Elizabeth Drew on *Richard M. Nixon*
John S. D. Eisenhower on *Zachary Taylor*
Paul Finkelman on *Millard Fillmore*
Annette Gordon-Reed on *Andrew Johnson*
Henry F. Graff on *Grover Cleveland*
David Greenberg on *Calvin Coolidge*
Gary Hart on *James Monroe*
Michael F. Holt on *Franklin Pierce*
Roy Jenkins on *Franklin Delano Roosevelt*
Zachary Karabell on *Chester Alan Arthur*
Lewis H. Lapham on *William Howard Taft*
William E. Leuchtenburg on *Herbert Hoover*
James Mann on *George W. Bush*
Gary May on *John Tyler*
George McGovern on *Abraham Lincoln*
Timothy Naftali on *George H. W. Bush*
Charles Peters on *Lyndon B. Johnson*
Kevin Phillips on *William McKinley*
Robert V. Remini on *John Quincy Adams*
Ira Rutkow on *James A. Garfield*
John Seigenthaler on *James K. Polk*
Hans L. Trefousse on *Rutherford B. Hayes*
Tom Wicker on *Dwight D. Eisenhower*
Ted Widmer on *Martin Van Buren*
Sean Wilentz on *Andrew Jackson*
Garry Wills on *James Madison*
Julian E. Zelizer on *Jimmy Carter*

# John F. Kennedy

Alan Brinkley

# John F. Kennedy

---

**THE AMERICAN PRESIDENTS**

ARTHUR M. SCHLESINGER, JR., AND SEAN WILENTZ

GENERAL EDITORS

Times Books

HENRY HOLT AND COMPANY, NEW YORK

Times Books
Henry Holt and Company, LLC
*Publishers since 1866*
175 Fifth Avenue
New York, New York 10010
www.henryholt.com

Henry Holt® is a registered trademark of Henry Holt and Company, LLC.

Frontispiece: © Bettmann/CORBIS

Library of Congress Cataloging-in-Publication Data
Brinkley, Alan.
   John F. Kennedy / Alan Brinkley.—1st ed.
      p. cm.—(The American presidents)
   Includes bibliographical references and index.
   ISBN 978-0-8050-8349-1
   1. Kennedy, John F. (John Fitzgerald), 1917–1963.   2. Presidents—United
States—Biography.   3. United States—Politics and government—1961–1963.
I. Title.
   E841.B734 2012
   973.922092—dc23
   [B]                                                        2011043747

Henry Holt books are available for special promotions and
premiums. For details contact: Director, Special Markets.

First Edition 2012

Printed in the United States of America
1   3   5   7   9   10   8   6   4   2

*For William Leuchtenburg*

*With gratitude for his friendship and for all I have learned from him*

# Contents

# Editor's Note

---

The president is the central player in the American political order. That would seem to contradict the intentions of the Founding Fathers. Remembering the horrid example of the British monarchy, they invented a separation of powers in order, as Justice Brandeis later put it, "to preclude the exercise of arbitrary power." Accordingly, they divided the government into three allegedly equal and coordinate branches—the executive, the legislative, and the judiciary.

But a system based on the tripartite separation of powers has an inherent tendency toward inertia and stalemate. One of the three branches must take the initiative if the system is to move. The executive branch alone is structurally capable of taking that initiative. The Founders must have sensed this when they accepted Alexander Hamilton's proposition in the Seventieth Federalist that "energy in the executive is a leading character in the definition of good government." They thus envisaged a strong president—but within an equally strong system of constitutional accountability. (The term *imperial presidency* arose in the 1970s to describe the situation when the balance between power and accountability is upset in favor of the executive.)

The American system of self-government thus comes to focus in the presidency—"the vital place of action in the system," as Woodrow Wilson put it. Henry Adams, himself the great-grandson and grandson of presidents as well as the most brilliant of American historians, said that the American president "resembles the commander of a ship at sea. He must have a helm to grasp, a course to steer, a port to seek." The men in the White House (thus far only men, alas) in steering their chosen courses have shaped our destiny as a nation.

Biography offers an easy education in American history, rendering the past more human, more vivid, more intimate, more accessible, more connected to ourselves. Biography reminds us that presidents are not supermen. They are human beings too, worrying about decisions, attending to wives and children, juggling balls in the air, and putting on their pants one leg at a time. Indeed, as Emerson contended, "There is properly no history; only biography."

Presidents serve us as inspirations, and they also serve us as warnings. They provide bad examples as well as good. The nation, the Supreme Court has said, has "no right to expect that it will always have wise and humane rulers, sincerely attached to the principles of the Constitution. Wicked men, ambitious of power, with hatred of liberty and contempt of law, may fill the place once occupied by Washington and Lincoln."

The men in the White House express the ideals and the values, the frailties and the flaws, of the voters who send them there. It is altogether natural that we should want to know more about the virtues and the vices of the fellows we have elected to govern us. As we know more about them, we will know more about ourselves. The French political philosopher Joseph de Maistre said, "Every nation has the government it deserves."

At the start of the twenty-first century, forty-two men have made it to the Oval Office. (George W. Bush is counted our forty-third president, because Grover Cleveland, who served nonconsecutive terms, is counted twice.) Of the parade of presidents, a dozen or so lead the polls periodically conducted by historians and political scientists. What makes a great president?

Great presidents possess, or are possessed by, a vision of an ideal America. Their passion, as they grasp the helm, is to set the ship of state on the right course toward the port they seek. Great presidents also have a deep psychic connection with the needs, anxieties, dreams of people. "I do not believe," said Wilson, "that any man can lead who does not act . . . under the impulse of a profound sympathy with those whom he leads—a sympathy which is insight—an insight which is of the heart rather than of the intellect."

"All of our great presidents," said Franklin D. Roosevelt, "were leaders of thought at a time when certain ideas in the life of the nation had to be clarified." So Washington incarnated the idea of federal union, Jefferson and Jackson the idea of democracy, Lincoln union and freedom, Cleveland rugged honesty. Theodore Roosevelt and Wilson, said FDR, were both "moral leaders, each in his own way and his own time, who used the presidency as a pulpit."

To succeed, presidents not only must have a port to seek but they must convince Congress and the electorate that it is a port worth seeking. Politics in a democracy is ultimately an educational process, an adventure in persuasion and consent. Every president stands in Theodore Roosevelt's bully pulpit.

The greatest presidents in the scholars' rankings, Washington, Lincoln, and Franklin Roosevelt, were leaders who confronted and overcame the republic's greatest crises. Crisis widens presidential opportunities for bold and imaginative action. But it does not guarantee presidential greatness. The crisis of secession did not spur Buchanan or the crisis of depression spur Hoover to creative leadership. Their inadequacies in the face of crisis allowed Lincoln and the second Roosevelt to show the difference individuals make to history. Still, even in the absence of first-order crisis, forceful and persuasive presidents—Jefferson, Jackson, James K. Polk, Theodore Roosevelt, Harry Truman, John F. Kennedy, Ronald Reagan, George W. Bush— are able to impose their own priorities on the country.

The diverse drama of the presidency offers a fascinating set of tales. Biographies of American presidents constitute a chronicle of wisdom and folly, nobility and pettiness, courage and cunning, forthrightness and deceit, quarrel and consensus. The turmoil perennially swirling around the White House illuminates the heart of the American democracy.

It is the aim of the American Presidents series to present the grand panorama of our chief executives in volumes compact enough for the busy reader, lucid enough for the student, authoritative enough for the scholar. Each volume offers a distillation of character and career. I hope that these lives will give readers some understanding of the pitfalls and potentialities of the presidency and also of the responsibilities of citizenship. Truman's famous sign—"The buck stops here"—tells only half the story. Citizens cannot escape the ultimate responsibility. It is in the voting booth, not on the presidential desk, that the buck finally stops.

—Arthur M. Schlesinger, Jr.

# John F. Kennedy

# Introduction

Among the many monuments to the memory of John Fitzgerald Kennedy, perhaps the most striking is the Sixth Floor Museum in Dallas, which more than three hundred thousand people visit each year. It is located in what was once the Texas School Book Depository from which Lee Harvey Oswald waited on November 22, 1963, to shoot at the president's motorcade. The museum is an oddity in itself in its close physical association with Kennedy's death, although the impressive exhibits trace much more than the history of the assassination. But the most memorable (and eerie) moment of a visit to the museum is when visitors turn a corner on the sixth floor and suddenly look out over Dealey Plaza from the window through which Oswald fired his infamous shots. The space is cluttered with boxes, as it had been on that November afternoon.

Almost equally memorable is the guest book in which visitors have signed their names and identified the towns or cities or countries in which they live. Many of them write comments. Some are tributes to Kennedy himself: "Our greatest President." "Oh how we miss him!" "The greatest man since Jesus Christ." At least as many others write about the assassination itself and what they consider the mendacity of the Warren Commission and the government's effort to hide the conspiracies that lay behind Kennedy's death.

John Kennedy's legacy remains enormous decades later. The reality of his life may not have lived up to his global reputation. But in his short presidency this reticent and pragmatic man became, in the eyes of the world, a charismatic leader who in his life and in his death became a symbol of hope and purpose.

• • •

As a young boy growing up in Washington, D.C., during the Kennedy years, I was entranced by him. His visibility was remarkable—his press conferences, his speeches, his visits across the world that attracted hundreds of thousands of admirers. He was the first president I was old enough to care about, and I devoured stories about him in newspapers, in magazines, and on television. I stood on Capitol Hill in 1961 to watch his inauguration, and I stood on Pennsylvania Avenue in 1963 to see his funeral cortege move slowly to the Capitol Rotunda (while overhearing a transistor radio in the crowd describing the shooting of Lee Harvey Oswald). The drama of his life and the tragedy of his death left an indelible mark on my memory, as it did on millions of people of my generation—and even on many others who were born after he died.

From the beginning, Kennedy's presidency seemed different. He was hugely popular through most of his presidency, described constantly by such words as *charisma, grace, vigor, purpose.* He was young, rich, handsome, witty, eloquent. He published essays, articles, and a book that won a Pulitzer Prize. He had a beautiful wife and charming young children. He brought a kind of exhilaration to Washington. "The capital city, somnolent in the Eisenhower years, had suddenly come alive," Arthur M. Schlesinger Jr. wrote of Kennedy in 1965. "The air had been stale and oppressive; now fresh winds were blowing. There was the excitement which comes from the injection of new men and new ideas, the release of energy which occurs when men of ideas have a chance to put them into practice."[1]

• • •

A decade later, most historians were treating Kennedy more lightly. In the scholarly rankings of presidents since World War II, Kennedy has tended to rank mostly in the middle of the pack. The political scientist Richard Neustadt—a great admirer of Kennedy—remarked in the 1970s that "he will be just a flicker, forever clouded by the record of his successors. I don't think history will have much space for John Kennedy."[2]

Kennedy's image did not always match reality. His famous vigor and energy hid serious lifelong illnesses. The image of his attractive family disguised his almost pathological womanizing. His first year in office was, as he himself admitted, a disaster. He was unable to pass most of the legislation he proposed. He was slow to embrace the civil rights movement, conservative in his embrace of Keynesianism, aloof and ineffective in his dealings with Congress. Through much of his presidency, he was largely reactive, driven by external events rather than by his own goals. A plan by the Eisenhower administration drove him heedlessly into the fiasco of the Bay of Pigs. A decision by the Soviet leader Nikita Khrushchev, encouraged by what he considered Kennedy's weakness, drove him into the Cuban missile crisis. A decade of precedent led him reluctantly but decisively into Vietnam. That Kennedy was not always as bold as he wanted the world to believe was not, perhaps, a weakness. His worst decisions were often his boldest ones.

None of this seemed to hurt him politically. His rhetoric almost always got him out of trouble. He promised to "get the country moving again." He sought a "national purpose." He asked Americans to sacrifice for the good of all. Americans liked these challenges, even if they did little to meet them. And for much of his presidency, his public approval rating was at 70 percent or more.

Like most presidents, he had good times and bad times, successes and failures. His administration was dominated by the many problems and crises he encountered—in Cuba, Laos, Berlin, and Vietnam; and in Georgia, Mississippi, and Alabama. Some of these crises he managed adroitly and, at times, courageously. Others he could not resolve. It would be hard to call him a great president, but neither was he a failure. He contributed to a reshaping of the Cold War, making it somewhat less dangerous and somewhat more manageable. His presidency launched dramatic new programs: civil rights bills, Medicare, the outlines of the War on Poverty. None of them became law in his lifetime. But all of them became law after his death, and in part because of it. Perhaps most surprising of all, John Kennedy—who almost never revealed passion—seemed to many people a passionate and idealistic liberal. "For a time we felt the country was ours," Norman Mailer said after his death. "Now it's theirs again."[3] But Mailer missed the point. In his lifetime Kennedy was never "ours," but neither was he "theirs." Only after his death did he become the property of the world.

# 1

## The Irish Prince

John Fitzgerald Kennedy was born into an Irish American world that his family helped change forever. For generations, Americans of Irish descent had faced almost insuperable boundaries to their aspirations. Until the first decades of the twentieth century, most Irish Americans lived in insular communities and were largely excluded from many professions. They attended Catholic schools and—for those who chose to enter politics—ran for office in Irish wards and won votes from mostly Irish voters. Rarely did they attract support from outside their own communities. But the two families who gave birth to the first Irish American president broke new ground.

One of John Kennedy's grandfathers, John F. Fitzgerald, was himself a politician who crossed the boundaries that had limited Irish American ambitions. He was a charming, garrulous, energetic man who graduated from Boston College, enrolled briefly at Harvard Medical School, and was elected to Congress in 1894. Twelve years later, he became the first Irish American mayor of Boston, serving three terms between 1906 and 1914. For years, he remained one of the best-known political figures in the city. (He lived long enough to see his grandson elected to Congress, and he predicted that he would become president.) Fitzgerald's wife and second cousin, Mary Josephine Hannon, gave birth to six children. The eldest of them was Rose Elizabeth Fitzgerald, born in 1890.[1]

The future president's other grandfather was Patrick J. Kennedy, who left school at fourteen to support his large and struggling family. But despite his scant education and his impoverished beginnings, he saved his earnings and bought a small string of taverns and bars. Later he opened a liquor importing company and later still bought substantial interests in a coal company and a bank— enterprises that made him a wealthy and substantial figure in the Irish American community. His wife, Mary Hickey, was herself the daughter of a prosperous tavern owner. She had four children— among them Joseph P. Kennedy, born in 1888.[2]

Rose Fitzgerald and Joseph Kennedy were exceptional young people within this enclosed world. Rose's eminent political family made her something of a celebrity at a young age. She attended elite Catholic schools and took an extensive tour of Europe. By the age of eighteen she had abandoned her early hopes to attend Wellesley College to join her father's political life.[3]

Joe Kennedy, although from a less eminent family than Rose's, was more ambitious—and more successful—than almost anyone else in the Irish community. He attended the prestigious Boston Latin School, graduated from Harvard, and moved into banking. By the age of twenty-five, he was the president of Columbia Trust, a modest bank in which his father had once invested. Joe quickly doubled its accounts.[4]

Rose and Joe had become attracted to each other as early as 1906, when she was sixteen and he eighteen. Rose's father had another suitor in mind for his daughter—a wealthy contractor and friend of the family—and Fitzgerald tried for years to keep her apart from Joe. But Rose found Joe a much more compelling figure than her father's choice, and she wore him down. They were married in 1914, and they broke with tradition by moving to a house in Brookline, then an almost entirely Protestant community. Their first son, Joseph Patrick Kennedy Jr., was born in 1915. Two years later, on May 29, 1917, their second son—John Fitzgerald Kennedy— was born.[5]

· · ·

Life in the Kennedy family was dominated by Joe's social ambitions and his spectacular financial success. His marriage to the mayor's daughter was only one of many steps that would lead him and his children well beyond the Irish world in which they were born. Joe was smart, ambitious, and often ruthless—determined not only to accumulate wealth but also to gain power. Banking, he believed, was the key to the kind of success he sought. "I saw, even in my limited dealings, that sooner or later, the source of business was traced to the banks," he wrote later. Banking, he claimed, "could lead a man anywhere, as it played an important part in every business."[6]

It was not just power and wealth he sought. He could have had a prosperous career as the most eminent Irish banker in the city, but he aspired to rise higher. He wanted to move into the great world of finance—a world dominated by old Yankee families in Boston and New York. World War I interrupted his plans. He left the bank and became a manager of war production at the Bethlehem steel yards in Quincy, Massachusetts. When the army tried to draft him, the Bethlehem executives fought to keep him, calling him indispensable. His success in a world of Yankee businessmen helped draw him into larger and larger worlds. "The key to Kennedy's spectacular financial success," one of his colleagues later said, "was his anticipation of the future . . . his vision of what lay down the road, a vision that was always there, sustaining him and guiding him—that vision was simply phenomenal."[7] In the heady days of the stock market boom in the 1920s, he joined a Brahmin brokerage house, where he expanded his connections in the financial world and became one of the canniest and most successful investors of his era. By 1927, he had relocated his family to Riverdale, just north of Manhattan, where he could be closer to Wall Street. Even before the family's move, he had accumulated over $2 million, which was only the beginning of his extraordinary rise.

Joe's remarkable success created problems for Rose. She wanted an ordered and respectable domesticity. But Joe was not much of a partner in the home—traveling constantly, working late, and always looking for new connections and new opportunities. That left Rose alone in a large and complicated home. By the early 1930s, there were nine children: Joe Jr., Jack, Rosemary, Kathleen, Eunice, Pat, Bobby, Jean, and Ted. It was a loud, boisterous, and at times chaotic household that never lived up to Rose's hopes—perhaps in part because Rose herself was either pregnant or recovering from pregnancy for the first seventeen years of her marriage. After the family moved to Riverdale, they retained a foothold in Massachusetts. Joe purchased a large property in Hyannis Port that became the family's most enduring home. The celebrated pictures of the Kennedy family in later years—sailing off the coast of Cape Cod, playing touch football on the lawn—were a reminder of decades of outdoor activity and competitive sports. Long before the Kennedys became politically active, the family had already become among the most famous Irish American families in America—a result of Joe's enormous and conspicuous wealth, and also because of the attractive image of the Kennedy tribe.[8]

But the attractive, even idyllic, images of this apparently golden family disguised its share of troubles. Rose remained overwhelmed by her large family, particularly after their first daughter, Rosemary, was diagnosed as mildly retarded. Rose had few friends and few activities in New York beyond taking care of her growing family. She distanced herself from her husband sexually except for procreation and traveled extensively around America and Europe to escape the pressures of home. Her absence dismayed her children (and especially Jack). Joe Sr. was still mostly away, traveling on business and expanding his business empire—including an investment in the movie industry. He also maintained an extramarital sexual life—most conspicuously with the actress Gloria Swanson. The children grew up supervised for long periods by servants and relatives.[9]

Rosemary aside, Jack had the most difficult life of the family. He was under the shadow of his older brother, Joe Jr., who was the recipient of his father's greatest hopes. Jack developed a competitive relationship with his older brother, who almost always won whatever contests they waged. But a more important part of his youth—and indeed of much of his life—was the long history of illness that began shortly after birth. He was restless and fitful even as a baby, had trouble digesting milk, and suffered frequent stomachaches. By the time he was three, he had experienced scarlet fever, causing his mother "frantic terror" and leading his father to spend hours praying (uncharacteristically) in the Catholic Church, which he rarely attended.[10] This frightening illness was followed by other debilitating diseases (chicken pox, ear infections, and undiagnosed stomach, intestinal, and other ailments that made it difficult for him to eat and sometimes left him so weak that he could hardly stand). Sickness plagued him into adolescence and beyond, baffling his doctors, his family, and Jack himself. For months at a time, he was gaunt, pale, and weak. Multiple and often mistaken diagnoses added to his ordeal. Treatment for one problem created problems elsewhere, and there was no definitive explanation of what ailed him. Jack liked to joke about his frequent illnesses, and he tried to disguise the pain and fear that he often felt. But there were also periods of near despair, especially when he was in hospitals for weeks, submitting to endless tests, and still failing to get any answers to what his problems were.[11]

His illnesses inevitably affected his schooling. Shortly after the family's move to New York, Jack was enrolled in the Riverdale Country School. But at the age of thirteen, with his grades an undistinguished C+ average, his parents decided he should go to boarding school. Rose Kennedy was especially eager to get the boys out of the house because she felt so overwhelmed by her many children. Jack expected to follow Joe Jr. to Choate, the distinguished boarding school in Wallingford, Connecticut, but Rose—on her own—decided in the fall of 1930 to send him instead to Canterbury, a Catholic school for boys in New Milford, Connecticut. He suffered there not only from his chronic ailments but also from homesickness. He complained to his family about the "whole lot of religion" and the isolation of the school. ("The only time you can get out of here is to see the Harvard-Yale and Army-Yale [games].")[12] Much of the time he was in the local hospital, and he spent the last months of the academic year at home, with tutors.[13]

The following fall, he enrolled at Choate, which he found more tolerable because his brother Joe was already there. Jack remained a lackluster student. He was constantly reprimanded by his teachers and the headmaster, who considered him "one of the most undependable boys" in his grade. He lacked "application." He was "careless" with his work. He was notoriously "casual and disorderly" in a school committed to order.[14] He insisted that he was "trying to be a more socially minded person."[15] Everyone agreed that he was intelligent, but that made his scholarly "mediocrity" all the more damning.[16] Inattention was only one of his problems, for he fell victim soon again to his puzzling and often debilitating illnesses. At one point, according to his lifelong friend Lem Billings, he "came very close to dying."[17] He was in and out of the infirmary and local hospitals, trying to lead a normal life, and struggling to keep up with his work. Through it all, he forced himself to remain cheerful, funny, and almost irresistibly charming. "I've never known anyone in my life with such a wonderful humor—the ability to make one laugh and have a good time," Billings once wrote.[18] "Jack didn't like to be too serious," the Choate headmaster said long after Jack left the school. "He had a delightful sense of humor always . . . He was a very likeable person, very lovable."[19]

Living in the shadow of his older brother was difficult. Joe excelled in athletics, discipline, and leadership. Jack could not compete. He did not like Choate very much more than he had liked Canterbury, and he often described it as a prison. But he made his way through his school years with garrulous charm and wit. It was not surprising that his jokes were often dark, because his health continued to deteriorate. He spent weeks at the Mayo Clinic, where he submitted to what seemed endless, humiliating tests. But as usual in his letters to Billings he treated it all as a joke. "I'm still eating peas and corn for food and I had an enema given by a beautiful blonde," he wrote. "That, my sweet, is the height of cheap thrills."[20]

Partly to compensate for his inability to thrive in sports or academics, he developed a new sexual prowess that lasted through the rest of his life. Like his father, he treated sex as a kind of sport— casual, frequent, mostly unconnected to affection or romance. Most of his trysts were one-night stands, and he sometimes forgot the names of his sexual partners. The constricted world of Choate did not make sexual activity easy, but he found ways to get around the boundaries of the school in the same way he got around his illnesses.[21]

Jack's disaffection—his illnesses, his poor academic performance, and his disdain for the stuffy traditions of the school—led him to join a group of similarly alienated students to form "the Muckers Club." (*Mucker* was a term coined by the faculty to describe rebellious students with little respect for the "Choate culture." Jack's father, somewhat in sympathy with his son, later noted that if he had organized the club, its name would not have begun with an *M*.) The Muckers composed and sang vaguely obscene songs, sometimes about teachers. They organized pranks that mocked the staid habits of the school. The headmaster called them "a colossally selfish, pleasure loving, unperceptive group" and nearly expelled the entire group. Rose Kennedy, horrified by Jack's rebelliousness, liked to believe that this confrontation with the headmaster was a turning point in his life—that he had learned to respect authority and to live by the norms of the school. But Jack was far from tamed. He avoided the more dangerous behavior that had created trouble for the Muckers, but he could not resist a final challenge to the Choate establishment by launching a successful campaign for the title of "Most Likely to Succeed," using his popularity to defeat the more obvious candidates.[22]

• • •

Jack's path to college was as rocky as his path through prep school had been. He enrolled at Harvard for the fall of 1935, then withdrew before the term began to go to England to spend a year at the London School of Economics. But the onset of another mysterious illness, and his disappointment with the LSE, drew him back to America, where—weeks after the term had begun—he enrolled at Princeton, primarily because Lem Billings and other friends were already there. His enthusiasm for Princeton soon cooled. He found it provincial and oppressive—with its Protestantism, its small-town environs, and its eating-club culture that did not often welcome Catholics. "I think he was a little disenchanted with the country-club atmosphere of Princeton," one of his friends later wrote.[23]

Before he finished his first term, he was rushed to Boston and was hospitalized with yet another apparently undiagnosable illness.

After weeks of invasive and humiliating tests—"the most harrowing experience of all my storm-tossed career," he wrote to Billings—he was diagnosed with leukemia. "Took a peek at my chart yesterday and could see that they were mentally measuring me for a coffin," he reported.[24] But he refused to take the diagnosis seriously. He was vindicated when the doctors finally admitted that they had been in error. He spent the rest of his aborted academic year trying to restore himself to health—through vacations at Palm Beach, a few Teddy Roosevelt–like months on a ranch in Arizona, and a libidinous week in Los Angeles. In the summer of 1936, he was accepted again to Harvard. "To be a 'Harvard Man' is an enviable distinction," he wrote on his application.[25] The Admissions Committee said of him, "Jack has rather superior mental ability, without the deep interest in his studies . . . He can be relied upon to do enough to pass."[26] His father wrote the dean saying much the same: "Jack has a very brilliant mind for the things he is interested in, but is careless and lacks application in those in which he is not interested. This is, of course, a bad fault."[27]

He was happier at Harvard than he had been at any of his former schools. Although he left behind his closest friend, Lem Billings, he found new friends at Harvard—many of them through his older brother. Joe Jr. was, as usual, serious, ambitious, and hot-tempered, always striving to attract the admiration of his father. His greatest ambition was to win a Harvard football letter, a goal he never achieved. Jack was more easygoing. In better health than he had been in some time, he tried out for football himself but never expected to remain on the team. He was also an avid swimmer and boxer. As at Choate, he was a popular figure among his contemporaries—witty, lively, irreverent, and highly social. He was a more serious student in his first year at Harvard than he had been at Choate or Princeton. His mediocre grades obscured his avid reading, especially during his frequent hospital stays. (He remained a fervent reader, especially of history, throughout his life.)[28]

Despite his mother's belief that Jack's near-expulsion from Choate was a defining moment in his life, a more plausible turning point was his summer-long European trip in 1937 after his freshman year at Harvard. He and Billings sailed to Europe on July 1 and returned in September—the longest trip either of them had ever made. It revealed the multiple roles that were coming to shape Jack's young life. He was the privileged and dutiful son, who traveled with his way paved by his father to meetings with statesmen and audiences with the pope and with Cardinal Pacelli (soon to become Pope Pius XII). Joe Kennedy's friends and colleagues assisted him everywhere he went. Jack was also the reckless playboy, chasing fun, and women, in bars and cafés in Paris, the Riviera, and Biarritz. He was also becoming a serious and ambitious student of the political world. He kept a diary of the places he visited, showing a particular interest in the fascist countries. He was eager to see Spain, but the civil war there prevented him from entering the country. Instead, he sought out soldiers fleeing into France and asked them questions about the fighting. Kennedy and Billings found Italy impressively prosperous and orderly ("Fascism seems to treat them well," Jack wrote of the Italians).[29] In Germany, Billings wrote that they both "had a terrible feeling about . . . the 'Heil Hitler' stuff."[30] Jack was more ambivalent. He too hated the German arrogance and deplored the growing persecution of the Jews, but he was impressed by what he considered German efficiency. "All the towns are very attractive," he recorded in his diary, "showing that the Nordic races certainly seem superior to the Latins. The Germans really are too good—it makes people gang against them for protection."[31] "Isn't the chance of war less as Britain gets stronger?" Jack wrote after his return to Harvard. "Or is a country like Italy liable to go to war when economic discontent is rife? Wouldn't Mussolini go if there was a war—as in all likelihood Italy would be defeated in a major war?"[32] These questions would increase his serious study of history and politics.

Back at college in the fall, Jack was at least as eager to be a social success as to be a successful student. His greatest ambition in his sophomore year was to be elected to one of the university's exclusive final clubs. Neither his father nor his brother had succeeded in getting elected to a club—largely because of anti-Irish prejudice.

But Jack worked hard to be accepted. Despite his uncertain health, he continued to try out for football and the junior varsity swimming team, but failed to win letters. He became a member of the Hasty Pudding Club and wrote occasionally for the *Harvard Crimson*. But his most important strength was his popularity. His loyal friends helped him get elected to the Spee Club. He so valued his acceptance that he spent almost all of his free time in the elegant clubhouse.[33]

After a term taking courses in political science and international relations (and receiving better grades than in the past), he took a leave in the spring of 1939, his junior year, to do research for a senior thesis. But his thesis took second place to a great event in the Kennedy family. His father had been appointed the United States ambassador to Great Britain in 1938. It was a position of particular pride to Joe given the long tradition of Anglo-Saxon appointments of ambassadors. Jack was drawn to England for research for his thesis topic. But he was also drawn to the dazzling new life of his family in London. Jack toured the capitals of eastern Europe and the Middle East, cared for at each stop by American diplomats. He spent much of his time in Paris, "living like a king" and staying at the American embassy.[34] The beleaguered diplomats working feverishly in the shadow of war were often irritated to have to serve the needs of what seemed a pampered son of a wealthy and powerful man. But they gave him material and arranged interviews, nevertheless. Jack also found time, as he always did, for "recreation"—including a luxurious September vacation in Antibes, where he learned of the outbreak of war.[35] He returned to Harvard as determined as before to understand the crisis in Europe.

Joe Kennedy, like most Americans, was opposed to U.S. intervention in the European war. And, not surprisingly, Jack shared Joe's belief that neither Britain nor America was equipped to defeat Germany. Jack argued for a negotiated end to the war, mediated by President Franklin Roosevelt, which would allow the Third Reich to survive and grow but would permit Britain and France to remain independent. With this unpromising premise, Jack began to write his senior thesis, which he called "Appeasement at Munich." Characteristically, he enlisted help from a network of helpers: his father's diplomatic colleagues, who scoured libraries and research centers in Britain for materials to send him; research assistants, who did his legwork in Harvard's Widener Library; typists and stenographers, who helped him write the manuscript.[36]

The final draft of his thesis was respectable and impressively ambitious—better than most of his earlier, mostly undistinguished academic work. His advisers admired the importance of the topic and the intelligence that went into the thesis. But it was also cumbersome, with a somewhat muddled argument and a text filled with grammatical and punctuation errors. Some of his readers found it excessively wordy, and none of them imagined it to be a significant work of scholarship. "Badly written, but a laborious, interesting, and intelligent discussion of a difficult question," his advisers wrote. He received a magna cum laude grade for the effort.[37]

The thesis had two major assets. One was its timing. He finished it in the midst of a global crisis, and despite its weaknesses it addressed a critical question: "Why was England so poorly prepared for the war?" The other asset was his connections—the efforts by his father and many colleagues and friends who gathered around on Jack's behalf and helped him make a "typical undergraduate effort" (as one historian wrote at the time) into a published book.[38] Jack, somewhat presumptuously but characteristically, drew distinguished people to his assistance. "Arthur Krock . . . feels that I should get it published," he wrote his father.[39] Krock, an eminent columnist for the *New York Times* with many lucrative ties to Joe Kennedy, helped rewrite the thesis (how substantially is not known) and provided a new title—*Why England Slept*, derived from a contemporaneous book title of Winston Churchill, *While England Slept*.[40]

Jack, for his part, revised his argument about Britain's lack of preparedness. Originally, he had said that the British public was the source of the problem because voters were unwilling to support strengthening the military. Democracy "may be a great system of government to live in internally," he wrote, "but its weaknesses are great."[41] In the book, Jack shifted more of the blame to Britain's leadership—Prime Ministers Stanley Baldwin and Neville Chamberlain, both friends of Joe Kennedy. He was moving away from his father's increasingly controversial views. Even as most Americans were becoming more supportive of Britain, Joe was becoming an increasingly entrenched isolationist. Without informing Washington, Joe was looking for compromises with Hitler, even unsuccessfully seeking meetings with him. By November 1940, President Roosevelt recalled Joe from London—creating a deep and permanent rift between them and destroying what Joe had hoped would be a dazzling political career.

Jack, however, was moving along with most of the public toward a belief in the importance of supporting the war against Germany. He never openly repudiated his father, but he slowly distanced himself from Joe's unpopular stances on the war. His increasing internationalism encouraged Krock to provide Jack with an agent, who passed the manuscript around through many rejections until the small publishing house of Wilfred Funk agreed to publish it. The publishers were much encouraged by an admiring introduction from Henry R. Luce, the publisher of *Time*, *Fortune*, and *Life* magazines. "I cannot recall a single man of my college graduation," Luce wrote, "who could have written such an *adult* book on such a vitally important subject during his Senior year at college."[42] By then, the writing was smoother, the argument clearer. But its timeliness may have been its most important strength. It was well reviewed and widely read. It helped establish Jack Kennedy—after years of mediocrity in multiple schools—as a serious thinker and an emerging leader of his generation.[43]

At the core of *Why England Slept* were Jack's first significant steps toward the muscular vision of American power that would characterize his future career. Jack stopped short of advocating American intervention in the war (although he was beginning to see it as inevitable). He made a strong case that Britain and the United States could become together the great world powers to defend against the spread of totalitarianism. But most of all, he laid out what he considered the great challenge of democracy. How can a free society mobilize its citizens for war? How can it "compete with the new totalitarian system based on an economy of rigid state control?"[44] Britain's failure to prepare, he wrote, was in part "a great lack of young progressive and able leaders"—a statement that irritated some of Joe's friends in the diplomatic corps.[45] But again and again, Jack returned to the "weaknesses" of democracy in the face of crisis. Dictators, he warned, have almost always been ahead of democracies in preparing for war. "To say that democracy has been awakened by [the fall of France] . . . is not enough. Any person will awaken when the house is burning down. What we need is an armed guard that will wake up when the fire first starts, or better yet, one that will not permit a fire to start at all."[46]

It was a measure of how little intellectual power had been targeted toward the strengthening of democracy against totalitarianism that a young college graduate could attract so much attention to a modest book. But it was also an early sign of what would become a hallmark of Kennedy's mature career: his strong belief in the importance of a robust democracy for what he later called the "long twilight struggle" against the growing power of the communist world.

. . .

The success of his book did little to settle Kennedy's plans. He briefly considered enrolling in law school. He spent a few months at Stanford University, hoping to improve his once-again deteriorating health and applying to Stanford Law School (as he had done at Yale Law School before). He traveled with his family and vacationed at Hyannis Port. But like many other young men in the year before Pearl Harbor, he was waiting for what he now understood to be the inevitability of America joining the war. He worried that his poor health would bar him from the military, and his fears were justified when he failed the physical exams for both the army and the navy in early 1941. But a few months later, Joe Kennedy arranged for another physical exam for his son, this time clearly rigged, that found no serious health issues. In October, he entered the Office of Naval Intelligence in Washington.[47]

The work was dull, he told Billings, but he was enjoying an active social life, including his first serious romance—a relationship with a Danish journalist, Inga Arvad, who had become a friend of Jack's sister Kathleen. Arvad was a beautiful woman (rumored to have been a Miss Denmark). She was a few years older than Jack. She was married, but in the process of divorce—a fact that, had Rose Kennedy known, would have horrified her. More important, however, were the growing rumors that Arvad was a spy—a rumor that had emerged from her assignment as the German correspondent for a Danish paper and her appearance in a few photographs with Hitler and Göring. There was no evidence that she was engaged in espionage, but the likelihood of a scandal grew once the FBI became interested. With Joe Kennedy's encouragement, the navy quickly moved Jack out of Naval Intelligence and to the navy yard at Charleston, South Carolina, leaving Arvad behind. Their relationship soon ended painfully.[48]

By then, the United States was at war with the Axis powers, and Jack was eager to be assigned to combat duty. New bouts of illness—severe back problems, continuing stomach problems, and other ailments, some of them hidden from the naval doctors—kept him out of active duty. But in July 1942, he entered midshipman's school to train as a combat officer.

His hope was to be the commander of a PT boat, a small and flimsy wooden craft that carried torpedoes and searched for Japanese vessels to attack. It was a prestigious assignment for a young novice officer, in part because of the heroic record of earlier PT commanders and in part because of the danger in serving on the fragile boats. Jack's health problems seemed almost certain to bar him from active duty. But his father intervened, once again providing more misleading medical records and convincing the PT officers that his presence would bring publicity to the fleet. That was not the last of the influential interventions that helped Jack on his way. Unhappy to be assigned to the Panama Canal, far from the fighting, Jack appealed to Senator David Walsh of Massachusetts, who arranged for him to be assigned to the South Pacific. Jack believed it was his duty to fight. He also knew that action in the war would help him in whatever career he might choose. In his competitive, achievement-oriented family, it was almost unthinkable for him to spend the war anywhere but the front.[49]

In the spring of 1943, Kennedy took command of PT 109 and soon found himself in a fleet of fifteen PT boats sent to torpedo a Japanese fleet trying to escape from the American navy. The attack was disastrous. The PT boats failed to damage any of the Japanese ships. One night, Kennedy's boat—alone without radio or radar communication in the dark of night—was idling with only one of three engines running as it awaited the enemy. Suddenly, a Japanese destroyer, fleeing the U.S. attacks, appeared out of the dark on a direct path to PT 109. Kennedy had no time to move his sluggish, underpowered boat out of the destroyer's way, and the Japanese ship cut the U.S. craft in half—killing two of Jack's crew, with the remaining men clinging to the hull of the boat or floating aimlessly around it. Kennedy swam out to help guide the remaining men back to the hull, surrounded by oil fires, tugging a badly injured sailor with him. By the early afternoon of the next day, with the hull slowly sinking, Kennedy organized his men in groups to head toward the nearest island. It was a five-hour swim, during which he continued to drag his injured crewman with him, fighting exhaustion. The remaining crew made it to shore. When they encountered an English-speaking native with a canoe, Jack carved his location on a coconut shell and requested a boat to rescue them. Seven days after the collision, with the coconut message delivered, they were once again on a PT boat returning to their base.

Almost immediately, the PT 109 rescue became a highly publicized event—driven by the drama of the crew's harrowing ordeal and the eminence of Kennedy's family. (Headlines almost invariably referred to him as "Kennedy's Son.") The story of his heroism became a staple of the press for weeks after his rescue, enhanced by his famous family. John Hersey chronicled the PT 109 story in the *New Yorker* in 1944 (decades later it was the basis of a successful film); Hersey portrayed Jack as a modest, self-deprecating hero.[50]

Absent from these accounts were elements that did not fit with either Jack's or Hersey's needs. Jack's heroic rescue of the crew might have been even more impressive if his physical problems had become part of the story, but he had hidden his pain when he joined the navy and had no wish to reveal his chronic illness and his deceptive health report. Hersey also ignored the murky circumstances that led to the destruction of Kennedy's PT boat and ignored criticisms, many of them unfair, that—as Jack's superior officer later said—"he wasn't a particularly good boat commander."[51] It was in everyone's interest to shape the story as a tale of heroism and survival. Jack himself did little to tout his sudden fame. He had no need to do so. His shipmates, the navy, the press, and his father did it for him.

• • •

Only ten days after his rescue, Jack returned to duty, back on PT boats. But by December 1943, his health was deteriorating again, and he was ready to go home. His doctors agreed. He left the Pacific front in December, arrived in San Francisco in early January, and a few days later checked into the Mayo Clinic once again, the beginning of several months of off-and-on hospitalization to deal with his many problems. The worst, as usual, was his back—a problem that was not caused by the PT 109 ordeal (although it had aggravated the already-existing pain), nor by playing football at Harvard (as his mother told reporters). It was an earlier chronic problem made worse by several failed operations and frequent treatments with steroids. But he received a much greater blow that summer. On August 12, 1944, Joseph P. Kennedy Jr.—Jack's brother, role model, and avid competitor—piloted a bomber dangerously packed with TNT destined for Germany. The plane exploded before it left Britain. Joe's body was never recovered.[52]

The death devastated the family. Joe Sr. was inconsolable. For weeks, he stayed alone in his room in Hyannis Port, hardly seeing his wife and children. When he emerged from his solitude, he was a broken and embittered man who blamed his son's death on Roosevelt's march to war. Joe Sr. may also have feared that his son had taken this terrible risk in part to help restore his father's reputation. Jack was shattered too, perhaps worried that Joe's reckless flight was partly an effort to outdo him. ("Where the hell were you when the destroyer hove into sight . . . and where the hell was your radar?" Joe Jr. had written Jack after reading the Hersey *New Yorker* article, still competing.)[53] To console himself, Jack set out to assemble a privately published book of remembrances of his brother, *As We Remember Joe.*[54]

In the face of his grief over Joe's death, the end of his active duty in the war, the loss of his relationship with Inga Arvad, and his continuing health problems, Jack was uncertain what to do next. He was officially discharged from the navy in March 1945, somewhat aimless. A few months later, he traveled to San Francisco to write for the Hearst newspapers about the creation of the United Nations. And shortly after that he flew to Britain to begin a tour of Europe that, once again, drew him into the world of politics and diplomacy.[55]

He kept a diary of his experiences. He was skeptical of the United Nations treaty, which "suffered from inadequate preparation and lack of fundamental agreement among the Big Three . . . I doubt it will prove effective."[56] In Britain, he followed Winston Churchill's doomed campaign for reelection, noting that the Labour victory was "a good thing" because it would require the party to make peace with capitalism.[57] In Ireland, he was disturbed by reports of President Eamon de Valera's wartime hostility to Britain. And he joined a tour of the postwar ruins of Germany with Secretary of the Navy James Forrestal. He was impressed by the "perfect" discipline of the American occupation troops, and he noted the disappointment of Germans that the U.S. Army had not occupied eastern Germany before the Russians did: "One opinion here is that the Russians are never going to pull out of their zone of occupation but plan to make their part of Germany a Soviet Socialist Republic."[58] But he was not uncritical of the American troops in Germany either. "Americans looted towns heavily on arrival," he noted. He was fascinated by his visit to Hitler's destroyed home in Berchtesgaden, and he was strangely interested in Hitler himself.

You can easily understand how that within a few years Hitler will emerge from the hatred that surrounds him now as one of the most significant figures who ever lived.

He had boundless ambition for his country which rendered him a menace to the peace of the world, but he had a mystery about him in the way that he lived and in the manner of his death that will live and grow after him. He had in him the stuff of which legends are made.[59]

Kennedy was not an admirer of Hitler. But this strange diary entry suggests his interest in the exercise of power—an interest that almost allowed Hitler's historical importance to overshadow the horrors of his regime.

Kennedy returned from Europe still uncertain about what to do with his life, but gradually it dawned on him that his future might be in politics. Joe Jr.'s death inevitably elevated Jack to become the carrier of the family's hopes. Despite Joe Sr.'s doubts about his second son's political skills, he began encouraging him to take Joe Jr.'s place and run for office. Jack was skeptical at first, but he soon began thinking about a political career himself. He had considered and rejected a career in the law. He had tried journalism and decided it was not for him. ("A reporter is reporting what happened. He is not *making* it happen," he said years later.)[60] "Nothing could have kept Jack out of politics," Lem Billings wrote. "I think this is what he had in him."[61] Jack had spent his young years thinking about and studying politics and international relations, and he was now beginning to consider a life dealing with the great challenges facing the country in the aftermath of the war.

Jack may not have needed pressure from his father to choose a career in politics, but he continued to need Joe Sr. to make that career possible. Late in 1944, Joe began quietly negotiating with James Michael Curley, the colorful former mayor of Boston who was now serving in Congress. Curley, not for the first time, was having trouble with both money and the law. Kennedy offered to pay off Curley's debts and help him with his legal problems in exchange for vacating his seat in the House of Representatives. Jack may not have known about his father's intervention with Curley, but he understood that without his father's help the likelihood of political success would be slim. "I just called people," Joe later told a journalist asking about the beginnings of Jack's political life. "I got in touch with people I know. I have a lot of contacts."[62] In December 1944, his father's support assured, Jack wrote Billings, "I have my eyes on something pretty good now if it comes through."[63]

2

———

# The Uncertain Politician

As Jack Kennedy took his first steps into electoral politics, he was surrounded by the doubts of many friends and family members who were worried about his suitability for public life. He was not yet an effective public speaker; audiences found him awkward, stiff, and insecure. When he mingled with voters (which he was reluctant to do), he seemed aloof and uncomfortable. He was careless with his schedule; audiences were often left waiting an hour or more. His health remained poor, and he seemed to lack the strength for a rigorous campaign. When asked about why he was running for office, he often said that he was taking over from his brother Joe. Most of the people who became part of Jack's first campaign for Congress in 1946 were chosen by his father. They saw his son as a work in progress. Despite his achievements—the well-regarded book, the impressive war record, the prominent name—he remained a young, inexperienced political unknown. His opponents ridiculed him as a carpetbagging rich kid with no qualifications other than his father's money.[1]

But Jack had qualities that were not immediately visible. In the absence of his intimidating parents, he could be a charming, magnetic, sociable figure. He had a large circle of loyal and admiring friends from Choate, Harvard, the navy, and other places. In many ways, he was a more appealing young man than his serious, competitive, and temperamental older brother. And like other young men entering politics in 1946, he had the advantage of a heroic war record—a record already highly publicized (and to some degree romanticized) by an eager press. Once, when he attended a meeting of Charlestown Gold Star Mothers (women who had lost sons in the war), he told them, "I think I know how all you mothers feel because my mother is a Gold Star Mother, too." The remark seemed to create a "magical link" with the women in the room.[2]

Jack benefited as well from another and even more important advantage: his father's money and influence. Jack himself paid little attention to how his campaign was being financed. He focused on his speeches, rallies, and meetings. For a while, his grandfather, the former mayor, tried to help organize the campaign, but there was no room for him once Joe Kennedy took over. Joe did the dirty work—distributing money to ward bosses, paying for leaflets and billboards, hiring a public relations firm, creating phone banks. He staged elaborate events, including a vast "tea" at an elegant hotel in Cambridge where members of the Kennedy family—the men dressed in white tie and tails and the women in Paris dresses—stood in line to shake hands with fifteen hundred women. As much as $300,000 went into Jack's congressional campaign, far more than the money raised by all the other candidates combined. Joe's money remained a critical, indeed indispensable, element of his political rise. "We're going to sell Jack like soap flakes," Joe Kennedy is said to have boasted. He was "the mastermind" of Jack's campaign, a colleague recalled. "He was completely in charge of every detail."[3]

The campaign itself was largely contentless. Jack spoke often about his wartime experiences and the heroism of his navy friends, some of whom joined him at rallies. (Joe reprinted John Hersey's *New Yorker* piece on Jack's PT 109 ordeal and distributed a hundred thousand copies to voters.) Jack was mostly interested in international questions and tried to make the state of the world his principal theme. But his speeches—despite their occasional eloquence—were vague and unspecific: "The people of the United States and the world stand at the crossroads. What we do now will shape the history of civilization for many years to come. We have a weary world trying to bind up the wounds of a fierce struggle . . . The days which lie ahead are most difficult ones."[4]

Voters in 1946 were more concerned about economic issues, and so Jack began to respond by parroting standard New Deal positions. But the most frequent elements of his campaign were still his youth, his war record, and his slogan: "The New Generation Offers a Leader."[5]

Jack easily won the Democratic primary for Massachusetts' Eleventh District. But because of the presence of ten other candidates in the race, he ended up winning with only about 12 percent of the total vote. In the general election, in which Jack was a prohibitive favorite in the heavily Democratic district, he tried to speak more broadly about his goals. In a well-publicized speech, titled "Why I Am a Democrat," he continued to support the Democratic platform, but he provided new ideas of his own. For example, he relied on his warnings of the dangers of the Soviet Union and its "program of world aggression." But at this point, it hardly mattered what he said. In the midst of a Republican landslide through most of the country, he won his solidly Democratic congressional seat with 73 percent of the votes.[6]

. . .

The 1946 congressional elections produced Republican majorities. But they also brought a wave of young war veterans into Congress from both parties. Jack Kennedy was one of the most visible of this new crop. There were others who also made names for themselves rapidly—among them Republicans such as Representative Richard Nixon of California and Senator Joseph McCarthy of Wisconsin. But unlike Nixon and McCarthy, who would come to prominence for their work in congressional committees, Kennedy had almost no interest in the work of the House. He built a large and competent staff—one of the biggest of any office on the Hill, thanks to his father—which allowed him to evade the many political chores he disliked. He avoided meeting constituents. With the help of his father's intervention, he became a member of the House Education and Labor Committee and the House Veterans' Affairs Committee, both of them important and prestigious given the economic turmoil of the transitional years after World War II. But Jack in fact knew little about the work of either committee and came to their meetings late (or not at all). His own constituency was dominated by working-class people about whose needs Kennedy knew or cared little. To whatever degree he paid attention to domestic issues, he mostly denounced deficits and urged Congress to reduce appropriations to make sure there was enough funding for defense. A notable exception was his support for federally supported housing, a major issue in 1946 after the long Depression and wartime slump in construction—although he clumsily alienated the American Legion by denouncing the organization (not inaccurately) as a "legislative drummer boy for the real estate lobby."[7] He was a reliable but not very ardent opponent of the Taft-Hartley Act of 1947, which reduced the power of labor unions.

Kennedy remained primarily interested in international affairs, an area in which he had no responsibilities nor influence in Congress. He supported the Truman Doctrine, which laid the foundation of containment—the American response to the Cold War. Even before the end of his first term, he was already planning a statewide campaign—perhaps for governor, perhaps for the Senate. Both of them were up for election in 1948, and he based his plans for higher office on what he considered his strength on international affairs. But Jack abandoned his plans for higher office once it became clear that the odds were strongly against a largely unknown candidate with just one term's experience in the House of Representatives. He easily won reelection to his congressional seat, and he dutifully supported legislation that would help his constituents. But his heart was not in it.

· · ·

One of the things that distinguished Kennedy from most other representatives was his frequent absences from Washington. He spent long weekends in Hyannis Port (not in the Boston district he represented). He vacationed at the family home in Palm Beach. He traveled to California, Ireland, and England. And as always he spent much time in pursuit of women almost everywhere he went. But it was not only his restlessness that kept him from the Capitol. It was also, as always, his health. His back pain was getting worse. He continued to have multiple illnesses that still defied explanation.

During a 1947 trip to England, he became so ill that he received the last rites of the Catholic Church in a London hospital. But finally a British physician recognized his symptoms. Kennedy was suffering from Addison's disease, a rare and dangerous disorder that is a product of the adrenal glands not producing adequate hormones. Adrenal insufficiency causes multiple problems, which make diagnosis difficult—part of the reason Kennedy's problems went unknown for so long, despite the discovery of the disease in the nineteenth century. The identification of Addison's disease probably saved Kennedy's life. Untreated, it is usually fatal. But regular treatments of cortisone, although not without side effects, could keep the disease under control. And while Kennedy continued to experience severe back pain and other maladies, the life-threatening illnesses that he had experienced for much of his life seemed to recede not long after treatment began. The cortisone also contributed to what appeared to be his ruddy tan and his no-longer-scrawny body.[8]

Throughout his youth, Jack had surrounded himself with many friends. But once he committed himself to politics, he began to withdraw from them. With the exception of Lem Billings and a few others, he saw little of his former friends. Nor did he make many new ones, although he, like most famous people, had many acquaintances who posed as friends. Even in his own family, he had a distant relationship with most of his siblings, who were much younger than he and who had rarely seen Jack during his years in boarding school, college, and the navy. His closest sibling, after Joe Jr.'s death, was his sister Kathleen, who had settled in England during World War II. Her first husband, the Marquess of Hartington, had died during the war. Not long after the war, she began a romance with Peter Fitzwilliam, the eighth Earl Fitzwilliam. Their romance appalled Rose Kennedy, who promised to disown Kathleen should she marry Fitzwilliam, who was in the process of divorce and who was not a Catholic. Kathleen, with Jack's support, continued the relationship despite Rose's threats. But in the spring of 1948, she and Fitzwilliam—

despite warnings of perilous weather—insisted on taking a private plane to the south of France. En route in impenetrable weather, they were killed when their plane crashed into a mountain. It was the second grievous loss within the family. Jack spent weeks distracted and depressed. Over time, he would become closer to his younger siblings—especially his sister Eunice and his brother Bobby. But for a while, he felt especially alone.[9]

· · ·

In this dark moment of his life, Jack immersed himself as never before in the political world. After he won reelection to his congressional seat easily, he continued to find the work of the House of Representatives often tedious, and he remained a largely absentee congressman. He usually returned to Massachusetts for much of the week, delegating the work of his Washington office to his large and talented staff. He was mostly focused again on a run for statewide office—the U.S. Senate seat that was up for election in 1952. He began traveling around the state to make himself more familiar outside of his district, and he learned how to communicate more effectively with voters. When he talked about issues, he continued to speak mainly about foreign policy, communism, and the Cold War—subjects that were largely uncontroversial among Massachusetts voters. If anything, he was a more belligerent Cold Warrior than President Harry Truman, the leader of his party. He joined the attacks on such China experts as Owen Lattimore, John King Fairbank, and State Department officials for allowing the Chiang Kai-shek regime to fall in October 1949. "What our young men had saved [in the war]," he said, "our diplomats and our president have frittered away."[10] Kennedy was not an anticommunist demagogue, but for a time he loyally supported his friend Joe McCarthy, whom as late as 1952 he called "a great American patriot."[11] And he voted enthusiastically for the controversial McCarran-Walter Act, which Truman vetoed and liberals deplored. Congress overrode the president's veto of the law, which required communists to register with the government. And it required the Justice Department to investigate their activities. Such positions would come back to haunt

Kennedy years later when he was seeking support from more liberal Democrats.[12]

By early 1952, Kennedy had cleared his path for a Senate race against the Republican incumbent, Henry Cabot Lodge, grandson of the powerful Massachusetts senator of the same name who had battled Woodrow Wilson over the League of Nations. Lodge was seeking a fourth Senate term, and he appeared to be a formidable opponent. But he also had significant handicaps. He was the campaign manager for Dwight Eisenhower's 1952 presidential campaign, which reduced his ability to campaign for his own Senate seat. And his prominent support for Eisenhower had alienated some Massachusetts Republicans who had favored the more conservative Robert Taft for the party's nomination.

But Lodge faced an even larger disadvantage in 1952: Joe Kennedy. As before, he was active in almost every aspect of his son's campaign—sometimes unknown to the candidate himself. He organized his own, invisible campaign organization for Jack, largely separate from the public one. Joe's lifelong aides quietly managed Jack's appearances, published and distributed campaign materials, and most of all helped distribute the money that flowed to committees and interest groups that could turn out voters. Joe fired one of Jack's most trusted aides and replaced him with Jack's younger brother Robert—who quickly became a capable and indispensable political organizer in his own right. Bobby soon replaced Joe as the most visible campaign manager. But Joe did not rest. He quietly persuaded the publisher of the *New Bedford Standard-Times*, which had supported Taft, to urge conservative Republicans to vote for Jack. He also secretly met with John Fox, the publisher of the *Boston Post*, who had already promised to endorse Lodge. Joe persuaded him to change his mind. Shortly after the meeting, Joe provided the financially strapped Fox with a half-million-dollar loan.[13]

Jack complained occasionally about the role his father played in his campaign, but given his own lackadaisical campaigning style, he had little choice but to cede virtually all responsibility to his father. He almost never asked where the money came from or how it was spent. And he continued to use his family as props for his appearances.[14]

The careful, lavish efforts by Joe Kennedy and his colleagues were almost certainly decisive in Jack's narrow victory over Lodge in 1952—a 3 percent margin of victory, about seventy thousand votes. But it was an impressive triumph nonetheless. He had defeated one of the most prominent Republicans in the nation, and he had done so despite the Eisenhower landslide and the Republican landslide in congressional elections across the country. "I kept thinking about my father," Rose Kennedy said in an interview years later remembering John Fitzgerald, the former mayor. "In my mind, I kept picturing him as a little boy, huddled in the servants' quarters at old Henry Cabot Lodge's home as he warmed his shivering body from the cold of his newspaper route. In his wildest dreams that winter's night, could he ever have imagined how far both he and his family would come."[15] For Rose, and to a significant extent for Joe, Jack's victory was a vindication—a kind of revenge for all the many years of anti-Irish bigotry and for the invidious and humiliating limits imposed on Irish families. To Jack, however, such long-standing grievances meant almost nothing. As the son of a wealthy and powerful man, he took for granted the cosseted life he had led and his easy assimilation into the world of the American aristocracy. Rarely did he reminisce about the old days of his Irish family. Instead, he looked forward.

. . .

Even as he moved toward becoming a United States senator, Jack was slow to grow up. He continued to rely mainly on a few close friends, Lem Billings still among them. He maintained his almost sophomoric ribald humor, his penchant for wild evenings, and his obsessive womanizing. There was a sense of detachment from the world he had chosen to enter. Nigel Hamilton, the author of a partly admiring study of Kennedy's early years, concluded: "He had the brains, the courage, the shy charisma, good looks, idealism, money. Yet, as always, there was something missing—a certain depth or seriousness of purpose . . . Once the voters or the women were won, there was a certain vacuousness on Jack's part, a failure to turn conquest into anything very meaningful or profound."[16]

But while Kennedy never fully overcame his recklessness and detachment, he became a more serious person as he moved up the ladder of his aspirations. His health was still precarious, but he was no longer a young man who half expected to die within a few years. Evidence of the change was his decision to marry.

Jacqueline Bouvier seemed an unlikely match for Jack Kennedy. She was aristocratic, fashionable, socially sophisticated, interested in art and literature. Jack, even though he was twelve years older, continued to live in many ways like a college student. He shared a house with male friends. He had few of Jacqueline's intellectual interests, just as she had few of his political ones. They met in 1951 through friends of the family. Despite their differences, they shared many things. The Bouvier family was aristocratic, but without great wealth. The Kennedy family was perhaps not yet quite aristocratic, but enormously wealthy. Both had grown up with powerful fathers who dominated their lives and whose philandering humiliated their mothers—in Jacqueline's case, driving her mother into a second marriage to Hugh Auchincloss, a wealthy oil heir.

Jacqueline was different from any of the women Jack had known before. Almost all of them—from one-night stands to long-standing affairs—were mainly sexual partners and little more (with the exception of Inga Arvad). Jacqueline was certainly beautiful, which had always been a requirement for the women who were attractive to him. But Jacqueline interested him in other ways: her artistic interests, her willingness to challenge him, even her aloofness from the Kennedy clan. She had what Lem Billings described as "classiness." She was also, as it happened, a Catholic, which reduced at least some of the tension between her and Rose. They were married on September 12, 1953, at the lavish Auchincloss estate in Newport, Rhode Island. The ceremony was arranged almost entirely by the Kennedys—an early sign of the difficulties Jacqueline would have fitting into Jack's large, clannish family.[17]

Kennedy knew that as a rising political star his continued bachelorhood would be an obstacle to his ambitions. But he long remained reluctant to marry. As late as the spring of 1953, when he was thirty-six, already in a significant relationship with Jackie, he cooperated with the *Saturday Evening Post* on an article called the "Gay Young Bachelor."[18] And as things turned out, his marriage did not significantly change what Jacqueline would later call his "violent independence," which included his continued womanizing.[19] Jackie was philosophical about men and seemed to accept what she thought was their inevitable infidelity (a belief drawn from her own father). But the combination of Jack's aloofness and the extraordinary level of his philandering came as something of a shock to her. She was shaken as well by Jack's health problems. The most serious was his grave back problem, which led to several dangerous operations, in one of which in 1954 he was for a while close to death. (He told his doctors that he would rather die than live with the pain, although he had lived with it for years and would for years longer.) The surgeries were only partly successful, and Jack continued to struggle with back pain for the rest of his life. One friend later recalled that "after the first year they were together, Jackie was wandering around looking like the survivor of an airplane crash."[20] But the marriage was not a sham. Jack clearly admired Jackie, and she was fascinated by him. Both eventually learned to live with the other's flaws and differences. Becoming a husband, despite his frequent faithlessness, had strengthened Jack's sense of his own seriousness and ambitions.[21]

• • •

Once in the Senate, Kennedy built an impressive staff—most importantly in hiring Theodore Sorensen, a twenty-four-year-old attorney who, among other things, pushed the young senator into a greater commitment to liberalism. ("You've got to remember," he once told Sorensen defensively, "that I entered Congress just out of my father's house.")[22] Sorensen's greatest contribution may have been his skill as a writer—his ability to take Kennedy's ideas, add a few of his own, and turn them into elegant and often powerful speeches or articles. Thanks to Sorensen, articles published under Kennedy's name began appearing often in serious magazines, among them the *Atlantic Monthly* and the *New Republic*. Kennedy thought of himself as a man of the world and a committed, intelligent Cold Warrior.

But he also understood the need to create a credible commitment to the needs of the people of Massachusetts and, eventually, the nation. Sorensen helped provide Kennedy with ideas about domestic policy, something in which the senator had shown relatively little interest so far.[23]

Kennedy's first years in the Senate continued to be dogged by his back problems and led him again to long absences from Washington. He was absent from Congress for more than three months (during which he neglected to take a position on the censure of Joseph McCarthy, a failure that would trouble many liberal Democrats—among them Eleanor Roosevelt—for years). He kept in touch with his office through Sorensen and other aides, but he mainly focused on writing a series of profiles of political figures whom Kennedy considered men of courage—the kind of men Kennedy hoped to emulate. It became a best-selling book, *Profiles in Courage*.[24] Inevitably, he had help—probably a great deal of it—from Sorensen and perhaps others. It was, of course, hardly unusual for a politician to publish a book in collaboration with others while taking full credit for it. Kennedy's book, however, won the 1957 Pulitzer Prize for biography—even though the jury that proposed biographies for consideration to the Pulitzer board did not recommend it. There are several explanations for this surprising award. One was the official explanation of the Pulitzer board, which noted its value in "teaching patriotic and unselfish service to the people," a sentiment attractive at a time when there was much concern about an absence of patriotism and commitment. Another was the ubiquitous intervention of Arthur Krock, who began lobbying for the book even before it was published. Both explanations could be true. Debates over Kennedy's authorship remained relatively invisible during his lifetime. The success of the book, in the meantime, added prestige to a thirty-nine-year-old senator who had not yet distinguished himself as a legislator.[25]

Kennedy's newfound eminence did little to increase his engagement with the Senate, but it did a great deal to strengthen his political ambitions. With rumors circulating that he might be a candidate for vice president in 1956, Kennedy set out to make himself a stal-

wart supporter of Adlai Stevenson, the likely Democratic presidential nominee. He also sought to gain control of the Massachusetts
Democratic Party. Overthrowing the conservative political bosses
who had long dominated the state party was no easy task, and the
battle between Kennedy and the entrenched Irish politicians was
ugly. But the struggle mostly damaged the reputation of the incumbent bosses and in the end left Kennedy in charge of the party.

Jack's father worked hard to persuade him not to seek the
vice presidency, arguing that Stevenson would certainly lose and
the defeat might damage Jack. But Kennedy was undeterred. At the
Democratic National Convention, he narrated a film recounting
the modern history of the party (after which the *New York Times*
compared him to a movie star), and a few days later, he gave the
nominating speech for Stevenson. His speech was drafted by Arthur
Schlesinger Jr., who was working for the Stevenson campaign, but
it was significantly rewritten later by Sorensen and Kennedy himself. In it, they introduced themes that would characterize Kennedy's future career. He warned of "the ever-mounting threats of our
survival that confront us abroad, threats that require a prompt return
to firm, decisive leadership." He deplored "the absence of new ideas,
the lack of new leadership, the failure to keep pace with new developments." And as he praised Stevenson, he closed with a phrase he
would use again: "Let the word go forth that we have fulfilled our
responsibility to the nation."[26] In the end, Kennedy's gambit to
become the vice-presidential candidate fell short. Stevenson was not
enthusiastic about him as a running mate and wanted a southerner
instead, but he was also afraid of offending the Kennedys and risk-
ing the loss of Joe Kennedy's campaign contributions. So he protected
himself by asking the convention to choose his running mate. Kennedy ran a respectable second to Senator Estes Kefauver of Tennessee. Jack was disappointed, but his candidacy raised his profile in
the national party.[27]

. . .

Although Kennedy faced reelection to the Senate in 1958, he was
already positioning himself to run for president in 1960. To many

people, the idea that such a young and relatively inexperienced politician could be a realistic candidate for the nation's highest office seemed preposterous. But to Kennedy himself, running for president had seemed almost an obligation ever since Joe Jr. died in the war. For a time, early in his political career, he was not sure that he could, or even wanted, to become president. But because of his father's expectations and because of his own growing ambitions, it was not long before almost everything he did became part of his preparation for seeking the presidency: the march through three terms in the House and two elections to the Senate; the enormous publicity built by his family and his aides; the success of *Profiles in Courage*; his campaign for the vice presidency; even his marriage, without which he knew he would have had no chance of being elected. And when the 1956 Democratic convention adjourned, no one in the party could doubt that Kennedy would be a formidable figure in 1960.[28]

There were, to be sure, significant obstacles still to overcome (or disguise). His marriage was shaky from the start, and it reached a crisis shortly after the 1956 Democratic convention. Jack left his pregnant wife in her mother's home while he went on a European vacation—which included a sybaritic cruise on the Riviera with his Senate colleague George Smathers of Florida, his frequent companion in womanizing. When Jackie experienced a miscarriage, he remained out of touch for three days before he flew back to Newport and tried to mend fences. Jackie was so traumatized by the experience that they abandoned the spacious estate they had bought in McLean, Virginia—Hickory Hill—and sold it to Bobby Kennedy and his wife, Ethel. Jack and Jacqueline moved instead to a town house in Georgetown. She also insisted on their separating from the rest of the Kennedy family in Hyannis Port, no longer sharing a house with other members of the family.[29]

But there were other problems as well. If he succeeded, Kennedy would be the youngest elected president in history as well as the first Catholic president. No one knew how serious such handicaps might be. He had succeeded in presenting himself as an assimilated, sophisticated politician, unconnected to the traditional Irish

Catholic world, but his Catholicism remained a controversial issue for many Protestants.[30] Many liberal Democrats continued to doubt Kennedy, particularly for his failure to turn against McCarthy. Jack needed a substantial reelection victory for the Senate to ready himself for a presidential race. And in 1960 he would face strong competition from Hubert Humphrey, Lyndon Johnson, and Stuart Symington in his own party, and Vice President Richard Nixon, the likely Republican nominee.

But Kennedy was confident that he could overcome the obstacles to his election. Only days after the 1956 election—with the enthusiastic backing of his family—Jack privately decided to run for president. And as in his earlier campaigns, everything seemed to break his way. His marriage was strengthened by the birth of his first child, Caroline, in 1957—an event that finally provided Jackie with some contentment in her marriage. His Senate colleagues, aware of his burgeoning fame, appointed him to the Foreign Relations Committee, a prestigious Senate post and an appropriate one for a man who was building his reputation on international affairs. At the same time, Kennedy was becoming a darling of the press— with lavish and almost always gushing cover stories in *Life*, *Look*, *Redbook*, and others. Among them was a *Saturday Evening Post* story titled "The Amazing Kennedys," in which the author correctly predicted "the flowering of another great political family such as the Adamses, the Lodges, and the La Follettes. They confidently look forward to the day when Jack will be in the White House, Bobby will serve in the Cabinet as Attorney General, and Teddy will be the Senator for Massachusetts."[31]

In November 1958, Kennedy won reelection to the Senate with the greatest share of the vote in the history of Massachusetts—73.6 percent. "Jack is the greatest attraction in the country today," Joe said. "He can draw more people to a fundraising dinner than Cary Grant or Jimmy Stewart. Why is that? He has more universal appeal. That is why the Democratic Party is going to nominate him."[32] Joe Kennedy had been wrong about many things in his life. But on this, he was mostly right.

# 3

---

# The Great Ambition

As early as 1956, John Kennedy was already a possible future candidate for the presidency. By the end of 1958, after his landslide reelection to the Senate, he was more than that—a highly regarded figure who seemed to many people to represent a "new generation," the slogan that had launched his first campaign for Congress in 1946. His presidential efforts were well under way early in 1959 before he announced his candidacy on January 2, 1960, in the U.S. Senate office building.

Kennedy seemed to be a new kind of candidate. He was young, charismatic, wealthy, and eloquent. Hundreds of supporters had been fawning over him for years. The hundreds soon became thousands, and the thousands eventually became millions. His presence transformed the relatively staid presidential campaigns into what seemed to be a different kind of election—the "first modern campaign," one writer has argued.[1] Campaigns had been "modernizing" for years, but the 1960 campaign shaped a different era of politics and a new form of leadership. Theodore H. White's 1961 book, *The Making of the President 1960*, retrospectively helped elevate the campaign. It was, White wrote, "the most awesome transfer of power in the world," a race that "captured a momentary, yet precise, picture of the moods, the wills, the past and the future of all the communities that made America whole."[2]

It was, on the whole, a relatively civil campaign. At what was perhaps the summit of American global leadership, the election of a president seemed to many people to be of unusual importance.[3] But despite his rise to prominence, Kennedy was still unknown to many Americans. Questions and doubts abounded. Many people thought he was too young, not ready—a view shared publicly and tartly by Harry Truman. Lyndon Johnson raised questions about Kennedy's health. A significant group of determined Democratic liberals were, at best, uneasy about Kennedy's own liberalism. But what bothered them most was that he was not Adlai Stevenson, who publicly insisted that he would not be a candidate in 1960 but who privately maneuvered to be drafted. As Kennedy moved closer to his announcement of his candidacy, he was—despite his considerable strengths—far from certain of winning the nomination.[4]

The journalist Ben Bradlee, a friend and neighbor of Kennedy, asked him late in 1959, "Do you really think—way down deep— that you can pull this thing off?" "Yes," Kennedy replied, "if I don't make a single mistake."[5] And that became the creed of the campaign: never make a mistake (or at least never admit one), never lose a primary, never get outmaneuvered.

. . .

For a time, one of Kennedy's most dangerous problems was Eleanor Roosevelt, whose influence over the Democratic party was enormous. The former first lady was a longtime admirer and friend of Adlai Stevenson, and she hoped he would once again become the Democratic candidate. But even if Stevenson was not a possible nominee, she would have doubts about Kennedy. Her reservations reflected a range of issues about which many others were concerned: his youth, his inexperience, his religion, and his father. It was a great danger to his campaign that the most revered woman in America was expressing them. In December 1958, during a television interview, Mrs. Roosevelt stated that "Kennedy's father has been spending oodles of money all over the country and probably has a paid representative in every state by now."[6] The accusation was not far from the truth, but perhaps just far enough for Kennedy to refute it. "I am certain that you are the victim of misinformation," he cautiously responded in a letter.[7] Mrs. Roosevelt was not persuaded, and the back-and-forth on the disagreement continued for weeks. She eventually dropped the money issue.

But several months later, she made even more damaging comments. Publicly, if primly, she attacked Kennedy's greatest vulnerability. She said in an interview that she doubted he "would be suitable" as the Democratic candidate because "if a Catholic is elected, he must be able to separate the church from the state. I'm not sure Kennedy could do this."[8]

Kennedy suppressed his irritation and worked hard to earn Mrs. Roosevelt's respect, with some success. Her loyalty to Stevenson never stopped. But by the end of 1959 the public rebukes largely ceased, and she began to offer tepid approval: "Here is a man who wants to leave a record (perhaps for ambitious personal reasons . . . ) but I rather think because he is really interested in helping the people of his own country and mankind in general . . . he would make a good President if elected."[9]

Kennedy's most dangerous obstacle remained his Catholicism. Almost everywhere he went religion dogged his path. Arthur Schlesinger Jr.—who had recently shifted his loyalty (somewhat shakily) from Stevenson to Kennedy—warned him that any open defense of his Catholicism might strengthen the Protestant opposition, that he must make clear that he "[did] not regard intolerance as an exclusively Protestant failing," that there was Catholic bigotry too.[10] But Ted Sorensen saw the benefits of Catholic support in the big cities, which he argued were more important to the campaign than the "Southern/border vote or the farm vote."[11] Sorensen (himself a secular Unitarian) also mobilized Protestant clergy to defend a Catholic candidacy. The most significant response was on September 12, 1960, when Kennedy gave a speech before the Greater Houston Ministerial Association (a mostly Protestant organization). It was particularly important because he delivered it less than two months before the election. "I believe in an America," Kennedy said,

. . . where the separation of church and state is absolute, where no Catholic prelate would tell the President—should he be a

Catholic—how to act, and no Protestant minister would tell his parishioners for whom to vote . . . and where no man is denied public office merely because his religion differs from the President who might appoint him or from the people who might elect him.[12]

The religious issue never went away, and it undoubtedly affected the election. His Catholicism won him many new voters and undoubtedly lost him others. But his efforts to defuse the issue lowered the temperature of the campaign and persuaded many doubters to look past religion as a major factor in the race.[13]

• • •

While Kennedy was wooing the Democratic elite, he was also barnstorming through the smaller states speaking many times a day to local audiences large and small. It was a grueling task, especially for a man with health problems and a bad back. He traveled mostly in small airplanes—aware of the politicians, as well as his own brother and sister, who had died in plane crashes during similar trips. (In one short flight piloted by a well-meaning but inexperienced amateur, the plane flew upside down shortly before an aborted landing.) The Democratic presidential nomination, Kennedy knew, was mostly in the hands of party leaders. Only a few states held primaries, and many of them were uncontested. But Kennedy had to prove his ability to win. And the best way to show that was to win primaries, not so much to accumulate delegates but to show the party that he could succeed. Ted Sorensen organized a perhaps unprecedented research project on every state in the nation, which he used to prioritize Kennedy's travels. Kennedy successfully accumulated small batches of delegates in many small states because no other candidates had the time or the money to pursue them. But his advisers knew that to demonstrate Kennedy's strength, the candidate had to win some contested races too.[14]

He began with Wisconsin, a farm state with a few large cities and a strong progressive tradition. His principal rival was Senator

Hubert Humphrey, one of the most prominent liberals in the party. Many observers assumed that Humphrey, from neighboring Minnesota, would have a tremendous advantage against a wealthy New Englander. Humphrey worked the small farm towns dominated by Protestants, gamely speaking at small (mostly male) gatherings in American Legion halls and school auditoriums—always cheerful, always friendly. Kennedy, cool, attractive, and urbane, worked the cities. He attracted large, enthusiastic crowds and spoke seriously and elegantly, with something of the shy reticence that was especially attractive to women. He won by a sizable margin—56 percent of the vote and carrying six of the ten precincts. But both candidates knew that he had benefited disproportionately from Wisconsin's significant urban Catholic vote.[15]

Wisconsin may not have secured Kennedy's victory, but it ended any real chance for Humphrey to win the nomination after a defeat in his own region. Even so, the contest moved to West Virginia, a rural state with few Catholics. Humphrey hoped that he could stop Kennedy's momentum there and keep his own hopes alive. Kennedy believed that Humphrey's presence in the primary would be a boon to him, because without Humphrey Kennedy would have won an uncontested and thus unnoticed race. West Virginia politics was rife with corruption, and everyone knew that the political leaders in the state expected to be paid for their support—"hot money, under-the-table money, open money," Theodore White noted.[16] Paying politicians was something Joseph Kennedy did well. Rumors abounded of Mafia participation in the primary and of surreptitious transfers of cash well beyond the norm. But even Humphrey understood that everyone paid off the politicians in West Virginia, and he later conceded that he would have spent the money if he had had it.[17]

Kennedy began the West Virginia campaign with a large margin in the polls, but that was before most people in the state knew he was a Catholic. He responded with a speech—a precursor to his Houston address several months later—in an effort to assure doubters of his independence and help voters to see that Catholics, just as much as Protestants, could be patriotic citizens. "When any man

stands on the steps of the Capitol and takes the oath of President,"
he said, "he is swearing to support the separation of church and
state . . . And if he breaks his oath, he is not only committing a
crime against the Constitution, for which the Congress can impeach
him—and should impeach him—but he is committing a sin against
God . . . A sin against God, for he has sworn on the Bible."[18] At
about the same time, Joe Kennedy's deep pockets allowed the campaign to circulate a film widely shown across the state showing the
candidate's war experiences, his Pulitzer Prize–winning book, and
his attractive family. It also helped that Franklin Delano Roosevelt
Jr. campaigned with Kennedy in West Virginia, reminding voters of
the still cherished New Deal. Kennedy won 61 percent of the vote
and drove Humphrey out of the race. But the nomination was still
in doubt as the Democratic party delegates gathered for the unpre-
dictable and (for Kennedy) perilous convention in Los Angeles.[19]

·  ·  ·

Adlai Stevenson was sixty years old in 1960, about the same age as
Dwight D. Eisenhower had been when he was elected president in
1952. Twice nominated by the Democrats for president and twice
defeated, Stevenson was no longer willing to declare himself a candidate for a third nomination. Although he stuck to that position
almost to the end, not many people believed him. For a generation of
liberal Democrats who loved his urbane, intelligent demeanor and
his bold liberal rhetoric (which was not always matched by his actual
positions), he was still for many Democrats the ideal candidate. If
anyone was going to stop Kennedy, it would likely be Stevenson.[20]

For several months before the convention, Stevenson and Kennedy maintained a cordial, even warm correspondence. Stevenson
sent his "warmest congratulations" to Kennedy on his victory in
West Virginia, and he continued to send notes and short letters
encouraging his campaign. "You're doing fine!" he wrote warmly in
May.[21] The two men talked frequently by phone and, on occasion,
met in person to discuss the race. Stevenson gave no indication of
his own presidential ambitions and instead offered advice for

how Kennedy could ensure his nomination. Kennedy, in turn, wrote warmly to Stevenson, congratulating him on his speeches and thanking him for his advice and encouragement.[22]

But both men knew that beneath what Kennedy called their "extremely cordial relationship" was an intense rivalry of unusual complexity.[23] Stevenson still harbored ambitions for the nomination—although he was unwilling to ask for it. And as his many admirers began promoting him, his interest grew. While Stevenson was hoping to derail the Kennedy campaign, he was also working hard to persuade Kennedy to appoint him to a major post in the administration, preferably secretary of state if Kennedy were to become president. This mutual need, laced with rivalry, was evident in the urgent correspondence by others whose letters and telephone calls were flying around the campaign.[24]

Arthur Schlesinger was one of Kennedy's most important go-betweens—a longtime friend and supporter of Stevenson, but now an ally of Kennedy. Schlesinger wrote Kennedy cautiously about "our mutual friend" and recounted a conversation that illustrated Stevenson's ambivalence. "He seems to feel," he wrote Kennedy, "that he has told so many people (especially present active candidates) that he would remain neutral that it would be a violation of his word to them if he were now to come out with an endorsement."[25] But Schlesinger did not tell Kennedy everything. He wrote in his diary in May that he thought Stevenson was beginning to encourage a draft. "People called and said that Kennedy's youth and religion were too much of a burden," Stevenson had told Schlesinger. His supporters were insisting that "the only answer was a Stevenson-Kennedy ticket." Stevenson continued to refuse to seek the nomination, but he also refused openly to support Kennedy. "If you do anything about this," Stevenson told his political allies who were promoting a draft, "you must do it on your own."[26]

Schlesinger himself was still privately torn between the two candidates. The collapse of a U.S.-Soviet summit meeting in Paris (in the aftermath of the Soviets' downing of an American spy plane over Russia piloted by Francis Gary Powers) energized Stevenson supporters, arguing that he was better prepared than Kennedy to deal with a crisis. Schlesinger released a cryptic statement: "[Stevenson was] best qualified but . . . since he was not a candidate, I was for Kennedy." Schlesinger then flew off to Berlin, relieved to be away from the battle.[27]

• • •

The Democratic convention in Los Angeles in July began with continued uncertainty as to who would be nominated. Kennedy had the most delegates and seemed the most likely winner. But he did not yet have a secure majority, and he knew that others were working hard to defeat him—not least the supporters of Stevenson. By Tuesday of convention week, delegates were being greeted by enormous numbers of Stevenson supporters chanting with growing emotion. Everywhere Stevenson went, Schlesinger recalled, "the crowd went wild."[28] When Stevenson walked onto the convention floor to take his seat as an Illinois delegate, Theodore White wrote, "galleries and delegates alike erupted in affection, their applause overwhelming him, their enthusiasm crushing him, until he could be extricated and brought safely to the platform."[29] To make things even more difficult for Kennedy, Senator Eugene McCarthy of Minnesota gave a dramatic speech nominating Stevenson. He pleaded with the many Democrats who revered Stevenson. "Do not reject this man," he boomed. "Do not reject this man who has made us all proud to be Democrats. Do not leave this prophet without honor in his own party."[30] Even committed Kennedy supporters were shaken by the passionate reception—among them Schlesinger, who confessed in his diary that he had questioned his own loyalty to Kennedy.

The "Adlai" boom was dangerous to Kennedy not because Stevenson was likely to win the nomination. (In the end, Stevenson received only 5 percent of the delegates.) The threat was that a Stevenson challenge would unravel Kennedy's own majority and open the door to other candidates—the most serious being Senator Lyndon Johnson of Texas. Johnson had avoided the primaries and had organized no campaign. He had launched his own candidacy only a week before the convention opened. In doing so, he helped illustrate a battle between the old politics and the new. Johnson saw the convention as a place "to consider who can best lead a party and a nation."[31] The party leaders, he hoped, would determine who the candidate would be, regardless of the primaries and the polls. That was the way things had been done at almost every convention prior to 1960. Kennedy, on the other hand, had set out to win the nomination long before the convention began by mobilizing support around the country and winning primaries.[32]

In the chaos of the convention, no one could be sure where the nomination stood. Harry Truman chose the week before the convention to attack Kennedy. The convention was "fixed," he complained, and he announced that he would give up his seat in the Missouri delegation as a result. He accused Kennedy of "buying" the nomination and of improperly pressuring delegates, and he complained that Kennedy lacked the maturity for the presidency.[33]

But the well-oiled Kennedy machine, overseen by the indomitable Robert Kennedy and many young, idealistic, and determined campaign aides, proved too much for the opponents. Early on July 14, the day of the balloting, Robert Kennedy had assembled his troops and announced that there were 740 secure votes for his brother, with 21 votes still to go to gain a majority. No other candidate had anywhere near the delegates that Kennedy had accumulated; when the many favorite sons who were waiting on the sidelines broke, it seemed almost impossible that the last few votes would not be found. It was important to the campaign that Kennedy would win on the first ballot. Were it to go to a second ballot, they feared, the sense of inevitability might disappear. The nomination would be open to the other candidates, and the old system of party bosses and elected officials would have much more leverage.

As the balloting began, Kennedy held on to his committed delegates. Although the favorite sons did not break in large numbers— many were waiting to see if there would be a second ballot—enough delegates moved to Kennedy to win him the nomination at the end of the first roll call. Wyoming, the last state to vote, provided the delegates that put Kennedy over the top. Only Lyndon Johnson received more than one hundred votes, and his tally was only slightly more than half of Kennedy's. Breaking with tradition, Kennedy appeared before the convention after the balloting to thank the del-egates. It was only a few hours after the emotional afternoon recep-tion of Stevenson, who seemed already forgotten.[34]

• • •

There was little time for Kennedy to enjoy his triumph. In the fren-zied weeks leading up to the nomination, almost none of the cam-paign staff had taken much time to consider who would join the ticket, and they now had only twenty-four hours to decide. But while the staffers were frantically making lists of possibilities, Ken-nedy himself seemed to have already made up his mind. He would ask Lyndon Johnson to be his running mate.

There were good reasons to choose Johnson. He was a major figure in the party, a powerful and experienced Senate majority leader, and someone who could occupy the presidency if necessary. But more important to Kennedy was what he could contribute to the election campaign. Johnson would, he believed, help him carry Texas and other southern states—an important issue given that Kennedy, one of his aides said, had received "fewer southern dele-gates than any Presidential candidate in the history of the Demo-cratic Party."[35] It did not help him in the South that the Democratic platform—composed by Chester Bowles, a liberal Connecticut congressman—included a civil rights plank that proposed a broad and tough series of proposals to end segregation.[36]

Johnson could indeed help Kennedy with the South. But at the same time Kennedy would face problems with some northern liberals, who considered Johnson too conservative. The resistance was per-haps strongest within the candidate's own family. Robert Kennedy disliked Johnson intensely, blamed him (correctly) for the rumors about Jack's perilous health. He and others hoped (and at times believed) that Johnson would not give up his powerful position in the Senate for the notoriously dull job of vice president. But John-son had already decided to accept if Jack asked him. Many rumors floated around the convention hall about how Johnson came to join the ticket, and some have survived for decades—among them that Kennedy actually did not want Johnson, that he wanted to flatter him because he was confident that he would say no. Other accounts suggest that Robert Kennedy tried to persuade Johnson to turn the offer down. But it is far more likely that Kennedy genuinely wanted Johnson on the ticket, and that Johnson wanted it too. Despite a brief tsunami of criticism from union leaders, civil rights advocates, and intense liberals, the convention easily approved Johnson.[37]

On the early evening of July 15, before a vast outdoor crowd at the Los Angeles Memorial Coliseum and millions of television viewers, Kennedy accepted his nomination with a speech that was meant to be both healing (after the bruising nomination fight) and energizing (with his sharp criticisms of his Republican opponent and with his own bold promises and challenges). "After eight years of drugged and fitful sleep, this nation needs strong, creative Democratic leadership in the White House," Kennedy said. It was time for new energy and new ideas.

> We stand today on the edge of a New Frontier—the frontier of the 1960's—a frontier of unknown opportunities and perils—a frontier of unfulfilled hopes and threats.
>
> Woodrow Wilson's New Freedom promised our nation a new political and economic framework. Franklin Roosevelt's New Deal promised security and succor to those in need. But the New Frontier of which I speak is not a set of promises, it is a set of challenges. It sums up not what I intend to offer the American people, but what I intend to ask of them. It appeals to their pride, not to their pocketbook—it holds out the promise of more sacrifice instead of more security.[38]

•  •  •

In the aftermath of the Democratic convention, Kennedy—in keeping a promise to his wife, who was pregnant with their second child—secluded himself at Hyannis Port for what was supposed to be a family vacation. For a few days, he and Jackie sailed, read, and played with Caroline and their nieces and nephews—all filmed for use in the campaign. But before long he was huddled in the house, working on strategy and waiting for the Republican convention to end so that the real battle could begin.

The Kennedy national campaign was as strictly managed as the primary campaign had been. Robert Kennedy continued to run the day-to-day events and kept anyone who wavered from the plan in line. The campaign was well financed, as all of Jack's campaigns had been. Much of his time was spent on traditional events—the quadrennial opening speech in Cadillac Square in Detroit, the open cars driving through crowds in downtown cities, the dozens of stump speeches—each slightly tailored for the place or the event, but mostly repetitive. He continued to focus on his theme of "getting the country moving again," but he also continued to connect to the New Deal legacy and helped energize the many liberals who had doubted his commitment. As the fall campaign began, the Republican nominee, Vice President Richard Nixon, held a modest but significant six-point lead in the polls. That was not surprising. Nixon was still much better known than Kennedy, who had yet to reach large numbers of voters outside the Democratic party—independents, liberal Republicans, and others.[39]

Kennedy's well-oiled campaign did much to improve his standing. But he benefited even more from his opponent's problems and mistakes. Richard Nixon damaged his own campaign in multiple ways. Shortly after the convention, he was hobbled by a knee injury that soon became infected, keeping him in the hospital for two weeks and leaving him weak for much of the rest of the campaign. He made a promise to visit all fifty states, which turned out to be a tremendous burden, forcing him to fly to small states already in his column when he should have been campaigning in the swing states that were still up for grabs. Kennedy made sure to take time to rest, and he campaigned almost entirely in important swing states. Nixon was racing exhaustingly from one rally to another, looking gaunt and sounding hoarse.

But a greater handicap was Nixon's relationship with President Eisenhower—still the most popular politician in the country. Nixon mostly spurned the president's support, arguing that he needed to establish himself as a leader on his own. But Eisenhower's opinion of Nixon remained a major issue in the campaign. For a while, Eisenhower tried to avoid the many press queries about what Nixon had done as vice president and what decisions he had made. Eisenhower, correctly, made clear that the vice president did not make decisions. Only the president did. But as the questions continued, Eisenhower made a serious gaffe. When a reporter asked for "an example of a major idea [from Nixon] that you adopted," the irritated Eisenhower snapped, "If you give me a week, I might think of one. I don't remember." And although the president later apologized, he still refused to give Nixon credit for any decisions.[40]

The most important events of the 1960 campaign were the first presidential debates. Both Kennedy and Nixon had reason to avoid face-to-face presidential debates, if only because they were unprecedented and their effects were unknown. Kennedy had much to lose. A significant misstep might have destroyed his chances to win. Nixon was an experienced debater, confident of his ability to do well, but the fact of his experience discounted his advantage. Nixon's advisers insisted that he should avoid the debates, that they could only help Kennedy, but Nixon ignored their advice. "I felt it was absolutely essential that I had not only to agree to debate but enthusiastically welcome the opportunity," Nixon wrote in the first of his many memoirs. "Had I refused the challenge, I would open myself to the charge that I was afraid to defend the Administration's and my own record."[41]

The candidates went into the debates with the polls showing a tight race. Four debates later, the race remained equally tight. The first debate was, of course, the most important one—the first time that voters had a chance to compare the two candidates directly. It was particularly important because the audience was one of the largest in the history of television to that point: 70 million people, almost three-quarters of the American adult population.[42]

Kennedy's opening remarks echoed the issues he had been promoting throughout his long campaign: that America was threatened by the spread of communism, and that only a strong and healthy America could ensure the survival of freedom. "I should make it very clear," he said, "that I do not think we are doing enough. I am not satisfied as an American with the progress we're making." He went on to present a litany of unmet needs and social failures: a floundering economy, "fifty per cent of our steel-mill capacity unused," children starving, schools deteriorating. "I'm not satisfied until every American enjoys his full constitutional rights," he said, opening the issue of segregation and race that he had mostly avoided during the primaries. "I think we can do better," he said again and again. "I don't want the talents of any American to go to waste."[43]

That Kennedy spoke first was a considerable advantage for him. In response to Kennedy's ambitious agenda, Nixon found himself picking around the edges—claiming to agree with Kennedy on the big things but disagreeing on the details. "I subscribe completely to the spirit Senator Kennedy has expressed . . . the spirit that the United States should move ahead," he said. But much of the rest of his statement—and much of the remainder of the debate—consisted of defenses of the Eisenhower administration. For most of the debate, Kennedy had the initiative while Nixon was mostly on the defense. Almost everyone agreed that Kennedy had "won" the debate.[44]

How the candidates looked also played a role. Nixon had not yet fully recovered from his infected knee, and he was still gaunt and pale. He was wearing a pale gray suit that blended with the background and that accentuated the pallor on his face (not helped by his pasty, inadequate makeup). "I don't know when I have ever felt so weak," Nixon later wrote of the days just before the debates.[45] Kennedy was dressed in a dark suit that emphasized his youth and what seemed to be his vigor and good health. While the television ratings showed Kennedy the winner, radio listeners tended to think Nixon had been the more impressive candidate—a result that has long been used to suggest that the debate was determined largely by the candidates' appearance. But it is equally likely that radio listeners (a much smaller audience than the television viewers) represented a different, older, and more isolated cohort.[46]

The subsequent debates continued to attract large audiences, though smaller than those who watched the first broadcast. Over the following weeks, about 50 million people watched each of the remaining three debates, which did little to shift the opinions of voters, most of whom had already made up their minds. Pundits varied in their opinions of who won each of the debates, but most agreed that overall they had helped Kennedy more than Nixon. After the final debate, the Gallup Poll announced that Kennedy now led Nixon by 51 percent to 45, representing a twelve-point shift from the summer, when Nixon had led by six points.[47]

With the debates behind him, and with the Catholic issue at least dampened, the most explosive issue was one that both candidates had hoped to avoid. Henry Cabot Lodge, Nixon's running mate, promised an audience in Harlem that Nixon would appoint an African American to the cabinet if elected. It was a promise that Nixon discovered only after the event, and it created considerable turmoil within the Republican campaign. Kennedy, when asked about the "pledge," responded to Lodge's promise by saying that the best-qualified people should fill government jobs. But he added, "I do believe that we should make a greater effort to bring Negroes into participation"—a position he had made clear weeks before at, among other places, Howard University.[48] A few days later, the civil rights leader Martin Luther King Jr. was arrested in the aftermath of a sit-in at an Atlanta restaurant. He was taken to the DeKalb County jail and then moved in chains to a rural prison for hard labor—the kind of sentence that often led black prisoners into great danger. Kennedy ignored the strong opposition of many of his aides (including his brother) and decided to telephone Coretta Scott King, who was terrified that her husband might be killed. Kennedy told her that he would do whatever he could to help, and within a few hours King was released. Black voters—along with many white ones—were drawn to what they considered his courage and compassion. Nixon said nothing. In the meantime, Lyndon Johnson was working tirelessly, stumping mostly in the South—and in Texas in particular—helping to arouse traditional Democrats and to divert them from Kennedy's outreach to King.[49]

In the campaign's final week, Eisenhower jumped into the race and helped Nixon close the gap. As voters went to the polls on November 8, the race looked like a dead heat. On election night, the returns continued well past midnight without any clear victor. Kennedy went to bed after midnight and left others to follow the votes. At 9 a.m., he woke up and came downstairs to be told that he was, at last, the president-elect. It was one of the closest elections in American history—a popular vote margin of just over 100,000 votes and a slim margin of 84 electoral votes out of 537. After the large Kennedy family gathered together, they rode in a cavalcade to the Hyannis armory. The new president-elect thanked the voters, the people who had worked on his campaign, and the disappointed Eisenhower and Nixon, both of whom had sent congratulatory messages. He finished his two-minute speech with a characteristically self-effacing statement: "And now my wife and I prepare for a new administration—and for a new baby."[50]

# 4

---

# The Perils of the New Frontier

His hands were trembling as he made his short speech in the Hyannis armory the morning after the election. He was exhausted—so much so that he spent his first weeks as president-elect isolated at his father's house in Palm Beach. Even two weeks later, Kennedy seemed distracted and testy. He complained about the demands already being made of him.

"This one wants that, that one wants this," he said to his father as they drove to a golf course. "You can't satisfy any of these people." Joe had no sympathy. "If you don't want the job, you don't have to take it," he replied sharply. "They're still counting votes in Cook County."[1]

Kennedy's distemper was partly a result of his continued weakness, which he worked hard to disguise. He had made sure to tell reporters that he was in "very good" health and had denied the rumors of Addison's disease—a reassurance that the *New York Times* repeated. ("They're saying you take cortisone," his press secretary, Pierre Salinger, once told him. "Well, I used to take cortisone, but I don't take it anymore," Kennedy falsely replied.)[2] His doctors had known otherwise for years but kept their knowledge to themselves. During part of almost every day, he soaked in a hot bath to relax his severe back pain. Only the powerful drugs he took from several doctors allowed him to appear healthy.[3]

Gradually, Kennedy regained his energy and began to organize his administration. One of his first decisions was to have no chief of staff—unlike Eisenhower (and unlike most presidents since). "He saw no need for staff meetings," Sorensen later wrote, "preferring the directness and increased confidentiality of one-on-one sessions." He chose familiar people as White House aides—young men like himself, many of them with long associations with him. There were the Boston friends and colleagues, semi-jokingly known as the Irish mafia: Kenneth O'Donnell, Lawrence O'Brien, and Dave Powers (one of the most senior White House advisers at the age of forty-eight). His closest friend, Lem Billings, had no official appointment, but he remained part of the inner circle, with his own bedroom in the White House. Ted Sorensen continued as Kennedy's principal aide; he wrote most of Kennedy's speeches and reviewed domestic policy (and later foreign policy) issues. McGeorge Bundy, a forty-one-year-old former Harvard dean, was appointed national security adviser and was clearly the most important foreign policy figure on the staff. Pierre Salinger, a thirty-five-year-old California journalist, took control of public information as the president's press secretary.[4]

If friends and contemporaries dominated the White House staff, men of experience and stature, some of them little known to Kennedy, filled most of the cabinet. Dean Rusk, his secretary of state, was a long-serving diplomat and former deputy secretary of state who would serve for eight years as a capable, if bureaucratic, pilot of the complex State Department. Douglas Dillon, secretary of the treasury, was an experienced and conservative investment banker and a lifelong Republican who had been undersecretary of state in the Eisenhower administration. Robert McNamara, secretary of defense and also a Republican, had little military experience but was known as a brilliant administrator in the Ford Motor Company, the kind of man Kennedy believed would be able to manage what seemed to be the unmanageable Pentagon. The remaining cabinet members were drawn from members of Congress, state governors, and the ranks of other politicians.[5]

The great exception was Robert Kennedy, the president's brother and his closest aide. Jack was determined to have him in the administration. He later explained his need for his brother to Ben Bradlee, in an interview for an article in *Newsweek* describing Bobby's qualities: "[Bobby has] high moral standards, strict personal ethics. He's a puritan, absolutely incorruptible. Then he has terrific executive energy. We've got more guys around here with ideas. The problem is to get things done. Bobby's the best organizer I've ever seen."[6] But most of all, Jack said, he needed Bobby's loyalty.

Everyone agreed that Bobby could not report to anyone other than the president. "It would be wholly impossible for any cabinet officer to have the President's brother as second in command," observed Dean Acheson, a former secretary of state under Truman. Nor could he serve in the White House. "Impossible," Bobby said. His presence would overwhelm the rest of the staff. Jack came up with the idea of making him attorney general, a post Bobby at first rejected. "It would be the 'Kennedy brothers' by the time a year was up," he warned, "and the President would be blamed for everything we had to do in civil rights."[7] Jack offered the post to Governor Abraham Ribicoff of Connecticut and to Adlai Stevenson, both of whom refused. Bobby continued to balk and finally called his brother to turn down the appointment. "I had to do something on my own," he said.[8] But Jack would not take no for an answer. He knew almost no one in the cabinet, he complained. "I need to know that when problems arise I'm going to have somebody who's going to tell the unvarnished truth, no matters what." Jack's most powerful argument was family. "If I can ask Dean Rusk to give up a career; . . . if I can ask Bob McNamara to give up a job as head of that company—these men I don't even know . . . certainly I can expect my own brother to give me the same sort of contribution."[9] Bobby finally agreed.

The opposition was considerable. At the University of Virginia Law School, where Bobby got his law degree, his former teachers let loose "a roar of incredulity." Newspapers were unimpressed, although most held their punches, reluctant to attack a president-elect so soon. Others complained of nepotism, inexperience, and ruthlessness (a term that would follow Bobby for many years). His testiness and diffidence did little to encourage his new colleagues in the Justice Department, or in the press. Byron White, his second in command, set out to staff the department with strong people, but he was worried about Kennedy's commitment and ability—and his youth. He was thirty-five when he became attorney general and had never practiced law. Over time, however, Bobby became comfortable in the job and won the respect of his colleagues.[10]

In many ways, the new president had the most trouble with his own constituents—the ardent New Dealers who bridled at any deviance from their liberalism. Arthur Schlesinger was one of them. He had supported Kennedy's campaign for the presidency, but his journals were filled with his dismay when Kennedy appointed Republicans to his administration. John Kenneth Galbraith, another committed liberal and an ardent Keynesian, wanted to fight the lingering recession by proposing government spending to stimulate the economy, but he lost the battle before Kennedy entered the White House. His colleague and more conservative rival Walter Heller, also a Keynesian, persuaded Kennedy to support a tax cut instead, to Galbraith's dismay. Even more disturbing to the liberals were the people they feared Kennedy was leaving out. "What about Averell? What about Orville?" Schlesinger asked, referring to the longtime diplomat and former New York governor Averell Harriman and Orville Freeman, the governor of Minnesota, also a stalwart liberal.[11] Kennedy remained cordial and supportive to the liberals, but he was not much interested in placating them. He brought Schlesinger into the administration with no real portfolio. ("I settled down in the East Wing of the White House and tried to find out what I was supposed to do," he later wrote.)[12] Almost all the liberals in the Kennedy circle were dismayed by the president's decision to retain J. Edgar Hoover as director of the FBI and Allen Dulles as director of the CIA. Kennedy's narrow election margin, and his own relative moderation, had led him down the path from the liberal true believers.[13]

• • •

The election was over, but the permanent campaign continued. Kennedy's aides suggested that he meet with Richard Nixon for what was essentially a photo shoot to demonstrate the statesmanship of both men. A few days after Election Day, Kennedy—tired as he was—helicoptered from Palm Springs to Nixon's retreat at Key Biscayne. It was an awkward meeting. Nixon did most of the talking.

A few weeks later, there was another, more important bipartisan meeting. Kennedy flew to Washington in early December to meet with President Eisenhower. Neither man had much respect for the other when they sat down in the Oval Office together for the first time. But to their mutual surprise, they were much more impressed with each other than either had expected. Kennedy said afterward that he now understood why Eisenhower had been elected president, that "there was a surprising force to the man."[14] Eisenhower was pleasantly surprised by Kennedy's knowledge and intelligence. He explained in great detail how he had organized his staff. But he sensed, correctly, that Kennedy was not interested in an organized chain of command.

At their second, and last, joint meeting at the White House, a day before Kennedy's inauguration, Eisenhower was blunter. Kennedy would have to put troops in Laos, he warned, to stop the otherwise inevitable fall of all the Southeast Asian nations: Thailand, Cambodia, Laos, and Vietnam. Toward the end of the meeting, the outgoing president turned to Cuba. "We cannot let the present government there go on," Eisenhower insisted.[15]

• • •

It was snowing heavily in Washington the night before Inauguration Day, January 20, 1961. But the snow stopped the next morning, and the weather turned bright, if still bitterly cold. People began filling up the stands early along Pennsylvania Avenue, bringing blankets and warm canteens. Kennedy attended services at a Catholic church in Georgetown, after a long night that included a gala organized by Frank Sinatra and parties with other friends and celebrities. (Friends claimed that he ended the evening with a private tryst with a young actress.)[16]

At eleven o'clock, the Kennedys had coffee with the Eisenhowers in the White House before the two presidents rode together up Pennsylvania Avenue. Chief Justice Earl Warren led Kennedy through the oath of office. The new president—his overcoat and hat abandoned on his chair—gave his much-praised inaugural address. It has often been said that the speech was entirely devoted to international issues: the Cold War, the threat of nuclear weapons, the dangers ahead, the menace of communism. But his characteristic call for energy, for moving forward, and for sacrifice was not just to combat communism. His most memorable phrase, "Ask not what the country will do for you—ask what you can do for your country" (adapted from a slogan at Choate) was also a call to Americans to elevate the nation's culture and to do more for the common good.[17] Kennedy had asked Robert Frost to write a poem for the event, but the aging poet could not read his own manuscript because of the glaring sunlight. Lyndon Johnson stood up and used his hat to protect him from the brightness, but to no avail. Instead, Frost recited another poem, from memory. It was a long day—hours of marching bands and floats during the inaugural parade and multiple inaugural balls. By the time the Kennedys returned for their first night in the White House, the staff had already sent Eisenhower's possessions off to Gettysburg and had unpacked the Kennedys' possessions and put them away.[18]

. . .

The Kennedy White House was organized like few other presidencies. The highly regarded book *Presidential Power*, by the political scientist Richard Neustadt, became a guide to Kennedy's White House structure. With Neustadt's advice, Kennedy relied upon what they considered Franklin Roosevelt's model. They rejected Eisenhower's rigid military management style and saw him as the slave of organization. Kennedy embraced what Schlesinger called "a fluid presidency."[19] He wanted to be involved with almost everything that was happening in the White House. He could as easily walk into the office of a junior staff member he had never met to discuss a policy issue as he could ask advice from his most senior advisers. "He abolished the pyramid structure of the White House staff," Sorensen wrote. "He paid little attention to organization charts and chains of command which diluted and distributed his authority."[20]

Despite the "fluid" quality of Kennedy's administration, there was a sharp divide between the White House and the rest of the government. The president considered most federal employees narrow-minded bureaucrats who stood in the way of progress. He seldom saw most of his own cabinet secretaries, and he had little interest in what they did—with the significant exceptions of Robert McNamara and Robert Kennedy. He called cabinet meetings "a waste of time." Through most of American history, secretaries of state had been among the most powerful officials in government. But Dean Rusk was clearly a secondary adviser to the president as McGeorge Bundy became the most powerful figure in managing Kennedy's foreign policy. Nor did Kennedy have much respect for Congress, despite his own fourteen-year service there. Only rarely did he engage directly with his former colleagues.[21]

The Kennedy administration's nonhierarchical character allowed many ideas to flow through the Oval Office. It also undermined the power of many established officers of government—both in the White House and in the federal government as a whole. Garry Wills, the journalist and historian, called it a "guerrilla government," an "attempt to rule *against* the government . . . delegitimating the very office they held." Wills portrayed Kennedy as a man who disdained organization and hierarchy and was drawn to "charismatic leadership," which made him alone the center of power.[22] This was something of an exaggeration. Most twentieth- (and twenty-first-) century presidents have seldom seen cabinet secretaries. Most have relied primarily on the White House staff. Most have used their own personalities to enhance their power.

But Kennedy's impatience with bureaucracy, his undisciplined eagerness to be at the center of almost all decision making, his desire for the broadest power possible to shape the contours of the world— these were the things that made him different from most of his predecessors. Kennedy wanted to "get things done," and to get them done in a hurry. That was what made him such an exciting figure to many Americans and to many people around the world. It also often frustrated many of his colleagues. Bundy wrote a remarkably sharp memo to the president in May 1961:

We do have a problem of management; centrally it is a problem of your use of time . . . We can't get you to sit still . . . Calling three meetings in five days is foolish—and putting them off for six weeks at a time is just as bad . . . Right now it is so hard to get to you with anything not urgent and immediate that about half of the papers and reports you personally ask for are never shown to you because by the time you are available you clearly have lost interest in them . . . If we put a little staff work on these and keep in close touch, we can be sure that all your questions are answered and that when they ask a big one, the expert himself is brought to recite. Will you try it?[23]

Kennedy tried, and he began to tolerate organized meetings more often. But he was easily bored, and he never met Bundy's hope of bringing consistent discipline to policy decisions.[24]

• • •

"The currents of vitality," Arthur Schlesinger wrote retrospectively of the first days of the Kennedy administration, "radiated out of the White House, flowed through the government and created a sense of vast possibility . . . Washington seemed engaged in a collective effort to make itself brighter, gayer, more intellectual, more resolute." There was a "flood of buoyant optimism. The Presidency was suddenly the center of action . . . thirty-nine messages and letters to Congress calling for legislation, ten prominent foreign visitors . . . nine press conferences . . . such promise of hope."[25]

But the first months of the Kennedy administration were less a triumph of politics and leadership than of style. Not since Theodore Roosevelt had a presidential family so fascinated the nation. Kennedy, unlike the bullish TR, attracted attention through his elegance and glamour. He was himself a handsome, articulate man—"that special grace," his friend Ben Bradlee once described his demeanor.[26] And he made up for his personal reticence with a sharp, intelligent wit and occasional self-effacement. He notably introduced himself at a luncheon in France in 1961 by saying, "I am the man who accompanied Jacqueline Kennedy to Paris."[27]

The first lady herself dazzled much of the world, with her beauty, her fashion, and her cultured, aristocratic demeanor. In Paris, she spoke fluent French and talked with cultural and intellectual figures. In Washington, she redecorated the White House and then, in early 1962, gave a televised tour that—despite her breathy, hushed voice—attracted an enormous audience. In the White House, she entertained frequently and lavishly, almost always including great cultural figures as well as diplomats and politicians. Her dresses and her recipes were widely copied. Her frequent unhappiness with the demands of her position was seldom visible to the public. But she spent much time away from the White House (and from her husband) at an estate in Middleburg, Virginia, where she could ride horses.[28]

At Hickory Hill in McLean, Virginia, Robert Kennedy's estate became another center of glamour, if a much more chaotic one. Bobby invited experts to talk about guerrilla warfare and nuclear strategy, while his many young children and his large dogs raced through the house. On summer days, large crowds of Kennedy "friends"—which included politicians, diplomats, journalists, writers, actors, singers, and liberal business leaders—floated across the broad lawn and gathered around the swimming pool. Often, some unlucky guest at the party would be pushed into the water. "It was all great fun," Schlesinger wrote, "a perfect expression of the rowdier aspects of the New Frontier." (He felt differently when he himself was pushed into a pool at another party filled with Kennedys.)[29]

The rest of the extended Kennedy family added to the fascination. The notorious Joe stayed out of the limelight (and late in 1961 was stricken by a severe stroke that left him an invalid for the rest of his life). But the president's siblings were constantly visible. Ted, the youngest of the family, was preparing to run in 1962 for his brother's former Senate seat in Massachusetts. The Kennedy sisters were similarly visible. Pat was married to the actor Peter Lawford. Eunice's husband, Sargent Shriver, became the first director of the Peace Corps. Jean was married to Stephen Smith, who managed the family's substantial finances. Comedians and television celebrities made jokes about the size and the ambitions of the family, but they added to the public's curiosity and fascination.

The president himself was more aloof than the other members of his family—in part because of his own temperament and health, and also because of the nature of the White House. But he nevertheless dazzled much of the public in the early months of his presidency—not least through his entertaining press conferences. Eisenhower, who was a dull and uncomfortable speaker, had met with the press in a cramped hearing room in the Executive Office Building next to the White House. Kennedy moved the press conferences to a large auditorium in the State Department, where they could be televised and where more reporters could be accommodated. He was adept at answering questions he wanted to answer, and even more adept at evading those he wanted to avoid. His quick, witty, and often eloquent responses were due partly to his own elegance and partly to massive research and support.[30]

• • •

The abounding optimism, the hope, the gaiety, and the vigor of the New Frontier was particularly important to Kennedy in his early months in office, because there were few significant achievements in the first year of his presidency.

Kennedy's inaugural address had been largely concerned with the Cold War. But his first State of the Union address on January 30 focused on the economy, which was emerging from a seven-month recession—preceded, Kennedy said, by "three and one half years of slack, seven years of diminished economic growth, and nine years of falling income." Having said very little about poverty and unemployment during his campaign, or indeed during his political career, he spoke about "those who are without jobs" and who "live almost without hope." He listed other problems: excessive government spending, inadequate education, juvenile crime, and the absence of medical care for the aged. He justified many of these efforts by alarmist warnings that the American economic growth rate was lagging behind that of the Soviet Union.[31]

But Kennedy's ambitious domestic programs made little progress in his first two years. At first, he blamed his lack of achievements on the House Rules Committee, which determined what bills could be brought to the floor. Despite the Democratic majority in the House, conservatives—Republicans and southern Democrats—dominated the committee and kept bills they disliked from going to a vote, which included many of Kennedy's initiatives. Against the advice of House leaders, Kennedy set out to reshape the committee so as to create a liberal majority in the Rules Committee. He proposed increasing the number of members of the committee so as to allow new members to create a liberal majority. He put enormous pressure on Democratic members of the House, and he won the battle narrowly (by a vote of 217 to 212).[32]

The victory did not help him very much. Democrats had a nominal eighty-nine-seat majority in the House of Representatives, but the real majority consisted of the same coalition of Republicans and southern Democrats that had stubbornly blocked most of his liberal measures in the Rules Committee. The closeness of Kennedy's election—he had run far behind most Democratic members of Congress in 1960—gave him little leverage. Kennedy still had to battle with the conservative coalition. And he was not very good at battling. He surrendered under pressure from fiscal conservatives and pledged a balanced budget. That promise made it almost impossible for him to stimulate the economy either by increasing spending or by lowering taxes. Not until 1963 did he propose a tax cut as an economic stimulus, and not until 1964, after his death, did Congress approve it, by which time the economy was already robustly expanding. Other programs—aid to education, health insurance for the aged, college scholarships, the creation of a department of housing and urban development, and many others—were all thwarted. And despite growing pressure for civil rights for African Americans, Kennedy believed there was insufficient public support and did not even submit a bill to Congress. He did succeed in raising the minimum wage and strengthening Social Security. He also won a modest education bill. But his successes were rare in a year of much frustration.[33]

Kennedy tried to compensate for his slim legislative successes by using executive orders (a strategy presidents often fall back upon when facing an obdurate Congress). He issued sixty-nine executive orders in his first year—some of them effective, others mostly symbolic. Among them was his creation of the first-ever Presidential Commission on the Status of Women. Most of the orders were largely unpublicized, but many of them were significant. Later, executive orders would play a large role in Kennedy's cautious civil rights agenda.

Not surprisingly, international initiatives were the most important issues to Kennedy. "It really is true that foreign affairs are the only important issue for a President to handle," he told Richard Nixon (who privately agreed with him). "I mean who gives a shit if the minimum wage is $1.15 or $1.25 in comparison."[34] Among these initiatives (a result of an executive order) was the highly popular Peace Corps, which sent young men and women across the globe to fight poverty and oppression in less-developed regions. "The vast task of economic development urgently requires skilled people to do the work of the society," he said. It would be "an organization which will recruit and train American volunteers, sending them abroad to work with the people of other nations." And he proposed a new initiative in Latin America, which he named the "Alliance for Progress." Kennedy called it "a vast cooperative effort, unparalleled in magnitude and nobility of purpose, to satisfy the basic needs of the American people for homes, work, and land, health and schools."[35] But despite its bold ambitions, the Alliance met with skepticism among Latin American nations; many people believed that it was simply another anticommunist effort to isolate Castro and other left-leaning regimes.[36]

. . .

In his discussions with Eisenhower shortly before his inauguration, Kennedy first heard about plans for overthrowing the communist regime of Fidel Castro in Cuba. It was no secret that Cuba was not only a geopolitical problem for the United States, but a commercial one as well. "Large amounts of capital now planned for investment in Latin America are waiting to see whether or not we can cope with the Cuban situation," Eisenhower's secretary of the treasury, Robert Anderson, had told Kennedy.[37]

Planning for the overthrow of the Castro regime was already under way in the fall of 1960. Even before he took office, Kennedy was under great pressure to take over the Eisenhower administration's plan—sending armed Cuban refugees back into Cuba, equipped by the American military and supported by American air attacks. The goal was to undermine and possibly overthrow the regime, or, if that failed, for the armed refugees to fade into the mountains and continue the insurgency. That pressure increased when Kennedy's aide Richard Goodwin provided the *New York Times* information that appeared on the front page under the headline "Kennedy Asks Aid for Cuban Rebels to Defeat Castro, Urges Support of Exiles and 'Fighters for Freedom.' "[38] The statement was an attempt to get ahead of Nixon's own efforts to take advantage of the proposed invasion. Kennedy was not informed and was troubled by the story. The press announcement increased the pressure on him to continue the invasion once he was in office.[39]

By the time he entered the White House, Kennedy had been fully briefed by CIA agents and outgoing Eisenhower staffers. Émigré Cubans were already being trained and equipped, and the momentum behind the effort seemed almost unstoppable. Kennedy remained uncertain about the likelihood of success, but he tentatively agreed to move forward because Allen Dulles, his deputy Richard Bissell, and other CIA officers seemed so confident. The key to success would be Cubans themselves, who—they assured him—would rise up to join the invasion because of their supposed hatred of the Castro regime. "They now know all the details of the plan and are enthusiastic," a CIA memo wrote of the émigré invaders. "The young officers are young, vigorous, intelligent and motivated with a fanatical urge to begin battle . . . Without exception they have utmost confidence in the ability to win."[40]

But others involved in the planning were skeptical about anticommunist sentiment in Cuba. Sherman Kent, a prominent CIA figure in the planning of the invasion, warned, "We see no signs that such developments portend any serious threat to a regime which by now has established a formidable structure of control over the daily lives of the Cuban people," he wrote.[41] Claiborne Pell, a former foreign service officer and newly elected senator from Rhode Island, also disputed the CIA's belief that the population of the island would turn against Castro. After a visit to Cuba, he told the *New York Herald Tribune*, "The people of Cuba that I saw and spoke to . . . were not sullen or unhappy or dissatisfied . . . they were still tasting the satisfaction of Castro's land reform, of his nationalization of United States companies and of the other much-touted reforms put into effect by Castro. The dispossessed and disgruntled were in jail or in exile."[42] Arthur Schlesinger, who had been asked by the president to look into the Cuban situation, was also highly skeptical ("a terrible idea," he once said)—as were Adlai Stevenson and even Dean Rusk.[43] But they mostly kept their reservations to themselves. William Fulbright, the chairman of the Senate Foreign Relations Committee, had no such reticence and argued intensely against the operation. "To give this activity even covert support is of a piece with the hypocrisy and cynicism for which the United States is constantly denouncing the Soviet Union," he insisted. His views were brushed aside.[44]

Most CIA officers continued to insist that the Castro regime was "tottering" and that the opposition forces in Cuba were "enjoying great popularity."[45] Perhaps the most influential supporter was McGeorge Bundy. There were risks, Bundy told the president, but he insisted that the risk of allowing the Castro regime to stay in place was even more dangerous. Although the invasion was still mostly secret, Kennedy knew it would not stay that way. If he canceled the operation, the émigrés would certainly complain publicly, and he feared that the CIA would leak damaging information. The new, young, untested president who had presented himself as a tough fighter against communism had much to lose if he were to back out of the mission now.[46]

. . .

By early April, the invasion was beginning to take shape. Little time remained for debate. But as the operation drew closer, Kennedy became more ambivalent. On the one hand, he was bombarded by optimistic CIA memos. "Sabotage and organized resistance are continuing to increase throughout Cuba," one intelligence memo said. "Opposition to the Castro regime is becoming more open," said another.[47] And yet he was fearful of a large American military presence, and he ordered the CIA to trim down the operation—no longer an "invasion," he said, but an "infiltration." No American troops would land in Cuba, Kennedy insisted, and only a small cadre of American pilots would fly secretly over the country. The Joint Chiefs of Staff were appalled at what they considered the "totally inadequate" transportation and the weakness of the proposed air support, but the absolute ban on American troops in Cuba left them little room for maneuver. Most of them quietly assumed that if the operation were to go badly, the American military would have to intervene to save it. Kennedy had no such intentions.[48]

At a climactic and disorganized meeting in the White House shortly before the operation began, the president was still unsure. He was worried about the chiefs of staff's pessimism. But he was encouraged that among his other advisers, only Senator Fulbright had opposed the invasion. "We'd better sleep over it," Kennedy said.[49] But by the next morning, he was committed. The *New York Times* and other newspapers were beginning to receive information on the invasion, and only under tremendous pressure from the White House did they refrain from printing what they knew. It was already clear that an operation was under way. "If they get into trouble," James Reston wrote in his influential column, "will [the administration] continue to supply them?"[50] It turned out to be an important question.

The invasion itself finally began on April 17, and from the start it was a fiasco. The expected spontaneous uprising of anti-Castro forces did not emerge in significant numbers. It took two days for the émigrés to get on shore, after finding themselves barred by rocky shores and high winds. Ammunition ships failed to reach the beaches. Castro's Cuban forces were already in place to prevent the U.S.-supported brigades from making any real progress. The invasion rapidly unraveled—a result of bungled planning, bad information, and the lack of sufficient soldiers and weapons. By the second day, the mission had changed from overthrowing the Cuban government to rescuing the émigrés. The Castro regime was never in serious danger. Kennedy tried to minimize the damage and make the failure "an incident, not a disaster." But there was no way to avoid what the operation really was—a catastrophe.[51]

An important element of the disaster was the role of the air attacks. The disguised American planes did damage to some Cuban military sites before the invasion, but not enough to weaken Castro's air capacities. Kennedy remained determined to disguise the American role in the invasion, and he refused to send in American planes. But it was, of course, virtually impossible to hide the fact that the invasion was an American project, and the cancellation of air strikes ensured the American defeat. "Everything is lost," Allen Dulles said in despair. "The Cuban invasion is a total failure."[52] Even so, the CIA quietly continued planning for another effort to defeat the Castro regime.[53]

What Kennedy tried to label the "incident" included the death of four American pilots and sixteen anti-Castro Cubans. The Cuban military lost almost two hundred soldiers. An unknown number of other Cubans, some of them civilians, were also casualties of the battle. Other anti-Castro Cubans were executed, tortured, or imprisoned in the aftermath of the invasion, as were several American CIA operatives caught on the island. (The CIA appeared not to have obeyed Kennedy's order that no Americans should join the operation in Cuba itself.)[54]

As what came to be known as the Bay of Pigs venture deteriorated, Kennedy—distraught and angry—invited Richard Nixon to visit him in the White House. Nixon expressed shock that Kennedy had not allowed American forces to intervene once the battle had begun, and he encouraged the president to do so. Kennedy refused. On April 20, he spoke to the press. "There's an old saying that victory has a hundred fathers and defeat is an orphan," he said, invoking a phrase from Galeazzo Ciano, Mussolini's foreign minister. Kennedy blamed no one but himself and insisted, "I am the responsible officer of the government."[55]

Maxwell Taylor, a former army chief of staff and friend of Kennedy, faulted what he considered the sloppy decision making. He told the White House aides who had supported the invasion: "You have to look him in the eye and say, 'I think it's a lousy idea, Mr. President. The chances are about one in ten.' And nobody said that." But to many of his disappointed colleagues, and to the majority of the American people, this simple admission of failure—far from damaging his popularity—significantly enhanced his stature. His popularity polling reached the highest level of his presidency—83 percent approval. "It's just like Eisenhower," the president said dismissively. "The worse I do, the more popular I get."[56]

Outside the United States, however, the aftermath of the Bay of Pigs was a major blow to Kennedy's international reputation—and nowhere more than in the Kremlin, where Nikita Khrushchev, the Soviet premier, began a remarkable correspondence with the now-chastened American president. In the first months of his presidency, Kennedy had corresponded with Khrushchev through a series of cordial messages congratulating him on the Soviet space program and other achievements. Khrushchev had responded in kind, hoping that Kennedy would reduce the tensions between the two nations. He had even published Kennedy's inaugural address in the Soviet newspapers and had told his colleagues that the new president had "disapproved of the policy of Cold War and worsening international relationships." But in the aftermath of the Bay of Pigs the tone of the messages from the Kremlin changed dramatically.

I send you this message in an hour of alarm, fraught with danger for the peace of the whole world. Armed aggression has begun against Cuba. It is a secret to no one that the armed bands invading this country were trained, equipped and armed in the United States of America. The planes which are bombing Cuban cities belong to the United States of America, the bombs they are dropping are being supplied by the American Government. All of this evokes here in the Soviet Union an understandable feeling of indignation on the part of the Soviet Government and the Soviet people.[57]

Kennedy responded with a combination of evasiveness and defiance.

> You are under a serious misapprehension in regard to events in Cuba. For months there has been evident and growing resistance to the Castro dictatorship . . . I have previously stated, and I repeat now, that the United States intends no military intervention in Cuba . . . While refraining from military intervention in Cuba, the people of the United States do not conceal their admiration for Cuban patriots who wish to see a democratic system in an independent Cuba. The United States government can take no action to stifle the spirit of liberty.[58]

Late at night after the failure, Kennedy left his crowded office and walked for an hour on the White House lawn, still wearing the white tie he had worn for a congressional reception earlier in the evening. According to Jacqueline Kennedy, he

> came back over to the White House to his bedroom and he started to cry, just with me . . . just put his head in his hands and sort of wept. . . . And it was so sad, because all his first hundred days and all his dreams, and then this awful thing to happen. And . . . all those poor men who you'd sent off with all their hopes and promises that we'd back them and there they were, shot down like dogs going to jail. He cared so much about them.[59]

In the Oval Office the next morning, Kennedy's first appointment was with Senator Albert Gore of Tennessee. The president was still distraught, at times in tears, Gore later recalled. "His hair was disheveled . . . his tie was askew, he talked too fast and he was extremely bitter, especially at Lemnitzer"—General Lyman Lemnitzer, the chairman of the Joint Chiefs of Staff. Privately, Kennedy felt he had been "framed," a self-pitying excuse for his own mistakes.[60] And his trust in the military was much reduced in the aftermath. Shortly after, he met with the cabinet. Robert Kennedy waited until the president had left the Cabinet Room and let loose his own distress. "We've got to do something," he told his colleagues. "All you bright fellows have gotten the President into this, and if you don't do something now, my brother will be regarded as a paper tiger by the Russians." That, of course, is what the members of the cabinet (few of whom had even known about the invasion) feared. Dean Rusk, perhaps the least emotional member of the cabinet, pounded his hand on the president's empty chair and said, "What matters now is this man. We have to save this man!"[61]

Despite his statement that he alone was responsible for the fiasco, Kennedy quietly told Allen Dulles and Richard Bissell that they would have to resign. He also had to placate the Cuban refugee officers who, they believed, had been abandoned by the president. He dispatched Adolf Berle and Arthur Schlesinger, presidential aides with a Latin American portfolio, to Miami to meet with them. ("I can think of happier missions," Berle said.)[62] But the anger was too great for middle-level officials to calm the storm. Instead, the Cuban officers were flown to Washington to meet with Kennedy in person.

Kennedy also had to deal with Adlai Stevenson, who had defended the invasion in the United Nations even though he had personally opposed it. He had told the United Nations (not knowing otherwise) that "the United States has committed no aggression against Cuba . . . No Americans were involved."[63] He was furious when the cover story unraveled and he learned that his words had been untrue. "He was disgusted," a colleague said. "He felt that this had tarnished his image." He considered resigning but thought better of it.[64] And Kennedy had to placate Eisenhower, who chided him for not hearing all views: "Everybody [should have been] in front of you debating the thing so you [got] the pros and cons yourself."[65] Kennedy's aversion to formal meetings had not served him well.

After a tempestuous week of discussions, he agreed to produce a "Record of Action," which said that "the United States should not undertake military intervention in Cuba now, but should do nothing that would foreclose the possibility of military intervention in the future."[66] But he faced another humiliation. He had to provide

American farm equipment to Cuba in exchange for some of the imprisoned anti-Castro soldiers.[67]

· · ·

"The Cuban affair," Schlesinger wrote privately at the time, "has produced . . . a profound prejudice against the taking of risks anywhere . . . there is now a general predisposition against boldness in all fields."[68] The press was more critical. "As John Kennedy closed out the first 100 days of his Administration," *Time* magazine's editors wrote, "the U.S. had suffered a month-long series of setbacks rare in the history of the Republic." Republicans in the House of Representatives spent a long day criticizing the president for "going from crisis to crisis."[69]

Kennedy's bold public response to the defeat hid the darkest period of his presidency. He had changed course in the midst of the battle for fear of revealing America's participation—a participation that was already known throughout the world. Most disturbing to the president was the image of weakness, something Kennedy loathed. He was shattered by the reality of his failure. "It was the worst experience of my life," he told Nixon.[70] It was not only the failure of the Bay of Pigs that distressed him. It was the prospect of his imminent summit meeting with Khrushchev in Vienna, where he would have to confront the most dangerous issue of the time: the status of Berlin. Back from a visit to the Kremlin, Walter Lippmann, the influential columnist, told Kennedy that Khrushchev was feeling very cocky. Despite Kennedy's occasional bravado about going back into Cuba, he knew that the opportunity was gone. "There is a good chance," he said, "that, if we move on Cuba, Khrushchev will move on Berlin."[71]

# 5

---

# "Flexible Response"

Late in May 1961, Kennedy decided to present a second State of the Union address—only four months after his first. He explained the unusual timing as a result of "extraordinary times." His January speech had focused mostly on domestic affairs. But his May speech included only a cursory call for "economic and social progress at home." Instead, he devoted the bulk of his long speech to international issues. He called for America to help economic progress abroad; for military reorganization and disarmament; and for the exploration of space, which he saw as part of how to "win the battle that is now going on around the world between freedom and tyranny." These were all goals consistent with his bold rhetoric. But such a speech, only a month after the Cuban catastrophe, almost certainly grew out of the unhappy results of his first hundred days, which included the Bay of Pigs disaster and a series of legislative defeats as well. It was as if he was trying to relaunch his presidency as he set off on another momentous challenge. "I have long thought it wise to meet with the Soviet Premier for a personal exchange of views," Kennedy concluded his speech as he announced that he would meet with Khrushchev in Vienna in early June. "We will make clear America's enduring concern is for both peace *and* freedom—that we are anxious to live in harmony with the Russian people—that we seek no conquests, no satellites, no riches—that we seek only the day when 'nation shall not lift upward against nation, neither shall they learn war any more.'"[1]

. . .

Among the many proposals in Kennedy's second State of the Union address was a call for "achieving the goal, before this decade is out, of landing a man on the moon and returning him safely to the earth." There were many reasons for this ambitious goal. Kennedy was still shaken by his first-year failures, and he saw space exploration as a way to raise American prestige and to revive his own claim of boldness. But the space program was not just a dazzling scientific achievement. It was also, he believed, a way of bolstering the nation's military strength. Falling behind the Soviets in space was a sensitive issue to him and many others. The Soviet Union had launched the first satellite in 1957, and Yuri Gagarin had become the first man to travel into space and to orbit the earth in April 1961, before the United States had yet to launch any manned space flight at all. "I saw a survey taken the other day of young French students, asking which countries they regarded as ahead in various areas of which systems," Kennedy noted testily. "About 67 or 68 percent regarded the Soviet Union as being first in science and technology."[2]

There was some skepticism in Congress and in the press about the cost of such an effort, but Kennedy insisted. "I do not think the United States can afford to become second in space," he told an informal press conference on June 14, 1962, "because I think that space has too many implications militarily, politically, psychologically, and all the rest . . . I think the United States cannot permit the Soviet Union to become dominant in the sea of space. There are many military implications to it which are still yet unknown."[3]

On May 5, 1961, Alan Shepard became the first American astronaut to travel into space—a relatively short trip of 300 miles, but 115 miles high, well outside the earth's atmosphere. The Shepard flight was a sufficient success to embolden Kennedy to make his pledge to reach the moon in his speech to Congress later that month, and it only intensified his eagerness to send out an astronaut who could orbit the earth, as Gagarin had already done. Nine months later, on February 20, 1962, more than 100 million Americans would watch as the rocket carrying John Glenn, a seasoned marine pilot, took off

from Cape Canaveral, Florida. Kennedy was extraordinarily tense
as Glenn navigated three times around the earth, but he was jubi-
lant once he landed safely in the Atlantic near Bermuda.[4]

• • •

The foreign policy of the Kennedy years, as the Cuban failure suggested, was a work in progress in the spring of 1961. But it was clear
that he would be simultaneously more cautious and at times more
reckless than Eisenhower had been. In 1956, Secretary of State
John Foster Dulles described the American Cold War strategy of
the 1950s as "brinkmanship": a risky strategy that rested on "the
ability to get to the verge without getting into the war. If you cannot master it, you inevitably get into war. If you try to run away
from it, if you are scared to go to the brink, you are lost."[5] The
Eisenhower administration would, in short, rely on nuclear weapons to intimidate the nation's adversaries, the Soviet Union most
importantly. They believed that Khrushchev would back down
before armaggedon. Dulles liked the idea because it was "tough"
and intimidating. Eisenhower supported the strategy (which was
known at the time as the "New Look") in part because it would avoid
the creation of a "garrison state" and would provide a less expensive
approach to the Cold War.[6]

    Kennedy was skeptical of the Eisenhower-Dulles strategy. He had
a much greater aversion to nuclear weapons than his predecessors
did, especially after the tests of the first hydrogen bombs. He had
long wanted to slow down the growth of nuclear weapons. But he
also wanted an alternative—a way to deal with problems around
the world without relying on global war. This new approach came
to be known as "flexible response": a strategy that would give the
United States a greater ability to intervene against aggression using
conventional arms with limited goals. Although he had dismissed
Allen Dulles and Richard Bissell, the top leaders of the CIA, in the
aftermath of the Bay of Pigs, he continued to rely on the agency
even more than Eisenhower had done. He also took a particular interest in the Special Forces (known as the Green Berets), an elite
military force inspired by British troops who were trained to fight

unconventionally, including guerrilla warfare. Kennedy expanded the Special Forces and gave them significant publicity. Robert Kennedy, also a champion of counterinsurgency, kept a green beret on his desk in the Justice Department.[7]

· · ·

Among the many costs of the Bay of Pigs failure was the deterioration of Kennedy's relationship with Khrushchev as he was preparing for the Vienna summit meeting. Many issues awaited him in Europe, but the most dangerous was the future of Berlin. At the end of World War II, the Western and Soviet armies had temporarily divided defeated Germany. Gradually, these makeshift boundaries became a lasting separation, with the Soviet-occupied area becoming the nation of East Germany and the Western allies' area becoming West Germany. "All of us know," Kennedy said in Paris, "that Germany will probably never be reunified."[8] But the future of Berlin, located in the middle of East Germany and divided into two cities, remained a sore point within the communist world. The Soviet leaders considered partitioned Berlin an insult. More important, the division had created a problem for East Germany, whose citizens were fleeing in vast numbers into West Berlin. Khrushchev had insisted that Berlin must be united under the control of East Germany. Kennedy wanted to evade the issue, aware that there was no visible solution to the dilemma. Both leaders knew that Berlin would be the most important question at the summit that was scheduled for Vienna in June.[9]

The president's first stop on his European trip was Paris, where Kennedy received an ecstatic reception as he rode through the streets with French president Charles de Gaulle. "Side by side, the two men moved all day through Paris," the *New York Times* wrote, "age beside youth, grandeur beside informality, mysticism beside pragmatism, serenity beside eagerness."[10] The great banquet for the Kennedys dazzled not only the Parisians but also the Americans at home. The *Washington Post* wrote gushingly that it was "indescribably elegant" (largely because of Jacqueline's enormous popularity there).[11] More important to Kennedy, however, was to seek advice from de Gaulle about how to deal with Khrushchev. "It is important," the French president told him forcefully, "to show that we do not intend to let this situation change. *Any* retreat from Berlin, *any* change of status, *any* withdrawal of troops . . . would mean defeat. It would result in an almost complete loss of Germany." That was not what Kennedy wanted to hear, especially when de Gaulle announced that if Khrushchev wanted war "we must make clear to him he will have it."[12]

Privately, de Gaulle expressed only tepid confidence in Kennedy's ability to match wits with Khrushchev in Vienna. Others were not even that certain. William Fulbright expressed "great nervousness" about Kennedy's readiness for the summit.[13] The journalist Richard Rovere observed, "Mr. Khrushchev may not see in our young President quite all that Theodore Sorensen and Charles Bohlen see in him."[14] The diplomat George F. Kennan was concerned that the Soviets would deliberately undermine the summit meeting to weaken America's "world position and influence . . . [by] an all-out propaganda attack that could include an effort to eclipse and embarrass at their summit talks."[15] Khrushchev himself worried that the president might proceed from what he called a "completely wrong basis" and would repeat what he considered Eisenhower's "many errors" (which Khrushchev defined as Eisenhower's intransigence). That, Khrushchev said, would be "absolutely unacceptable."[16] Unknown to all but a few intimates, Kennedy approached the summit in weak health and great pain, soaking for hours in a hot bath to make it possible for him to walk or even to sit for a few hours—another problem that his closest colleagues feared might weaken his negotiating.[17]

The American ambassador to the Soviet Union, Llewellyn Thompson, warned Kennedy that if there was no progress on Berlin, Khrushchev might unilaterally move to incorporate West Berlin into East Germany. That event, Thompson warned, would produce an unthinkable humiliation to the West, and perhaps war. At the least, Thompson predicted, Khrushchev would "seal off the sector boundary in order to stop what they must consider the intolerable continuation of the refugee flow through Berlin."[18] Kennedy was not yet ready to settle the Berlin issue. His plan was delay—

perhaps for as long as five years—to avoid having to make a difficult decision in Vienna. It was an unrealistic hope.

Kennedy and Khrushchev arrived in Vienna early on June 3—Khrushchev with little attention, Kennedy in a large motorcade that moved through great throngs of cheering Austrians. After arriving at the American embassy, the two leaders spent a few minutes of awkward small talk and then began their first serious conversation— although one that Ambassador Thompson had warned the president to avoid. It was a discussion of the relative strengths of communism and democratic capitalism, a tedious debate that Thompson had correctly predicted would go nowhere. "Communism exists and has won its right to develop," Khrushchev argued, noting that former secretary of state Dulles "had based his policy on the premise of liquidation of the Communist system." Kennedy responded that "the Soviet Union was seeking to eliminate free systems in areas that are associated with us." Khrushchev said that "ideas should be propagated without the use of arms or interference in the internal affairs of other states. If Communist ideas should spread in other countries, the USSR would be happy, just as the US would be glad if capitalist ideas were to spread." The conversation came to a testy end when Kennedy warned about what turned out to be a very sensitive word for Khrushchev: "miscalculation." He responded with a tirade. He accused Kennedy of wanting the USSR "to sit like a school boy with his hands on the table," and he insisted that "the term 'miscalculation' should be stored away." Perhaps the most useful comment of this conversation was Khrushchev's suggestion that he "would not try to convince the President about the advantages of Communism, just as the President should not waste time to convert him to capitalism."[19]

Kennedy was on the defensive from the start, and so it continued through the afternoon, as Kennedy tried and failed to find common ground. Khrushchev pounded on the "miscalculations" of the United States. During an informal walk after lunch (according to Kenny O'Donnell and Dave Powers, watching from the window), "Khrushchev was carrying on a heated argument, circling around Kennedy and snapping at him like a terrier and shaking his finger."[20]

He "treated me like a little boy," Kennedy later complained.[21] By the time their second session came to an end, Kennedy was exhausted (it was rare for him to go so long without rest and medication). So far, he had made little progress. Never did Kennedy challenge Khrushchev on the USSR's greatest flaws: the use of violence against uprisings in Hungary and East Germany, the secret prisons for dissidents, the 3.5 million refugees fleeing East Berlin. "This man is very inexperienced, even immature," Khrushchev told his interpreter. "Compared to him, Eisenhower is a man of intelligence and vision."[22] On other issues—Iran, China, Korea—the awkward parrying between the confident Khrushchev and the defensive Kennedy continued.[23]

· · ·

Both men understood that the real issue of the summit was Berlin, by far the most difficult question they would encounter in Vienna. On that issue there would be no agreement. Khrushchev was adamant that West Berlin must be incorporated into East Germany through a peace treaty—with or without American agreement. He tried to soften his demands by suggesting that a united Berlin would become a "free city," with open access from Western nations. But he was insistent that East Germany would have "sovereignty" over the city. He wanted to "sign a peace treaty and the sovereignty of the GDR [German Democratic Republic] will be observed. Any violation of that sovereignty will be regarded by the USSR as an act of open aggression against a peace-loving country with all the consequences ensuing therefrom."[24]

Kennedy responded with equal determination. "We fought our way [into Germany] during World War II," he said. "We are in Berlin not by agreement of East Germany but by contractual rights."[25]

In this long and difficult day, what Khrushchev rightly called "this sore spot . . . this thorn" led to an intractable dispute. Both leaders claimed that they were in danger of unacceptable humiliation. "US intentions did not bode anything good," Khrushchev said. "The USSR considered all of Berlin GDR territory . . . if the US should start a war over Berlin there was nothing the USSR could do about it . . . This constitutes a threat of World War III which would be even more devastating than World War II." Kennedy replied that Khrushchev wanted to "precipitate a crisis . . . by seeking a change in the existing situation." He told Khrushchev that even though he was a "young man," he had "not assumed office to accept arrangements totally inimical to US interests." He had "come here to prevent a confrontation face to face between our two countries," and he "regretted to leave Vienna with this impression." But Khrushchev called his decision on Berlin "irrevocable." Kennedy replied, "If that's true, it's going to be a cold winter."[26]

Kennedy was disappointed by what he considered his failure at the summit. "Worst thing in my life," he told the *New York Times* columnist James Reston. "He savaged me . . . I've got two problems. First, to figure out why he did it, and in such a hostile way. And second, to figure out what we can do about it." Reston, whose interview was off the record, nevertheless wrote in the *Times* that Kennedy "was astonished by the rigidity and toughness of the Soviet leader."[27]

On his return to Washington, Kennedy was brooding about an imminent doomsday, fearful that Khrushchev would move against West Berlin. His aides told him that their only plan for the defense of Berlin was to use nuclear weapons. "Goddamit . . . use your head," Kennedy snapped at Roswell Gilpatric, the deputy secretary of defense. "What we are talking about is seventy million dead Americans."[28] Bundy's conclusion was equally bleak: "The only plan the United States had for the use of strategic weapons was a massive, total, comprehensive obliterating attack upon the Soviet Union. . . . [and] the Warsaw Pact countries and Red China."[29] It was not only casualties that worried Kennedy. It was also his own credibility. "There are limits to the number of defeats I can defend in one twelve-month period," he told his aides.[30] The columnist Joseph Alsop wrote an article for the *Saturday Review* about a meeting he had with Kennedy and titled it "The Most Important Decision in U.S. History." He asked "whether the United States should risk something close to national suicide in order to avoid national surrender."[31] In early August, Kennedy announced a civil defense program "to stiffen public willingness to support U.S. use of nuclear weapons if necessary."[32]

Throughout much of the summer, Kennedy spoke publicly and often about the crisis. "West Berlin," he said in a televised speech in July, "has now become—as never before—the great testing place of Western courage and will, a focal point where our solemn commitments stretching back over the years since 1945 and Soviet ambitions now meet in basic confrontation . . . We have given our word that an attack upon that city will be regarded as an attack upon us all."[33] The speech was more for Khrushchev than it was for the American audience.

Kennedy's powerful rhetoric on defending West Berlin bothered, and even outraged, some of his colleagues and many West Germans because he seemed to be ready to abandon the communist sector of the city. Once again, he faced accusations of "weakness." The postwar treaty of 1945 called for a united Berlin, and there were many Germans—and some Americans—who considered his position a surrender of half the city. William Fulbright complicated the debate by asking "why the East Germans don't close their border, because I think they have a right to close it."[34] Kennedy did not refute Fulbright's claim, and he told Deputy National Security Adviser Walt Rostow that Khrushchev "will have to do something to stop the flow of refugees. Perhaps a wall. And we won't be able to prevent it."[35]

A few days later, in the early hours of August 13, 1961, the border between East and West Berlin was closed—and would remain so for twenty-eight years. The barrier began with barbed-wire fences but quickly evolved into tall concrete walls, ending the complicated relationships that had shaped Berlin since 1945. There was outrage in West Berlin and fear of what might happen next. But Kennedy's response was calm and unruffled. He went sailing after he learned of the events in Berlin, and he told Dean Rusk to go to a baseball game. The State Department released a cursory protest but added that further comments would come only through appropriate channels. Kennedy's most telling remark was a private statement that "this was the end of the Berlin crisis . . . The other side panicked—not us. We're not going to do anything now."[36]

. . .

What Kennedy called the "end of the Berlin crisis" was, of course, not the end of the tensions between the United States and the Soviet Union. The Berlin Wall may have been a relief to Kennedy, but his casual acceptance of the wall, and the absence of any strong criticism of it, added to the anger of the right and of much of western Europe.

In the United States, Kennedy was accused of not investing enough in weapons, including nuclear weapons. To some degree, this charge was a result of his earlier, and mostly false, claims of a "missile gap" and his assertion that America was "falling behind." The issue became so toxic in October that Deputy Secretary of Defense Roswell Gilpatric responded to a Khrushchev speech with an incendiary one of his own. At a meeting in Hot Springs, Arkansas, he spoke of "our confidence in our ability to deter Communist action, or resist Communist blackmail . . . The Iron Curtain is not so impenetrable as to force us to accept at face value the Kremlin's boasts . . . The United States does not intend to be defeated."[37] The Kremlin responded with equal bombast: "The imperialist powers are hatching mad plans of attack on the Soviet Union . . . The threat does not frighten us."[38]

As Kennedy's first year in office neared its end, the Cold War was still the central issue facing the United States. Conservatives in the United States were unhappy, as the editor of the *Dallas Morning News*, Ted Dealey, made clear. At a White House luncheon, Dealey read a statement to the president: "You and your Administration are weak sisters . . . We need a man on horseback to lead this nation and many people in Texas and the Southwest think that you are riding Caroline's tricycle."[39] Kennedy was so shaken (and furious) by Dealey's tirade—and others like it—that he made a rare speech attacking his opponents. While endorsing Democratic candidates in the coming midterm elections, he spoke harshly about "the discordant voices of extremism . . . who are unwilling to face up to the danger from without are convinced that the real danger is within . . . So let us not heed the counsels of fear and suspicion."[40]

· · ·

In the aftermath of so many frustrations in 1961, Kennedy tried again to destabilize the Castro regime through a program named "Operation Mongoose." It was a response, in part, to Maxwell Taylor, the general the Kennedys most revered. Taylor's secret report not only explained the failure of the Bay of Pigs operation but also concluded that "there can be no long-term living with Castro as a neighbor . . . His continued presence within the hemispheric community as a dangerously effective exponent of communism and anti-Americanism constitutes a real menace."[41] With another invasion out of the question, the only option was a covert counterinsurgency. The president assigned Robert Kennedy to oversee the project. Among the few officials who were aware of the operation, a significant number were opposed, including Arthur Schlesinger and Chester Bowles, the deputy secretary of state. "The question that concerns me most about this new administration," Bowles wrote, "is whether it lacks a genuine sense of conviction about what is right and what is wrong."[42] His opposition led to his replacement by George Ball, who was more amenable to the plan. That the Berlin crisis was easing made the possibility of a new effort against Castro more attractive. "My idea," Robert Kennedy said, "is to stir things up on the island with espionage, sabotage, general disorder, run & operated by Cuban themselves . . . Do not know if we will be successful in overthrowing Castro but we have nothing to lose in my estimate."[43]

By the end of 1961, the new operation was stalled. Robert Kennedy, speaking for the president at a small meeting, "expressed grave concern over Cuba" and called for "immediate dynamic action."[44] The president, frustrated by the lack of progress, asked Tad Szulc, a *New York Times* reporter deeply engaged with the Cuba issue, "What would you think if I ordered Castro to be assassinated?"[45] Szulc was strongly opposed, on both moral and practical grounds. Kennedy claimed to agree with him but complained that he was under great pressure to act. Reckless talk of assassination was already under way within Operation Mongoose. Robert McNamara brought up the idea of killing Castro, and his comments were included in the record of the meeting to the alarm of some of the CIA participants in the project. It is clear that at least some CIA operatives believed that assassination was one of the options for Mongoose. (John McCone, soon to be the director of the CIA, was enraged at the open discussion of assassination and demanded that it be "expunged from the record.")[46] Whether or not assassination was part of the agenda, Robert Kennedy said in a meeting in October that the president wanted "massive activity."[47] There is little doubt that the Kennedys wanted a clandestine program to bring down the regime. A new operation would, Kennedy hoped, restore his reputation as a strong leader against the communist world.

· · ·

President Kennedy continued to hope for progress on disarmament. At the Vienna summit, he had made no specific proposals, but he had hoped that a conversation might begin about how to reduce the danger of nuclear war. Khrushchev had made no proposals of his own. Kennedy believed that his only realistic hope was to persuade the Soviets to approve a nuclear test ban treaty. Such a treaty, its supporters claimed, would slow and perhaps even stop the development of new atomic weapons. Kennedy envisioned a gradual reduction of arms, but Khrushchev continued to insist that complete nuclear disarmament throughout the world had to be a precondition of any agreement. Kennedy knew that so broad a proposal had no chance of success, but he continued to push for a ban on testing. Khrushchev responded that "the test ban alone would not be very important to the national security of the people. The danger would remain." But he did say that "the USSR would not resume testing if the United States did likewise."[48]

Encouraged by Khrushchev's informal pledge not to test any more bombs, Kennedy sought an agreement among the American military, the Congress, and the scientific community. Jerome Wiesner, one of Kennedy's science advisers, argued for a comprehensive ban. Without it, according to another White House adviser, "this dilemma of steadily increasing military power and steadily decreasing national security has no technical solution."[49] But given Kennedy's reputation for political weakness on armament matters, his opponents were many. The military was reluctant to agree to a test ban without rigorous inspection, but Khrushchev insisted on only three inspections a year. "A larger number would be tantamount to espionage," he claimed.[50] Some of the Russian scientists were against any limitations on testing; others believed that testing should be only underground, to reduce the spread of radioactivity in the atmosphere. A lack of trust on both sides made the issue difficult. In the end, there was no agreement in 1961, and even Khrushchev's informal promise at the Vienna summit not to test new atomic weapons if the United States did the same did not last for even a year. The USSR successfully tested a fifty-megaton hydrogen bomb in the atmosphere in August. "Fucked again," Kennedy barked. The issue of a test ban did not arise again until 1963.[51]

. . .

Among the many crises Kennedy faced in his first year in office was his inheritance of the issue of Laos, a problem Eisenhower introduced to him in their meetings in late 1960. Laos is a small, landlocked country that had 3 million people in the early 1960s and was bordered by Burma, China, Cambodia, and primarily Thailand, North Vietnam, and South Vietnam. Throughout the 1950s, there were battles between the weak royal government of Laos and the growing strength of the Pathet Lao (the Laotian communist Popular Front) with ties to North Vietnam. In the Eisenhower years, there were many CIA efforts to undermine the Pathet Lao, including occasional military support. When Kennedy took office, the instability in Laos was still growing.[52]

Kennedy devoted much of a March 23, 1961, press conference to what he called "the most immediate of the problems that we found upon taking office." The Pathet Lao "have had increasing support and direction from outside. Soviet planes, I regret to say, have been conspicuous in a large-scale airlift into the battle area . . . plus a whole supporting set of combat specialists, mainly from Communist North Viet-Nam." But Kennedy was not inclined to go to war in Laos, and he was quietly determined to downgrade the U.S. role there. He insisted instead that "we strongly and unreservedly support the goal of a neutral and independent Laos, tied to no outside power or group of powers, threatening no one, and free from any domination."[53]

Seeking neutrality for a nation threatened by communism enraged the many Americans who believed in aggressive responses to communism anywhere in the world. *Time* magazine's editors described Kennedy's effort as "the sickening realization that U.S. backed Laos was about to go down the communist drain."[54] But Kennedy was determined not to get drawn into a war, and the more he learned about Laos the more determined he became. He consulted with five American generals, and each one had a different point of view; the president was so frustrated that he "threw up his hands and walked out of the room."[55] He recalled advice from Charles de Gaulle, who—remembering France's failed efforts in Indochina after 1945— had warned him that "intervention in this area will be an endless entanglement."[56] Both Kennedy and Khrushchev agreed in Vienna that "Laos was of no strategic importance." Once back in Washington, Kennedy confided to his aides, "If we have to fight in Southeast Asia, let's fight in Vietnam."[57]

But strategic importance or not, Kennedy could not afford another public defeat—and "pulling out of Laos" was not an option. He chose instead, as Ted Sorensen later wrote, to "combine bluff with real determination . . . in proportions he made known to *no one*."[58] He refused to send troops into Laos, but he put American soldiers along the Thai-Laotian border, in the hope that their presence would intimidate the Pathet Lao. At the same time, he dispatched the veteran diplomat Averell Harriman to Moscow to ensure that North Vietnam would not intervene in the conflict. Kennedy's bluff seemed to succeed. In mid-June, shortly after the Vienna summit, the Pathet Lao and the Laotian government agreed to talk. "Good news has come from Laos," Khrushchev boasted to Kennedy. "There is no doubt that this may be the turning point not only in the life of the Laotian people but in the Consolidation of a peace in Southeast Asia."[59] A year later, the cease-fire led to a "Declaration of Neutrality of Laos" at a conference in Geneva.[60]

In the end, the cease-fire and the Declaration did little to stabilize Laos. The always-shaky coalition of the Laotian government and

the Pathet Lao collapsed in the fall of 1962. Laos remained a problem for Kennedy, who tried in vain to solve it through continued
clandestine interventions by the CIA, diplomatic efforts in Moscow
and Washington, and a constant, if reluctant, willingness to use
military measures if necessary. Only the insignificance of Laos and
the weakness of both sides in the civil war kept the tiny nation from
becoming an active ally of its communist neighbors.[61]

* * *

As 1961 came to an end, Kennedy had little good to say of his first
year in office. When the NBC correspondent Elie Abel told the president he wanted to write a book about his first year, Kennedy replied,
"Who would want to read a book about disasters?"[62] But Kennedy
also looked ahead and wrote to Khrushchev on December 30: "It is
my earnest hope that the coming year will strengthen the foundations
of world peace and will bring an improvement in the relations
between our countries, upon which so much depends." Khrushchev
replied, "The Soviet people regard the future optimistically. They
hope that in the coming New Year, our countries will be able to find
ways toward closer cooperation for the good of all humanity."[63]

The editors of *Time* magazine chose Kennedy as their annual
"Man of the Year." Despite many disagreements between *Time* and
the president, the article portrayed his first year in a much more
positive tone than Kennedy himself did. He had, the editors wrote,
"made 1961 the most endlessly interesting and exciting presidential
year within recent memory . . . [He] has always had a way with the
people . . . His popularity has remained consistently high . . . 78%
of the American people said that they approved of the way he is
doing his job." The article concluded by calling Kennedy "the most
vigorous President of the 20th century . . . In his first year as President, John Fitzgerald Kennedy showed qualities that have made him
a promising leader . . . Those same qualities, if developed further,
may yet make him a great President."[64] It was a hard portrait to live
up to, and Kennedy knew how difficult it would be.

6

---

# Freedom

It was no secret to those who knew him that John Kennedy had relatively little interest in domestic issues. But he understood that he could not focus on foreign policy efforts alone. As 1962 began, he hoped for a year in which the Cold War would be less dangerous, and he looked ahead to a growing prosperity, which he knew would shore up his already strong approval ratings. The recession that plagued his first year in office had receded, and in his 1962 State of the Union address he spoke of "the high road of recovery and growth . . . racing to new records in consumer spending, labor income, and industrial production."[1] But the economic growth was not entirely positive. The nation was now facing another economic concern in early 1962—no longer recession but inflation. It was time, Kennedy decided, for Americans to sacrifice for their country at home—a sacrifice that he believed would help hold down inflation. He called on companies and unions "to apply the test of the public interest" to their wages and profits. By the spring of 1962, he felt confident that his call for restraint on prices had been accepted by the corporate world.[2] The steel industry, in particular, appeared to be cooperating with the president's request to postpone any price increases.[3]

But only a few days later, Roger Blough, the president of U.S. Steel, came to the White House to tell Kennedy that his company would raise the price of steel by 3.5 percent. All of the smaller steel companies were following suit. Kennedy furiously told Blough, "You double-crossed me." Arthur Goldberg, the secretary of labor who had worked hard to hold down prices, was even harsher: "This is war." And a kind of war it was for the Kennedy White House. The president encouraged Congress to investigate antitrust violations. Robert Kennedy convened a grand jury to see if there was evidence of price fixing. "We were going to go for broke," the attorney general said, "—their expense accounts and where they'd been and what they were doing."[4] The national press was largely on the president's side, and Blough received little sympathy from the public. Clark Clifford, Kennedy's trusted lawyer and fixer, had private conversations with Blough and other executives to make sure they understood the price they would pay. But perhaps most powerful of all was the president's harsh public denunciation of the steel price hikes.

> The simultaneous and identical actions of United States Steel and other leading steel corporations . . . constitute a wholly unjustifiable and irresponsible defiance of the public interest . . . At a time when restraint and sacrifice are being asked of every citizen, the American people will find it hard, as I do, to accept a situation in which a tiny handful of steel executives whose pursuit of private power and profit exceeds their sense of public responsibility can show such utter contempt for the interest of one hundred and eighty-five million Americans.[5]

It did not take long—under the weight of the White House, the press, and the public—for the steel magnates to back down. Three days after the announcement of the price hike, Blough stated that he would cancel the increases, followed quickly by the smaller steel companies. Kennedy prudently resisted public celebrations—and for good reason. It was no small thing for a president to declare war on the business world.[6]

It was unusual for Kennedy to speak so harshly in public, but it was not at all unusual for him to speak in that way privately. His intimates were accustomed to his foul-mouthed rage. ("God, I hate

the bastards." "They fucked us, and we've got to try to fuck them.")[7]
He exploded at critical comments in the newspapers. ("The fucking *Herald Tribune* is at it again," he once said, after which he canceled all subscriptions to the paper in the White House.)[8] His
short-lived fury against the businessmen was a rare public hint of a
dark element of his temperament.[9]

As it happened, inflation turned out not to be Kennedy's problem. By the spring of 1962, the seemingly strong recovery sagged
once again. In mid-March, the markets fell significantly (by 22 percent), a result of a decline in manufacturing and (according to the
Council of Economic Advisers) "governmental hostility to business."[10] He was careful not to antagonize the business world again.[11]

The slump revived Walter Heller's proposal for the long-delayed
tax cut that he believed would create a stimulus to the sluggish
economy. Heller proposed a reduction in the top tax bracket from
70 percent to 50 percent. Kennedy—who had little knowledge of
or interest in economics—held no strong views of his own on how
large it should be. He quickly acquiesced in Heller's solution, and
he dutifully supported the proposal in his 1963 State of the Union
address: "I am convinced that the enactment this year of tax reduction and tax reform overshadows all other domestic problems in
this Congress, for we cannot for long lead the cause of peace and
freedom, if we ever cease to set the pace here at home."[12] The House
approved the tax cut by a large majority, but a coalition of Republicans and southern Democrats in the Senate blocked it, fearful of a
growth in the deficit.[13]

. . .

Kennedy's broad personal popularity among the American people
compensated to some degree for his apparent lack of clout with
Congress. But there were other reasons to worry that his popularity, and even his presidency, might be in danger. Kennedy had spent
most of his adult life seeking sexual partners almost everywhere
he went. The presidency—unsurprisingly—made him a particularly
attractive catch. Friends, aides, and other (similarly randy) politicians
all conspired to provide Kennedy with women. His sexual partners

included movie stars, models, relatives of friends, high-end call girls. The trysts were often arranged through second and third parties, who escorted his women to public events.[14]

Kennedy was brazen about his sexual escapades. When he traveled to Paris, the French ambassador arranged for women to meet him during his visit. He shocked British prime minister Harold Macmillan during a meeting in Bermuda when he said, "If I don't have a woman for three days, I get terrible headaches."[15] In New York, where he maintained an apartment, he evaded his Secret Service agents and slipped away on his own to meet other partners. One of the many side effects of daily cortisone treatments was increased sexual desire. But that was one thing for which Kennedy had never needed medical help.[16]

Early in 1962, a particularly serious threat began to appear. J. Edgar Hoover, the director of the FBI, had made himself almost invulnerable by collecting information on presidents, members of Congress, and many others. He reveled in providing Kennedy with salacious information he had gathered about the president's habits, claiming that he was protecting him. But Hoover also made clear that he could seriously damage Kennedy's presidency. Among the president's many "companions" (as Hoover delicately wrote) was Judith Campbell, a frequent visitor to the president in the White House when Jacqueline was away and to other places when she was not. Hoover's memo to Kennedy was titled "Judith E. Campbell, Associate of Hoodlums." Campbell, he wrote, was "a free-lance artist" who had "associated with prominent underworld figures such as Sam Giancana of Chicago and John Roselli of Los Angeles," both believed to be important figures in the Mafia. Hoover listed the many telephone calls that Campbell had made to the White House and to other places where Kennedy stayed when he was outside of Washington. These relationships were particularly dangerous because the CIA had recruited Giancana and Roselli to help organize their persistent (if inept) efforts to assassinate Castro—perhaps unknown to Kennedy. The president was shaken by Hoover's obvious threats, which he knew could be leaked to the press at any moment, and he quickly severed his relationship with Campbell. But relationships with other women continued.[17]

Equally dangerous to Kennedy was his continued precarious health. By 1962, his Addison's disease (which he had kept from the public) was mostly under control with daily injections of cortisone. But that had not brought his illnesses to an end. His health problems were carefully hidden, but there were claims that he suffered from colitis, prostatitis, sleeplessness, and venereal diseases. He was treated daily by multiple doctors. Kennedy made sure that at least one of them—Max Jacobson, who often provided him with amphetamines several times a day—was for a time unknown to his other physicians. Other doctors gave him daily injections of a broad array of pharmaceuticals.[18]

Kennedy's most serious problem remained his back. It was often the source of almost unbearable pain. The Kennedy family continued to explain his back pain as the result of Jack's wartime ordeal in the South Pacific, but they knew that his problems long preceded the war. Things became worse when he was away from the White House, where it was harder for him to rest. In Ottawa, in 1961, he participated in a tree-planting ceremony at the request of the Canadian prime minister John Diefenbaker (whom Kennedy loathed). Kennedy strained his back shoveling, which left him with especially severe pain for some weeks afterward. He often was nearly incapacitated by the pain and had to spend time on crutches. He did so usually out of sight of the public, leaving the crutches behind during his short walks into his office to meet visitors. At least one of his doctors, and several of his Secret Service agents, predicted that he might spend a second term in a wheelchair.[19]

Did Kennedy's health affect his ability to govern? It is certainly possible that, had he lived, his health might have reached a point where his ability to serve as president would have become severely compromised. Several of his doctors, and his brother Robert, warned him of the dangers of his excessive use of medication—especially amphetamines. But the president brushed these concerns aside. His daily injections of cortisone might have produced a common side effect—"an enhanced sense of confidence and personal power."[20] The same traits, however, can be found among many politicians, with or without cortisone.

Whatever the future might have held had he lived, there is no persuasive evidence that his health interfered with his leadership. He lived in pain and in the knowledge of likely future illnesses, but for the most part he continued his presidency in such a way that few Americans were aware of his health problems. Indeed, he seemed to most people around the world to be a vigorous, dynamic, active young man. That he was significantly limited in his physical activities was not an impediment to making important decisions, just as Franklin Roosevelt's hidden disabilities did not significantly interfere with his leadership until near the end of his life. "Despite almost constant stress generated by international and domestic crises," the historian Robert Dallek wrote after extensive reading of Kennedy's medical records, "he survived a presidency that was more burdened with difficulties than most . . . It seems fair to say that Kennedy courageously surmounted his physical suffering. His medical difficulties did not significantly undermine his performance as president on any major question."[21] As with almost anything connected with the Kennedy era, much was hidden. But Dallek is likely right that Kennedy was able to function effectively during his short time in office.

. . .

Through most of his political career, Kennedy was a supporter of civil rights for African Americans. There was little he could do to advance this goal while he was in Congress in the 1950s, few of whose members were prepared to fight for racial justice. But Kennedy supported the Supreme Court's decision in *Brown v. Board of Education* when it was announced in 1954. He included references to civil rights in his speeches in the 1950s. He made positive statements through the early years of the civil rights movement, and he spoke positively about the Montgomery bus boycott, the Greensboro sit-ins, and the emergence of Martin Luther King Jr. (whom he helped release from jail in 1960). Supporting civil rights was, of course, a logical and politically useful position to take as a liberal Democrat in Massachusetts. Kennedy also made civil rights part of his first, and most important, televised debate in September 1960. "If a Negro baby is born . . . he has one-third as much chance to get through college as a white . . . student. He has a third as much chance to be a professional man, about half as much chance to own a house . . . I think we can do better. I don't want the talents of any American to go to waste."[22] He offered no path to solving these problems, but he at least made reference to them.

Yet once in the White House, preoccupied with foreign affairs and fearful of political opposition, he pulled back from civil rights. Occasionally, he would encourage his advisers to find ways to promote civil rights—mostly through Harris Wofford and Louis Martin, White House aides whom he had chosen to focus on the issue. But almost every time they proposed ways to move forward, Kennedy backed away. This pattern of rhetorical activism followed by resistance and delay began on his very first day in office. Wofford and Martin had proposed a bold civil rights passage in the inaugural address. It remained in the speech until almost the very last moment. But by the time Kennedy delivered his speech, the passage was gone, replaced with a more opaque phrase that said nothing directly about race.[23] Caution had already set in.

Kennedy did take small steps forward. He made sure that African Americans had jobs within the White House and in the rest of the federal government—and unlike earlier presidents, he placed black men and women in positions unconnected to race or civil rights. (The numbers of African Americans in the government were larger than in any previous presidency, but they were still a very small percentage of the staff and an even smaller percentage of high-ranking federal employees.) Kennedy invited African American leaders to receptions and meetings at a larger rate than any earlier president. Both John and Robert Kennedy also spoke of the international implications of the civil rights movement, even if briefly. In his first State of the Union address, the president said: "The denial of constitutional rights to some of our fellow Americans on account of race—at the ballot box and elsewhere—disturbs the national conscience, and subjects us to the charge of world opinion that our democracy is not equal to the high promise of our heritage."[24]

Robert Kennedy, speaking at the University of Georgia shortly after, said bluntly that "in the worldwide struggle, the graduation at this University of Charlayne Hunter and Hamilton Holmes [the first two African American students to enroll] will without question aid and assist the fight against communist political infiltration and guerrilla warfare."[25] Even these modest efforts had a significant impact on black voters. "In readily identifiable Negro precincts," *Frontier* magazine reported in early 1961, "the Democratic ticket rolled up amazing pluralities."[26] But the strong black support of the president worried Kennedy, fearing a backlash from white southerners.[27]

Kennedy's skittishness about the issue began to lose the support of some African American leaders. The president resisted meeting with Martin Luther King Jr., who, after many delays, said that he would "never again request an appointment personally."[28] The leaders of the moderate National Urban League also met resistance from the White House, despite Harris Wofford's persistent effort. A presidential proposal to accelerate school desegregation met with the argument that it "would doom aid-to-education."[29] An effort to "prohibit discrimination in direct Federal Housing programs" was answered with the argument that "quite clearly the bill to create the Dept. of Urban Affairs would be lost if ordered."[30] For a time, Kennedy resisted taking action on any of those issues. He was much more comfortable tackling discrimination in employment and voting.

In March, he signed an executive order "Establishing the President's Committee on Equal Employment Opportunity." It reaffirmed the 1955 executive order (weakly enforced during the Eisenhower administration) banning "discrimination against any employee or applicant for employment in the Federal Government because of race, color, religion, or national origin." Kennedy expanded the earlier order "by taking affirmative action to ensure that applicants are employed, and that employees are treated during employment, without regard to their race, creed, color, or national origin."[31] But the full implications of the order emerged slowly, and serious efforts to desegregate employment would wait until legislation was passed several years later.[32]

Harris Wofford, the most passionate civil rights figure in the White House, did not take public positions without the agreement of the president. Through 1961, he kept mostly quiet on controversial racial issues because of Kennedy's fears. But the president was more open to promoting voting rights through executive orders and the enforcement of existing laws. And so in March 1961, Wofford gave a speech promoting voting rights—titled "New Frontiers in Civil Rights"—that was consistent with Kennedy's concerns. Would it be better, he asked, "to avoid a tendency to prefer to lose a long, loud fight for a Congressional civil rights bill rather than to win a quiet, steady campaign for effective executive action?" Wofford argued that he (and the president) preferred the latter. Much of what he offered sounded like a speech from Booker T. Washington: "What must happen now is that Negroes consciously prepare themselves for the new frontiers of science and technology, of industry, of foreign service, of economic and social development around the world." But Wofford decried "the fact that millions of colored Americans" lived in "a rural blackbelt county in the South where even the right to vote is not yet secured."[33] At the same time, the Justice Department began enforcing the relatively weak civil rights laws passed in 1957 and 1960 to ensure voting. "It is the responsibility of the Department of Justice," Robert Kennedy said late in 1961, "to investigate and to bring legal action when citizens are denied the right to register and vote without distinction on account of race."[34]

Two years after his campaign promise of an executive order banning housing discrimination ("with a stroke of the pen," he had said in 1960), the president had not yet signed it. But by 1962 there was growing pressure for him to do more. Kennedy had hoped to sign the housing order alongside the creation of a new Department of Urban Affairs. Robert Weaver would be its secretary and would have become the first black member of the cabinet. (He later became secretary of housing and urban development under Lyndon Johnson.) But congressional conservatives blocked the passage of the department, and thus Weaver's ascent, and further delayed the president's executive order. Kennedy waited until after the November 1962 midterm elections to sign the executive order on housing discrimination. Even then, he struggled over the scope of the order—fearful that it would damage the housing market and create dissension and violence. In the end, he restricted the new law to cover only public housing and homes financed by government guaranteed loans. It made no rules governing private financial institutions that provided mortgages—the institutions that had long discriminated against black borrowers. So weak was the executive order that both the president and Robert Kennedy spent days before the announcement trying to mollify Weaver, members of the administration, and civil rights activists. Even so, there was also considerable opposition from many local governments, especially in the white South. Kennedy's proposal for a constitutional amendment to abolish poll taxes for voting also lagged in Congress. (It was eventually enacted in the aftermath of his death.)[35]

Before Kennedy became president, Wofford said in 1961, the administration was "flying on only one engine in civil rights—the Federal Judiciary." But now, he said, "the Executive Branch is beginning to turn. This is a tremendous new source of power."[36] And the executive orders did have a significant impact in a few areas. But on the whole, the Kennedy strategy of using executive powers to promote civil rights was largely a failure. Despite the many boasts of "Civil Rights Achievements" and "Civil Rights Progress," progress was slow and modest. The executive orders were mostly impotent without strong broad support in and out of government. That support was not yet visible.[37]

• • •

The postwar civil rights movement had been growing steadily since the end of World War II, but not until after the *Brown* decision did it require the attention of the presidency. The violence that surrounded the 1957 integration of Little Rock Central High School in Arkansas was the first major presidential intervention in the South's slow movement toward desegregation since the end of Reconstruction. President Eisenhower federalized the Arkansas National Guard and ordered it to ensure the safety of the black students entering the school. But the movement grew slowly, mostly without presidential intervention. The Montgomery bus boycott had been settled as a result of a Supreme Court decision in 1956, with relatively little violence. The 1960 Greensboro sit-ins, similarly, remained mostly peaceful and mostly local—despite the significant national attention they attracted. But Kennedy's first year as president coincided with the growth of a much larger and more sustained movement that expanded steadily throughout his presidency and that created significant violence.[38]

It began in the spring of 1961, when "Freedom Riders" decided to ride interstate buses through the South. Their tactic was to sit in waiting rooms reserved for whites with a mixture of black and white men and women as a gesture of defiance in the face of segregation. The Supreme Court had recently ruled that segregation of interstate travel was illegal. James Farmer, the leader of the Congress of Racial Equality (CORE), wanted to test the new law.

Farmer had organized Freedom Rides almost fourteen years earlier, in 1947. He had called them a "Journey of Reconciliation." The early black and white protesters had also challenged segregated buses and bus stations and had been arrested quickly and often violently by the local police. Some of the demonstrators spent weeks in harsh labor camps, and CORE quickly abandoned the journey. They did not consider trying again until after Kennedy's election. Like many African Americans, Farmer believed that the new president would support challenges to segregation. And so in May 1961, another group of Freedom Riders began riding through the Deep South, with judicial support behind them. They rode regularly scheduled Greyhound and Trailways buses and tried, in each city in which they stopped, to use facilities reserved for whites. They expected violence. "We can take anything the white man can dish out," one of the Freedom Riders said, "but we want our rights. We know what they are—and we want them now."[39]

As a group of Freedom Riders approached Anniston, Alabama, on May 15, 1961, on a Greyhound bus, a white mob—fifty cars

driven by white men carrying clubs, chains, and other weapons—
surrounded the bus and slashed the tires. The bus wobbled along
en route to Birmingham as the tires deflated. The cars followed the
crippled bus until it could not continue. The white attackers then
threw a firebomb into the bus and beat the riders as they fled. Local
black supporters helped them escape in their cars. The local police
were nowhere to be found. A second bus, a Trailways, was carrying
other Freedom Riders into Birmingham. The same mobs followed
them there. They beat not just the riders, but also reporters, photographers, and even passersby, once again with no police at the
scene. Not until a *New York Times* reporter picked up an Associated Press account of the Anniston and Birmingham violence did
anyone in the White House have any information about the Freedom Rides.[40]

For all his image of vigor, for all his efforts to "get the country
moving again," John Kennedy was not one to get ahead of the public. This was his first encounter with violence as a result of antiseg-
regation demonstrations, and his initial reaction was irritation. No
one had told him of the Freedom Rides, he said—a reasonable
complaint. But he was more concerned about what he called "this
Goddamned civil rights mess" and how it would hurt his ability to
work with southerners in Congress and damage the image of the
United States abroad.[41] When it became clear that new Freedom
Rides would soon begin, the president tried calling the governor of
Alabama, John Patterson, who refused to take his calls. The president shunted the problem over to the attorney general. Robert
Kennedy finally reached Patterson, who promised to protect the
riders—a promise he failed to keep. When John Seigenthaler, the
Justice Department's negotiator, was beaten and hospitalized, Rob-
ert Kennedy finally sent out federal marshals to ride the buses to
protect the demonstrators. But they too met with violence.[42]

The Freedom Rides were a turning point in the emergence of
the civil rights movement, and they put new pressures on both the
Kennedys, neither of whom had paid very much attention to race
in their first months in office. The president, at the urging of his
brother, made no public statements about the Freedom Rides. But

he privately called Harris Wofford and told him to "call it off . . . Stop them. Get your friends off those buses"—an impossible task for Wofford and, indeed, for the president himself.[43] Robert Kennedy, on the other hand, told the marshals that he would be "very much upset if this group does not get to continue their trip." He was furious at the violence, especially the beating of Seigenthaler. But he too continued to encourage the Freedom Riders to curtail their efforts, and he seemed at times to blame the demonstrators more than the people who had brutalized them. "I wonder," he asked, "whether they have the best interest of their country at heart. Do they know that one of them is against the atomic bomb—yes, he even picketed against it in jail . . . Whatever we do in the United States at this time which brings or causes discredit on our country," he said, referring to his brother's impending summit with Khrushchev, "can be harmful to [the president's] mission."[44]

Five days after the violence in Alabama, President Kennedy released his first statement on events in the South. They were, he wrote, "a source of deepest concern to me as it must be to the vast majority of the citizens of Alabama and other Americans." He asked state officials to prevent further violence. But he expressed little support for the Freedom Riders. "I would also hope," he continued, "that any persons, whether a citizen of Alabama or a visitor there, would refrain from any action which would in any way tend to provoke further outbreaks."[45] When Eugene Rostow, the dean of the Yale Law School, urged the president to desegregate all public accommodations, Kennedy bridled. "What in the world does he think I should do?" he exploded once Rostow had left. "I've done more for civil rights than any President in American history. How could any man have done more than I've done?"[46] Less than a week later, when he gave his second State of the Union address, he pledged to put a man on the moon but made no reference to the events in Alabama or to civil rights in any form.[47]

• • •

In the aftermath of the Freedom Rides, the Kennedy brothers began, little by little, to come to grips with a civil rights movement that they realized would continue for years, with increasing force. The president was slow to accept the movement for a time, and when he did act, it was with cool, pragmatic caution. Robert Kennedy, however, understood the reality earlier than his older brother did, and he gradually embraced the movement with the kind of passion that he had once focused on his brother's campaign.

The president's continued timidity about addressing the problem of race was illustrated by the creation of a new initiative. He invited a group of business leaders to launch a program named "Plans for Progress," a voluntary effort to persuade businesses to hire African American workers. The leaders of the effort claimed that they would "open the doors of job opportunities," and the president called it a "historic step forward in the effort to secure equal employment opportunity for every American of every race, color and belief."[48] The program was connected to the Committee on Equal Employment Opportunity, and it produced some successes in drawing black workers into previously all-white companies. But the modesty of the program inevitably led to disappointment—and even contempt from some black leaders ("more publicity than progress," an NAACP labor specialist complained).[49] The program's amiable director, Robert Troutman (a prominent white Georgia lawyer), was someone the president trusted to handle the job with restraint. But despite Troutman's considerable efforts and his sincere concern about what he called "the real nature and gravity of the nation's Negro problem," the progress was frustratingly slow.[50] He resigned in June 1962, after a year, leaving few results behind him. The president soldiered on, keeping the program alive with slim results and with the mostly forlorn hope that "in six months or nine months or a year . . . we can really make a contribution in the best voluntary sense between the government and the people working for a very important national objective."[51] But those who were overseeing the program had little optimism. "The Plans for Progress program should be brought along rather slowly," concluded the White House aides who were managing the effort.[52] They understood that little would come from it, but that shutting down the effort altogether would be unacceptable to the president.[53]

This bland and mostly symbolic effort was typical of Kennedy's tepid commitment to civil rights in 1962, even as the civil rights movement began to take on bigger and more aggressive forms. He largely ignored his civil rights advisers, so much so that Harris Wofford finally asked to be moved to the Peace Corps. The president continued to be so worried about losing white southern support that he avoided even the the hundredth anniversary of the Emancipation Proclamation on January 1, 1963, which he acknowledged by a recorded message while he went sailing.

Robert Kennedy, however, was moving forward. The more problems he saw, the angrier he became, his Justice Department colleague Burke Marshall said. He had been slow to understand the civil rights leaders, and he had often been frustrated by their refusal to compromise. In the famous "Letter from a Birmingham Jail," Martin Luther King Jr. wrote, "I have almost reached the regrettable conclusion that the Negro's great stumbling block . . . is not the White Citizen's Counciler or the Ku Klux Klanner, but the white moderate, who is more devoted to 'order' than to justice."[54] It is likely that the Kennedys were included in that denunciation. But Robert Kennedy never stopped trying to understand the movement at the same time that he was trying to tame it.

For a short while after the Freedom Rides, the movement seemed to be relatively calm. The effort by King's Southern Christian Leadership Conference to desegregate Albany, Georgia, in 1961 and early 1962 was a dreary failure, without significant violence. But in the fall of 1962, new turbulence began with the desegregation of the University of Mississippi in Oxford, where James Meredith, after years of litigation, was to become the first black student admitted to the school. Ross Barnett, the governor of Mississippi, refused to allow him to enroll, despite court orders. Nicholas Katzenbach, one of Robert Kennedy's assistant attorneys general, negotiated an unofficial plan to allow Meredith to register without Barnett publicly acknowledging it. The agreement broke down several times in the face of likely violence. But two days later, Meredith was helicoptered into Oxford and escorted into the Ole Miss administration building, surrounded by conspicuously armed U.S. marshals.[55]

With Meredith seemingly safely in the building, the president made a nationwide address praising the federal marshals and the Mississippi police for keeping calm.[56] But at almost the same time that the president was speaking, the Mississippi police were quietly ordered to leave the scene. In their absence, thousands of students and other white southerners poured onto the campus. Violence rapidly escalated—rocks, bricks, acid stolen from university laboratories, and a Molotov cocktail were only part of the mayhem. Gunfire soon followed, injuring 160 U.S. marshals, 28 of them with gunshot wounds. A French journalist and a passing repairman were killed in the crossfire. The president sent in federal troops, fearful that the mob would storm Meredith's dormitory. Soldiers began to arrive late that night—2,300 in all after a few days. On October 1, Meredith was finally registered and began to attend classes. He was ignored by most of his fellow students except when they made racial taunts. The president's popularity in the South dropped temporarily (from 65 to 51 percent by mid-October, but it came back to 65 percent in November). In the rest of the nation, his popularity remained very high at 75 percent.[57]

. . .

In 1963, the civil rights movement shifted to Birmingham, Alabama, where the Southern Christian Leadership Conference set out to challenge segregation in the South's most robust industrial city. The Birmingham campaign was a turning point in the movement. It also became a turning point in John Kennedy's relationship to civil rights. The Birmingham protests were a daring effort to confront one of the largest cities in the Deep South, and one of the most deeply racist. The president, watching from afar, considered the SCLC campaign a provocation that might produce unnecessary violence. At a press conference in May, shortly after the protests had begun, the president called the Birmingham campaign "a spectacle which was seriously damaging the reputation of both Birmingham and the country," a statement that seemed to blame the SCLC and the white segregationists equally.[58]

Kennedy's pleas had no effect. The Birmingham protests

grew larger as the days went by, and the violence expanded steadily. The Birmingham sheriff, Bull Connor, jailed thousands of black protesters—so many that King's ability to sustain the protests was in danger. In response, King began a new and controversial tactic. He organized more than a thousand black elementary school children to join the protest marches. They received the same responses that the adults had encountered: police dogs, fire hoses, clubbing, arrests (nine hundred children were jailed). George Wallace, the governor of Alabama, sent state troopers into the city to prevent further protests, but they did little to settle the turmoil. King, one of the first to be jailed, spent Easter weekend in a cell in which he wrote his "Letter from a Birmingham Jail," one of the iconic texts of the movement. In it, he rejected the pleas of the city's white clergy and others to use the courts and not demonstrations. He said they were more committed to stability than to justice. " 'Wait' has almost always meant 'Never,' " he wrote in his letter. "When you are forever fighting a degenerating sense of 'nobodiness'—then you will understand why we find it difficult to wait."[59]

In the aftermath of the nationally televised violence in Birmingham, the city's civic leaders stepped in to try to settle the conflict, guided by the determined Burke Marshall, deputy attorney general, who worked laboriously to hammer out a compromise. Members of the president's cabinet pressured corporate leaders (among them Roger Blough of U.S. Steel) to hire more black employees. City officials agreed to desegregate public accommodations in stores and restrooms and at lunch counters and drinking fountains. Marshall hoped the agreement would satisfy King and the SCLC while avoiding a backlash from white segregationists. The president, in a press conference, was optimistic about the future, but no sooner had he spoken than more violence emerged. In the aftermath of a Ku Klux Klan rally, vigilantes moved into the city and battled the protesters with rocks, bottles, and clubs. Finally, African Americans (from Birmingham and from the SCLC) began to fight back—rampaging through much of the city, setting fires, damaging police cars, throwing rocks at state troopers who were carrying Confederate flags. "Let the whole fucking city burn," one protester said.[60] It was a remarkable event after so many decades in which black Americans were cowed by violence from white southerners. Marshall, in the midst of the crisis, described the situation succinctly. Previously, he said, "We had a white mob against a Negro. Here we have a Negro mob against whites."[61]

With tensions rapidly growing, Marshall, Robert Kennedy, and other prominent members of the administration urged the president to address all the issues of segregation in a televised speech that would confront not just the immediate crisis but the larger issue of racial justice. "One of the great moral issues of our time is the achievement of equal opportunities for all citizens," the drafters wrote. "Too long have Negroes been denied fair treatment and equal opportunity in all parts of our land." There were problems "which must concern all of us and to which we have a moral obligation to put right."[62] But the president balked. He continued to resist a moral argument, once again fearful of white southerners' anger. He called not for justice but for peace: "This Government will do whatever must be done to preserve order, to protect the lives of its citizens, and to uphold the law of the land."[63] He then ordered three thousand federal troops to a base near Birmingham to be used if needed. Gradually, the violence dwindled, and for several weeks the city was calm. No one—least of all John Kennedy—believed that the crisis was over.[64]

. . .

It was not only in the South that the president was fearful of embracing civil rights. An example was a large reception on Lincoln's birthday. The event was to celebrate a U.S. Civil Rights Commission report on a hundred years of progress since Emancipation. Eight hundred guests poured into the White House—perhaps the most African Americans to enter the building in its entire previous history. Most of the guests were thrilled to see the White House and to see the president and the first lady. But unknown to the visitors, the event was carefully organized to give the reception as little public attention as possible. Guests were greeted at an entrance that would keep them away from photographers. Sammy Davis Jr., the celebrated singer and dancer, came with his wife, May Britt, a white woman from Sweden. The president was horrified at the prospect of a photograph of an interracial couple, and he quietly urged an aide to "get them out of here!" That was clearly impossible, but Kennedy insisted that she not appear in any photographs—a decision that infuriated Jacqueline Kennedy, who left the reception in tears. This momentous event received almost no press coverage and no public acknowledgment that the guests were African American.[65]

But slowly Kennedy was becoming aware of the power of the movement, and of the moral issues behind it. The Birmingham violence had changed the outlook of much of the country, and Kennedy was increasingly carried along with it. "I can well understand why the Negroes of Birmingham are tired of being asked to be patient," he said in May.[66] And he began to educate himself. Through much of his life, Kennedy—like most white Americans—had considered Reconstruction an oppressive travesty, a vicious revenge on the supporters of secession. But reading books by the historian C. Vann Woodward and others helped him begin to understand Reconstruction differently. "I don't understand the South," Kennedy admitted to Schlesinger, who had recommended the books. "I'm coming to believe that Thaddeus Stevens [the Radical congressman from Pennsylvania] was right. I had always been taught to regard him as a man of vicious bias. But when I see this sort of thing [the violence in Birmingham], I begin to wonder how else you can treat them."[67]

Having mostly tiptoed around civil rights for more than two years, Kennedy finally began to understand that the movement was unstoppable and that he had to embrace its moral necessity. He was struck by the thousands of people—black and white—who were willing to travel to hostile places, to demonstrate in the face of dogs, clubs, and fire hoses, and to risk injury and death from White Citizens' Councils and the Ku Klux Klan. And he was aware that without significant government action, the battles in the South would become more violent and far more widespread.

At short notice, Kennedy decided to speak on television on the evening of June 11, 1963. No one had prepared a speech for him, and the script—hurriedly written by Sorensen, Marshall, Robert Kennedy, and the president himself—was unfinished when he had to face the cameras. He spoke for eighteen minutes, much of it spontaneous. It became one of the most powerful and important addresses of his presidency—perhaps among the most important of the twentieth century. After years of talking about civil rights in cool, legalistic language, he now spoke with a moral passion that the nation had rarely heard from him.

> We are confronted primarily with a moral issue. It is as old as the Scriptures and is as clear as the American Constitution.
>
> If an American, because his skin is dark, cannot eat lunch in a restaurant open to the public, if he cannot send his children to the best public schools available, if he cannot vote for the public officials who represent him . . . then who among us would then be content to have the color of his skin changed? Who among us would then be content with the counsels of patience and delay?
>
> We face, therefore, a moral crisis as a country and as a people.[68]

That same evening in Jackson, Mississippi, the civil rights leader Medgar Evers was walking up his driveway toward his home when he was shot and killed by a White Citizens' Council gunman who was not convicted of the crime for more than thirty years.[69]

Kennedy's powerful rhetoric could not stop either the demonstrations or the violence, as the Evers assassination made clear. In late August and early September 1963, only weeks after a pause in the turmoil in Birmingham, he was faced with another crisis—this time in Tuscaloosa, Alabama, where Governor George Wallace was attempting to prevent two African American students from enrolling in the University of Alabama. A tug-of-war between Wallace and Robert Kennedy continued for hours as they tried to negotiate a settlement. Wallace continued to obstruct the integration of the university. Marshall, Robert Kennedy, and the federal government were committed to following court orders to admit the students.

Wallace finally stood at a podium outside the administration building and spoke of the "unwelcomed, unwarranted and force-induced intrusion upon the campus" and of "a frightful example of the suppression of the rights, privileges and sovereignty of this state."[70] Wallace then stepped aside, and Nicholas Katzenbach from the Justice Department escorted the two students into the building. In the meantime, the president had federalized the National Guard and had called in troops from the regular army to ensure that there would be no more violence.

. . .

One of the most important parts of Kennedy's speech was his proposal to introduce legislation that would require the end of racial segregation in almost all areas of American life. The president had resisted such a bill throughout much of his administration, certain that it would fail and fearful that it would damage other legislation that he considered important. But in the aftermath of Birmingham and Tuscaloosa, he decided that it was time to introduce a civil rights bill to Congress. Some of his most trusted aides—Ted Sorensen, Larry O'Brien, Kenny O'Donnell, and others—wanted to continue to deal with the crisis through executive orders, persuasion, and existing law. Vice President Johnson shared their view. But the president was no longer content with slow, careful progress. "There comes a time," he said, "when a man has to take a stand and history will record that he has to meet these tough situations and ultimately make a decision."[71]

He knew that passing the bill would be a monumental task. He was certain that there would be a filibuster in the Senate against any civil rights legislation, and he doubted that he could mobilize the sixty-seven votes needed under the 1963 Senate rules to bring the bill to a vote. The president made moral and political arguments to persuade members of Congress to support the bill, and he recruited as many eminent leaders as he could find. He tried to persuade Eisenhower to endorse the bill, to no effect. Robert Kennedy testified before congressional committees for weeks, making much the same arguments again and again: "We believe . . . that the Federal

Government has no moral choice but to take the initiative . . . The United States is dominated by white people, politically and economically. The question is whether we, in this position of dominance, are going to have not the charity but the wisdom to stop penalizing our fellow citizens whose only fault or sin is that they are born."[72]

But their arguments were to little avail. Senator Sam Ervin of North Carolina, far from the most conservative member, recalled the "follies of Reconstruction" and compared them to the president's legislation. "I cannot forget," he said, "that under the Reconstruction Acts we had a federal garrison stationed in my hometown."[73] Even Mike Mansfield, the Democratic Senate majority leader, balked at the bill, convinced that legislating desegregation of public accommodations would be unconstitutional.

The most powerful support for the civil rights legislation did not come from the White House or the Congress, but from the hundreds of thousands of demonstrators who gathered on August 28, 1963, in front of the Lincoln Memorial—a crowd that stretched back across the mall almost as far as could be seen. It was called the "March on Washington for Jobs and Freedom." Although the great majority of the demonstration consisted of African Americans concerned about their rights, it also included a demand for jobs—as Walter Reuther, the president of the United Auto Workers, made clear as he marched to the Lincoln Memorial next to Martin Luther King Jr. Kennedy was worried about possible violence and embarrassment, but he did not try to stop it (although he intervened through his aides to soften some of the language). The organizers made sure that the march would not attack Kennedy, but rather would use the event to support the president's bill. King's extraordinary "I Have a Dream" speech galvanized the crowd on the mall and the vast television audience, overshadowing everything else that day.[74]

On September 15, 1963, in Birmingham, a bomb exploded in an African American church during a Sunday school class. Four young girls died and many others were injured. The vicious attack produced horror and shame, not least in Birmingham itself. "As we weep for the martyred children of Birmingham," the city's Community Relations Advisory Council responded, "we are oppressed by the knowledge that they were murdered by that official contempt for basic human rights which supported the hands of those who, without conscience or reason, performed the terrible act."[75] The bombing galvanized men and women across much of the nation and brought more public support for the president's civil rights legislation. But the bill continued to flounder in Congress and failed to pass in either the House or the Senate. Kennedy remained optimistic. In a November 14 press conference (his last), he made a prediction for the following summer: "However dark it looks now, I think that 'westward, look, the land is bright,' and I think that next summer it may be."[76]

. . .

Was John Kennedy a champion of racial justice? Or was he drawn reluctantly into a battle he wished to avoid? Did he delay so long that he lost his chance to pass the legislation that he did not live to see? Or did he need the growing turmoil to be able to act? Everett Dirksen, the Republican leader in the Senate (and a man who eventually supported the civil rights bill in 1964), criticized Kennedy for allowing "the crisis of demonstrations and violence" to force his hand. "Had the President kept his campaign pledge and sent his program to Congress in 1961," Dirksen implausibly said, "new civil rights statutes would have been on the books before demonstrations and violence were ever precipitated."[77]

There is little evidence to suggest that there was a "historic opportunity" in 1961 to transform the racial landscape, or that a strong civil rights bill was likely to succeed in a Congress dominated by a combination of southern Democrats and conservative Republicans. Kennedy was, to be sure, somewhat timid about embracing civil rights for much of his time in office. But at the end of his life, he had committed himself to both the political and the moral necessity of ending segregation. John Kennedy may have done more for civil rights than any president before him since Lincoln. But he faced a harsh and often violent opposition that made it unlikely that his civil rights legislation would succeed soon. His tragic death, and the political skills of Lyndon Johnson, made possible the passage of civil rights and voting rights legislation. But John Kennedy—and the great movement that he finally embraced—was essential to the great achievements.

---

# 7

# The Evolving Cold War

The Kennedys could not get untangled from Cuba. The Bay of Pigs disaster followed them for years. Covert operators continued to seek ways to overthrow the Castro regime. (Lyndon Johnson later said that the Kennedys "had been operating a god-damned Murder Inc. in the Caribbean.")[1] Of more concern to President Kennedy was the growing alliance between the Soviets and the Cubans; the Soviets were now providing Cuba, according to CIA memos, with "large quantities of transportation, electronic and construction equipment . . . possible limited quantity weapons."[2] The battle of Cuba had never stopped.

Despite the buildup in Cuba, Kennedy's concerns remained at a relatively low level. "The major danger is the Soviet Union with missiles and warheads, not Cuba," he said privately.[3] The Justice Department warned that a blockade of commerce would be illegal under international law. In a September press conference, Kennedy described Cuba as a country "in trouble . . . increasingly isolated from this hemisphere. [Castro's] name no longer inspires the same fear or following in other Latin American countries."[4] And so Kennedy and most of his advisers continued to believe that the Soviet military buildup in Cuba was modest and entirely defensive. (An exception was John McCone, the CIA director, who warned the president that the Soviet shipments could only mean they were planning offensive weapons.)[5]

Members of Congress were also becoming alarmed by the

presence of Soviet weapons in Cuba, and pressure for action was growing from the press and the public. There were rising calls for a blockade of Cuba. Kennedy resisted. "It's an act of war," he said, even though he had considered a blockade himself not long before. "There's no evidence that it would bring Castro down for many, many months. You'd have a food situation in which you'd have people starving."[6] Kennedy's focus was still primarily on Berlin, but he agreed to call up 150,000 reserve soldiers near the Florida coast in case events in Cuba became more dangerous. But Kennedy still considered the placement of offensive weapons in Cuba to be unlikely, and he left Washington for a long and grueling midterm campaign trip through the Northeast and Middle West for almost two weeks in October.[7]

In response to the growing anxiety in Congress, the president approved sending U-2 flights over Cuba to photograph the weapons that the Soviets were bringing into the country. Kennedy felt certain that the surveillance would confirm that the buildup in Cuba was entirely defensive. But after the first reconnaissance flight on October 14, and after the photographs were processed the next day, there was clear evidence that the Soviets were indeed placing offensive missiles in Cuba. The missiles had a range capable of reaching much of the United States, and it appeared almost certain that nuclear warheads were either already in Cuba or soon to arrive. Bundy, who worried about Kennedy's exhaustion from his campaign trip, waited until the following morning, October 16, to give him the news. The president quickly assembled a group of aides and military men to respond to the sudden crisis. It was a group that became known as ExComm (short for Executive Committee of the National Security Council), and it met daily, often several times each day, for nearly two weeks. The group included, in addition to the president, Vice President Lyndon Johnson, Secretary of State Dean Rusk, Secretary of the Treasury Douglas Dillon, Secretary of Defense Robert McNamara, Attorney General Robert Kennedy, Undersecretary of State George Ball, National Security Adviser McGeorge Bundy, Special Adviser to the President Ted Sorensen, CIA Director John McCone, recently former ambassador to Mos-

cow Llewellyn Thompson, and General Maxwell Taylor. Others—
mostly military and CIA figures—joined the meetings from time to
time. Kennedy's charge to them was to "set aside all other tasks to
make a prompt and intensive survey of the dangers and *all possible
courses of action.*"[8]

The first question that Kennedy pondered was why Khrushchev
would take such an aggressive step. "What is the advantage?" he
asked rhetorically. "Must be some reason for the Soviets to set this
up."[9] In fact, there were many rational (if risky) reasons for the Soviets to move offensive missiles into Cuba. The missiles were not placed
there to start a war, although in the tense first days of the crisis no
one could be sure. Khrushchev had several motives. Putting medium-
range missiles in Cuba would, he believed, ensure that the United
States would not dare to invade Cuba again. He also believed that
having missiles so close to the United States would give the Soviet
Union an easier and less expensive way to match the American missile arsenal. For Khrushchev, whose political power at home was
becoming shaky, the Cuban missiles could free him from an expensive arms race and allow him to invest more heavily on building up
much-needed domestic programs. Most conclusive to the Soviets
were the U.S. missiles in Turkey, near the USSR border, which the
Soviets considered comparable to the Cuban missiles. But Kennedy
feared more aggressive reasons. Was Khrushchev bringing missiles
to Cuba to force a U.S. retreat from West Berlin? Did Khrushchev
think that Kennedy was a weak leader who would give in to the
facts on the ground? If so, he underestimated the president, who
from the start believed that he had no choice but to remove the
missiles from Cuba.

The long, tense discussions of how to respond to the crisis
began with a meeting on the morning of October 16 in the Cabinet
Room, where the president was sitting with his young daughter,
Caroline, while the participants gathered. Once she was whisked
away, the meeting began—the start of two agonizing weeks that may
have been among the most important days of the twentieth century.[10]

The first decision was to send more U-2 planes over Cuba to
be sure of how many missiles there were. But perhaps the most

significant statement of this first meeting was the choice that Secretary of State Rusk set out that morning.

> This is, of course, a very serious development. It's one that we, all of us, had not really believed the Soviets could carry this far . . . Now, I do think we have to set in motion a chain of events that will eliminate the base . . . The question then becomes whether we do it by a sudden, unannounced strike of some sort or we build up the crisis to the point where the other side has to consider very seriously about giving in.[11]

The options that Rusk proposed determined how the administration would approach the crisis.

The first instinct of almost every member of ExComm, including the president, was to launch a military strike that would wipe out the Soviet missiles quickly. But Kennedy soon began to worry about the likelihood of success. "Let's say we just take out the missile bases," he said. "Then they have some more. Obviously they can get them in by submarine and so on. I don't know whether you just can't keep high strikes on."[12] And so his doubts began. Robert Kennedy added to the worries: the killing of many people, the tensions it would create in the hemisphere, the fear that the Russians would escalate. But despite these doubts, almost everyone still assumed that there would have to be some kind of air strike, followed by an invasion of Cuba that would overthrow the Castro government. The president ended the meeting saying, "We're certainly going . . . to take out these missiles."[13]

But by October 19, three days into the crisis, the idea of a blockade had begun to gather momentum. Some ExComm members saw the blockade as a companion to air strikes; others were considering a blockade without air strikes, accompanied by negotiations with Khrushchev. Knowledge of the Cuban missiles still remained a tightly guarded secret, and remarkably there had been no serious public leaks. But no one was confident that the secrecy could be kept for long. The military men continued to press for a quick air strike. Kennedy was still worried about the repercussions in

Europe—in particular, a Soviet move on Berlin. "They can't let us just take out . . . their missiles, kill a lot of Russians and not do anything," he warned.[14]

Air strikes and other military attacks on Cuba remained the strategy preferred by most of the participants. When the president had left the room, the military officers (unaware that they were being taped) worried aloud about Kennedy's commitment to the measures they believed were required. "You can't fiddle around with hitting the missile sites and then hitting the SAM sites," David Shoup, commandant of the Marine Corps, said angrily. "You got to go in and take out the goddamn thing that's going to stop you from doing your job." An exasperated Earle Wheeler, the army chief of staff, said, "It was very apparent to me . . . that the political action of a blockade is what [he prefers]." What most irritated them was Kennedy's use of the word "escalation," which they considered a "piecemeal" way of fighting. "That's our problem," Shoup said. "You go in there and friggin' around with the missiles. You're screwed."[15] Unknown to the generals, however, Kennedy was once again moving away from the blockade option himself, and he was now reconsidering a surprise air strike. But at the same time, Robert Kennedy was wavering in the other direction. He was uneasy about what could be seen as a "Pearl Harbor" sudden strike, which he said was "not in our traditions."[16] Instead, he was tentatively proposing a plan that would give Khrushchev a chance to change course. The president, in the meantime, was back on the campaign trail, trying to stick to his public schedule as a way to buy some more time while the committee debated the next steps.[17]

By the time the president returned from his trip that afternoon, the blockade-versus-air-strike debate was the central issue of the meeting. The military men were united in their preference for bombing. But McNamara, Sorensen, Robert Kennedy, and others were now leaning more toward a blockade (as were Adlai Stevenson and George Ball). In part because of their persuasion, the president finally decided on a blockade, combined with an effort to persuade Khrushchev to back down. He decided that the blockade would be called a "quarantine," to avoid being charged with an act of war under international law. If the blockade failed, air strikes might follow. The American navy was in a particularly strong position in the Caribbean, and no other nation could challenge it on the sea. But more to the point, a blockade left the Soviet Union with the "burden of choice." It gave the Soviets the option of backing down without "a humiliating defeat or a nuclear war," Kennedy explained at the time.[18]

By October 22, the secrecy of the crisis was beginning to unravel. The *Washington Post* on October 21 ran a front-page headline: "Marine Moves in South Linked to Cuban Crisis."[19] Kennedy pleaded with the journalists to hold off the story for another day until he was able to speak to the nation on television. The editors reluctantly agreed.

On the evening of October 22, Kennedy began briefing important figures who could help him strengthen his hand. He met with Eisenhower, who agreed with the blockade and promised his support. He met with congressional leaders, some of whom were skeptical about the effectiveness of the quarantine. But Kennedy had made up his mind, and that evening he spoke by television and radio to the American people, and much of the world, about the crisis. He explained the nature of the Soviet buildup in Cuba, and he responded:

> Neither the United States of America nor the world community of nations . . . can tolerate deliberate deception and offensive threats on the part of any nation, large or small . . . Nuclear weapons are so destructive and ballistic missiles are so swift, that any substantially increased possibility of their use or any sudden change in their deployment may well be regarded as a definite threat to peace.

He explained the character of the "quarantine," and he called on Khrushchev "to halt and eliminate this clandestine, reckless, and provocative threat to world peace . . . [and] to abandon this course of world domination."[20] The next day he issued a proclamation ordering

U.S. forces to stop all ships carrying offensive weapons to Cuba. The Cuban missile crisis was now visible to the entire world.[21]

. . .

The crisis produced anxiety and, for some people, near panic across the country and much of the world. Financial markets plunged in New York, London, and the European Common Market. The price of gold rose to a record high. There was a run on canned food, ration packs, and bottled water to supply makeshift fallout shelters. Sleeping bags and backpacks were in high demand in cities, where many people feared they would have to flee from bombing sites. Some grocery stores were emptied as terrified shoppers filled multiple shopping carts with food. A Columbia professor described his students as "literally scared for their lives."[22] But most people continued their work and their lives at home as usual, tense but not panicky. On the whole, Americans seemed remarkably confident in the president's response to the crisis.[23]

Not long after his television address, Kennedy began what would become a long and difficult correspondence with Khrushchev, which seemed oddly similar, in reverse, to their testy exchanges over the Bay of Pigs. The president referred to their conversations in Vienna and again insisted that "the United States could not tolerate any action on your part which in a major way disturbed the existing overall balance of power in the world . . . I must tell you that the United States is determined that this threat to the security of this hemisphere be removed."[24]

Khrushchev's first response was indignant. "By what right do you do this?" he said of the blockade. "You . . . are setting forth an ultimatum and threatening that if we do not give in to your demands you will use force . . . You are no longer appealing to reason, but wish to intimidate us . . . I cannot agree to this."[25]

Kennedy responded curtly:

I think you will recognize that the steps which started the current chain of events was the action of your government in secretly furnishing offensive weapons to Cuba . . . I am concerned that we both show prudence and do nothing to allow events to make the situation more difficult to control than it already is.[26]

The president told Khrushchev that the quarantine would go into effect on the afternoon of October 24. Almost everyone in ExComm felt certain that some kind of conflict would emerge from trying to block the Soviet ships. "The instruction from Khrushchev [to his ships] is very likely to be: 'Don't stop under any circumstances,'" McNamara predicted. Kennedy agreed, saying, "We're going to have one hell of a time getting aboard that thing [a ship approaching Cuba] and getting control of it, because they're pretty tough."[27] If anything, the members of ExComm believed, the crisis was now escalating. The Soviet ships were continuing to approach Cuba, although not yet breaching the quarantine line, and everyone in the White House felt certain that the ships were "going to go through."[28] And as always the president was concerned that whatever movement the United States made would lead to a response from Khrushchev in Germany. "There may be a Berlin squeeze," Kennedy said that evening.[29]

It was, they all thought, the most dangerous moment of the crisis. Early the next day, with the ships still approaching, there was talk of torpedoes and depth charges. At that point, Robert Kennedy noted, "These few minutes were the time of greatest worry by the president. His hand went up to his face & covered his mouth and he closed his fist. His eyes were tense, almost gray, and we just stared at each other across the table."[30]

But only a few minutes later, intercepts began to arrive showing that the ships were slowing or turning back. That evening, a message from Khrushchev to Dean Rusk was delivered by Bertrand Russell, the British philosopher and pacifist. In it, Khrushchev appeared to be softening his position: "The Soviet government will not take any decisions which will be reckless, will not allow itself to be provoked by unwarranted actions of the United States of America. We shall do everything in our power to prevent war from breaking out."[31] Khrushchev also called for a summit meeting to resolve all problems between the two superpowers. Kennedy brushed the summit idea away. Instead, he spoke harshly of what he considered Khrushchev's duplicity. He responded curtly: "While your messages are critical of the United States, they make no mention of your concern for the introduction of secret Soviet missiles into Cuba. I think your attention might well be directed to the burglars rather than to those who have caught the burglars."[32]

The president was unwilling to believe that the crisis was ebbing, still fearful that Khrushchev was considering action against West Berlin. He was particularly alarmed when another, more belligerent message came from Khrushchev late that night showing no willingness to change course. The president replied to Khrushchev early the next morning: "I regret very much that you still do not appear to understand what it is that has moved us in this matter . . . I ask you to recognize clearly, Mr. Chairman, that it was not I who issued the first challenge in this case . . . I repeat my regret that these events should cause a deterioration in our relations."[33]

But in the afternoon of October 26, the face of the crisis began to change. Soviet officials at the United Nations were suggesting that, as Dean Rusk said, "The Cubans may want to resolve this by getting their weapons out in exchange for some sort of assurance about their territorial integrity."[34] Later in the day, an ABC News reporter, John Scali, had a conversation with a Soviet officer in Washington who seemed to be making the same offer. And that evening, another message came from Khrushchev, with hints of conciliation and evidence of his own distress. "I see, Mr. President," he wrote, "that you are not devoid of a sense of anxiety about the fate of the world."[35] Khrushchev continued to insist that there were no offensive weapons in Cuba, but he did suggest that he was ready to embrace the deal that had emerged earlier in the day: "If assurances were given by the President . . . that the USA itself would not participate in an attack on Cuba . . . if you would recall your fleet, this would immediately change everything . . . the question of armaments would disappear."[36]

The next morning, however, another, longer message came from

Khrushchev with additional conditions, among them an agreement that the United States would remove its missiles in Turkey in return for the Soviets removing their missiles in Cuba. There was speculation that the second message was written not by Khrushchev but by more militant members of the Politburo; whatever the case, the proposed deal had suddenly become more complicated. "How can we negotiate with somebody who changes his deal before we even get a chance to reply," McNamara asked, "and announces publicly the deal before we receive it?"[37]

While the Joint Chiefs of Staff were chafing to launch air strikes on the missile bases in Cuba, and while U-2s were being shot down in Siberia and over Cuba, Kennedy was working on a response to the Soviets that would give Khrushchev a way out. The demand that American missiles in Turkey must be dismantled in exchange for the dismantling of the Cuban missiles seemed unacceptable. Bundy warned that if they were "trading the defense of Turkey for a threat to Cuba, we'll just have to face a decline [in the alliance]."[38] For a time, the negotiators felt stymied—trying to find a way to reach agreement while struggling to find a way around the missiles in Turkey. But gradually the group began to focus on another tactic: replying to Khrushchev's first letter (the proposal to remove the missiles in return for a promise not to invade Cuba) and ignoring the second, more difficult one (which included trading the missiles in Turkey). Sorensen, Robert Kennedy, Rusk, and eventually the president began to coalesce around this plan. Llewellyn Thompson was the most emphatic supporter. He described Khrushchev's behavior as "almost incoherent and showed that they were quite worried."[39] And so the group agreed that they would respond to Khrushchev's first communication and mostly ignore the second.[40]

At 8 p.m. on October 27, the president sent the response, accepting Khrushchev's first proposal. He did not mention the missiles in Turkey, but he made general reference to "other armaments" and to "a détente affecting NATO and the Warsaw Pact."[41] Quietly and secretly, Kennedy also agreed on a proposal Rusk had made: an oral message to Khrushchev saying that the United States was determined to remove the missiles in Turkey once the missile crisis was over.

The next morning, October 28, the ships that had seemed to be approaching the quarantine line had now stopped or turned back. At the same time, Khrushchev sent a public message in response to Kennedy's October 26 message. It included assurances that the Russians would dismantle "the weapons which you describe as 'offensive,' and their crating and return to the Soviet Union . . . I regard with respect and trust your statement in your message of October 27, 1962, that no attack will be made on Cuba—that no invasion will take place."[42]

In the Pentagon, the Joint Chiefs were still skeptical of the Soviets' intentions. They suspected that the Russians were delaying to give themselves time to make the missiles operative, and they continued to urge an air strike before the Russians had time to embed themselves. But in the White House, there was something close to euphoria. Kennedy called all three living presidents—Eisenhower, Truman, and Hoover—all of whom congratulated him on his handling of the crisis. And he sent a conciliatory message to Khrushchev: "I welcome this message and consider it an important contribution to peace . . . Perhaps, now, as we step back from danger, we can together make real progress in this vital field [of nuclear weapons]."[43] He urged Khrushchev to cooperate with him to limit proliferation of nuclear weapons and to agree on a test-ban treaty. Kennedy acknowledged the shaky agreement with a broadcast over Voice of America.

> I welcome Chairman Khrushchev's statesmanlike decision to stop building bases in Cuba, dismantling offensive weapons and returning them to the Soviet Union . . . This is an important and constructive contribution to peace.[44]

Knotty questions continued for several weeks, and there were many tense moments as the crisis slowly unraveled. But for the most part, the Cuban missile crisis was moving toward its end. Three weeks later, in a November 20 press conference, Kennedy publicly declared success. "The evidence to date indicates that all known offensive missile sites in Cuba have been dismantled. The missiles and their associated equipment have been loaded on Soviet ships . . . There is much for which we can be grateful as we look back to where we stood only 4 weeks ago—the unity of this hemisphere, the support of our allies, and the calm determination of the American people."[45]

. . .

John Kennedy's management of the Cuban missile crisis has become the most revered accomplishment of his presidency—much burnished, of course, by his colleagues, friends, and contemporary admirers. "The President saw more penetratingly into the mists and terrors of the future than anyone else," Arthur Schlesinger wrote in his 1965 memoir.[46] "He had earned his place in history by this one act alone," noted Harold Macmillan, the British prime minister during much of Kennedy's presidency; Macmillan called his leadership of the crisis "one of the great turning points in history."[47] "The 10 or 12 people who had participated in all these discussions were bright and energetic people," Robert Kennedy wrote shortly after the crisis, "and if any one of half a dozen of them were President the world would have been very likely plunged in a catastrophic war."[48] Elie Abel, an NBC News journalist, who wrote the first serious account of the missile crisis, summarized Kennedy's achievement.

> Kennedy succeeded in steering a safe course between war and surrender, remembering always that Khrushchev too was a politician, who must never be put in the position of risking discredit at home. . . . "Above all, [Kennedy later said] while defending our own vital interests, nuclear powers must avert those confrontations which bring an adversary to the choice of either a humiliating retreat or a nuclear war."[49]

For many years, few people disputed this view. But a decade after Kennedy's death, an alternative argument began to emerge that was far less heroic. Some scholars and critics argued that Kennedy himself was responsible for the missiles in Cuba. It was the Bay of Pigs imbroglio that triggered the missile crisis. The continuing threat of another invasion of Cuba seemed still very much alive, and the Russian missiles were not placed in Cuba to threaten the United States but protect Cuba from another American attack. Other scholars criticized the missile crisis as an example of Kennedy's Cold War obsessions and his tendency toward conflict—his belief that he had to display his "toughness" despite the great dangers it helped create. He stubbornly refused to compromise by removing the unnecessary American missiles in Turkey (missiles closer to the Soviet Union than the Cuban missiles were to the United States). Eisenhower, who had put the missiles in Turkey, had privately admitted in 1959 that

> putting the Jupiters in Turkey was like the Soviets putting intermediate-range missiles in Cuba or Mexico. He said, privately again, that for once Khrushchev was absolutely right in accusing the United States of provocations; that if Soviets had done something like that, the United States would have had to take military action.[50]

Eisenhower was surprised that Khrushchev did not protest.

Unlike Eisenhower, Kennedy's critics claim, the president displayed no such understanding of Khrushchev's point of view on this question. The historian Richard Walton argued that his "machismo" caused him to embrace "an anti-communist crusade much more dangerous than any policy Eisenhower ever permitted." It was Khrushchev, not Kennedy, other historians said, who risked (and not long after lost) his job to avoid a nuclear confrontation. "Had Khrushchev not done so," Walton argued, "there might well have been no later historians to exalt Kennedy."[51]

But as more time passed, and as the archives of the former Soviet Union became available, Kennedy's efforts have become more understandable, and in many ways more impressive. Unknown for some time, Kennedy and Khrushchev together worked diligently through the crisis to avoid a catastrophic confrontation. They communicated with each other almost every day, not only during the crisis but well beyond. They quietly agreed that Kennedy would remove the missiles in Turkey shortly after Khrushchev removed the missiles in Cuba. Kennedy did not make the deal public, fearing it would damage him politically. And while almost any course Kennedy might have chosen would have been risky, he avoided the most dangerous ones. He rejected the strong preference of the military to "take out" the Cuban missiles with air strikes and chose instead a relatively passive alternative: a naval blockade, during which the United States never fired a shot. Nor did Kennedy take action when the Soviet air force shot down two U-2 planes during the crisis.

No American president could have allowed nuclear missiles to remain in Cuba without losing his political and military support; and no Soviet leader could have pulled back from the brink of the crisis without a compromise—the public promise not to invade Cuba and the secret promise to withdraw the missiles from Turkey. In the end, Kennedy and Khrushchev dealt with this difficult crisis cautiously, deftly, and safely.

· · ·

In the aftermath of the missile crisis, significant geopolitical changes emerged in the Cold War. To the president's surprise, the "Berlin crisis," which had troubled him for so long, turned out no longer to be much of a crisis at all; the Soviet Union (if not perhaps East Germany) was apparently resigned to the wall. There was no significant pressure for unification until 1989. At least equally encouraging was that Khrushchev and Kennedy began a serious effort to negotiate a treaty to ban the testing of nuclear weapons.[52] The proposed treaty had multiple goals. One was to reduce or eliminate radioactive materials in the atmosphere; another was to slow down the arms race and prevent proliferation of nuclear weapons in other nations.[53]

At first, both sides wanted a "comprehensive" test ban—in which no atomic weapons would be detonated for tests either above ground or below. But continuing, if reduced, mistrust between the two superpowers made the problem of verification an almost insuperable obstacle. It was not difficult to detect atmospheric atomic tests, but underground testing was much more difficult—if not impossible—to verify. Such a treaty would require frequent American inspections on Soviet territory, and Russian inspections on American soil in return. There was resistance in each government to such an agreement. Kennedy said he understood why these inspections gave Khrushchev "considerable difficulty." But the president tried to assure his Soviet counterpart that "arrangements could be worked out."[54] He was especially eager for the treaty because he believed it would impede other nations—China, France, Germany, Israel—from building atomic bombs of their own.

By early April, the obstacles to inspections seemed impossible to overcome, and the treaty, which had looked so promising a few months earlier, now seemed on the road to failure. At times, the Kremlin appeared to have returned to the harsh Cold War relationship of several years before. "Who did we think we were in the United States trying to dictate to the Soviet Union?" the Soviet government replied (as the State Department awkwardly translated). "The United States had better learn that the Soviet Union was as strong as the United States and did not enjoy being treated as a second-class power."[55] For a moment, it seemed that the treaty was doomed. But the president worked hard to recover from the hostile response, and he realized that he would need to make a strong effort to improve Soviet-American relationships. He was encouraged by subsequent messages from the Kremlin that the Soviet Union wanted to work for "peaceful coexistence"—and that it was "the sincere desire of our government, of our people, and of our party."[56]

Encouraged by this conciliatory message, Kennedy decided to take advantage of a planned speech at American University in Washington, D.C., in June 1963 to propose a new approach to the Cold War. Few people in the government, and even fewer elsewhere, were aware in advance of the startling message of his speech. Kennedy did not allow the State or Defense departments to participate in the drafting of his remarks—or even to see them before he spoke. "I suppose that, from the viewpoint of orderly administration," Arthur Schlesinger wrote in his diary at the time, "this was a bad way to prepare a major statement on foreign policy. But the State Department could never in a thousand years have produced this speech."[57]

"I have chosen this time and this place," Kennedy began, "to discuss a topic on which ignorance too often abounds and the truth is too rarely perceived—yet it is the most important topic on earth: world peace." He described a peace "that makes life on earth worth living, the kind that enables men and nations to grow and to hope to build a better life for their children—not merely peace for Americans but peace for all men and women—not merely peace in our time but peace for all time."

He spoke of the dangers of atomic weapons, and he described peace as "the necessary rational end of rational men." But he also spoke of America's own role in the world and of the "possibilities of peace, toward the Soviet Union, toward the cold war and toward freedom and peace here at home." In a strikingly conciliatory statement that noted the important achievements of the Soviet Union, he said:

> No government or social system is so evil that its people must be considered as lacking in virtue. As Americans we find communism profoundly repugnant as a negation of personal freedom and dignity. But we can still hail the Russian people for their many achievements—in science and space, in economic and industrial growth, in culture and in acts of courage.

He repeated his desire for a test-ban treaty that "would check the spiraling arms race . . . It would increase our security—it would decrease the prospects of war." And he spoke of an end of war—a "world of peace where the weak are safe and the strong are just. We are not helpless before that task or hopeless of its success. Confident and unafraid, we labor on—not toward a strategy of annihilation but toward a strategy of peace."[58]

The speech was a success but not a sensation. Kennedy was praised more abroad than at home. ("One of the great state papers of American history," the British *Manchester Guardian* called it.) The *New York Times* barely covered it. *Time* magazine tepidly called it "fresh and worthwhile." Letters to the White House did not spike up. Craig Hosmer, the senior Republican on the Joint Atomic Energy Committee, called it "a soft line that can accomplish nothing." Senator Barry Goldwater called it a "dreadful mistake." It probably did not help Kennedy with members of Congress that the most enthusiastic reception to the speech came from Khrushchev himself, who called it "the best speech by any president since Roosevelt."[59]

What made the speech significant—and why it is remembered more vividly now than it was in 1963—was its break from the usual attacks on communism and the Soviet Union. It was a vision of a peaceful world that might reduce (and perhaps end) the danger of war in the atomic age. And although the speech had little public traction, it was an important contribution to the revival of the test-ban treaty within the American government and the Kremlin—and perhaps more important a contribution to a peaceful world.[60]

Over the summer, Averell Harriman (at the president's request) negotiated a treaty with the Kremlin that would stop all atmospheric tests of atomic weapons, but would remove underground tests from the treaty. The Comprehensive Nuclear Test Ban Treaty that Kennedy had proposed became the Limited Nuclear Test Ban Treaty. It was not what Kennedy had hoped for, but it was a step forward. Yet even this relatively small step created strong opposition. Many former American military leaders, not to mention defense contractors, were dismayed. General Thomas S. Power, chief of the Strategic Air Command, denounced the treaty in an appearance before the Senate. Senator John Stennis of Mississippi doubted that "the U.S. can or would maintain its present undisputed superiority in nuclear power if it ratified the treaty. General Power believes this is the only present deterrent to war."[61] Edward Teller, one of the "fathers" of the atomic bomb, told the Senate Foreign Relations Committee that signing the treaty "was a mistake. If you ratify it you will have committed an enormously greater mistake." It would be, he wrote, "a step away from safety and possibly . . . toward war."[62]

But despite the doubters, the Senate ratified the treaty on September 24, 1963, by a margin of 80–19. Kennedy signed the treaty in the White House and said: "This small step toward safety can be followed by others longer and less limited, if also harder in the taking. With our courage and understanding enlarged by this achievement, let us press onward in quest of man's essential desire for peace."[63]

Ted Sorensen later said that no accomplishment "gave Kennedy greater satisfaction."[64]

· · ·

If the American University speech attracted relatively little attention in 1963, less than two weeks later Kennedy delivered perhaps the most famous speech of his life: a brief address in Berlin outdoors near the now famous Wall. An estimated two-thirds of the population of West Berlin poured into the plaza in front of the city hall, spreading out into the streets behind, to hear it. Kennedy was so stunned by the size and enthusiasm of the crowd that he joked with one of his aides, "If I told them to go tear down the Berlin Wall, they would do it."[65]

The brief speech itself was on the verge of demagoguery at times, and the massive crowd was almost ecstatic. "There are some who say communism is the wave of the future," he said. "And there are some who say in Europe and elsewhere we can work with the Communists . . . And there are even a few who say that it is true that communism is an evil system, but it permits us to make economic progress." He refuted each of these statements by saying, "Let them come to Berlin." He closed with a vision of the future.

Freedom is indivisible, and when one man is enslaved, all are not free. When all are free, then we can look forward to that day when this city will be joined as one and this country and this great Continent of Europe in a peaceful and hopeful globe . . . All free men, wherever they live, are citizens of Berlin, and, therefore, as a free man, I take pride in the words, *"Ich bin ein Berliner."*[66]

The speech was a rhetorical triumph, and a contrast to his tempered call for peace two weeks earlier at American University. There were few hints of conciliation in his words in Berlin as Kennedy rolled out the failures of the East and the triumphs of the West. But the exhilaration of the crowd overcame any backlash that might have come. "We'll never have another day like this one, as long as we live," Kennedy told Sorensen.[67] But later that day, in a speech to the Free University of Berlin, he tempered his harsh words about the Soviet Union to avoid insulting Khrushchev.[68]

The Berlin speech was part of a grueling nine-day trip in which Kennedy spoke in Germany, Ireland, England, and Italy—sixteen speeches, remarks, and toasts altogether. Everywhere he went, he was met by large and enthusiastic crowds. Arthur Schlesinger said, only partly in jest, that "in the summer of 1963, John F. Kennedy could have carried every country in Europe."[69] He had made progress with the allies and even with Khrushchev. And he had helped reshape the Cold War, moving it toward a less confrontational relationship between the two superpowers. But as the clash between the United States and the Soviet Union was declining, he was being drawn into other, even more difficult challenges—America's growing role in Third World nations threatened by local communist insurgencies. That effort, which continued for decades, was most prominent in the emergence of the war in Vietnam.

# 8

---

# Quagmire

In the spring of 1954, Senator John F. Kennedy gave a speech to the Executives Club of Chicago about France's colonial war in Indochina. His remarks were filled with ambivalence and doubt about the course the United States was taking. "The West is reaping a bitter harvest of decades of mistakes," he told his audience, thinking of the fall of China, the unpopular Korean War, and the French fiasco in Vietnam. He warned that an American military engagement to support the French might not be winnable.[1]

Two years later, Kennedy spoke again about Indochina before the American Friends of Vietnam, an organization created to publicize and support the relatively new anticommunist regime of Ngo Dinh Diem in South Vietnam. But this time Kennedy spoke with far more certainty, proclaiming that "[South] Vietnam represents the cornerstone of the Free World in Southeast Asia, the keystone to the arch, the finger in the dike." Its survival "represents a test of American responsibility and determination in Asia . . . And if it falls victim to any of the perils that threaten its existence—Communism, political anarchy, poverty, and the rest—we will be held responsible and our prestige in Asia will sink to a new low."[2]

These unremarkable speeches are significant because they suggest two different responses to what would become Kennedy's view of the Vietnam War. One suggested doubt about the wisdom of intervention. Another suggested strong commitment to a free

South Vietnam. The statements, of course, were among Kennedy's earliest remarks about South Vietnam, a country already becoming reliant on American support. For the next seven years, the United States slowly increased its role in Indochina until, in the last months of Kennedy's life, there was a significant American political, economic, and military presence in South Vietnam.

• • •

Few Americans knew anything about Vietnam until the end of World War II. It had been a colony of France since the late nineteenth century and had fallen to the Japanese during the Pacific conflict. When the war ended, the French returned to Vietnam and attempted to restore the colonial government. But by then, a nationalist movement, driven by the communist Viet Minh party, had organized a military effort to expel the French. In what is now known as the First Vietnam War, the Viet Minh defeated the French in 1954 and established an independent nation in northern Vietnam. But in southern Vietnam, there was significant opposition to the Viet Minh. And so the southerners, with encouragement from the United States, sought to create their own independent nation. A conference in Geneva in 1955 established a supposedly temporary partition of the country—North Vietnam, led by the Viet Minh and its charismatic leader, Ho Chi Minh, and South Vietnam, led by Ngo Dinh Diem, a Catholic who quickly allied himself with the United States.

Despite his occasional comments on Indochina in the 1950s, Kennedy entered the White House knowing relatively little about Diem or about the Second Vietnam War that had begun in 1959. Ho Chi Minh's goal was to unite all of Vietnam under the Viet Minh. To undermine the Diem regime, North Vietnam and its allies in South Vietnam created the National Liberation Front. It was based mostly in the South, but it was closely allied with the North. Eisenhower's national security team, in their last day in office, told Kennedy that his first priority should be Laos. Later, Kennedy noted, "Eisenhower never mentioned the word Vietnam to me."[3]

But it did not take long for him to understand the magnitude of the problem in Vietnam, especially when he read Eisenhower's last, pessimistic briefing on the war.

> Beginning in December 1959, there has been a mounting increase throughout South Vietnam of Viet Cong terrorist activities and guerilla warfare . . . If the GVN [government of South Vietnam] does not take immediate and extraordinary action to regain popular support . . . the Viet Cong can cause the overthrow of the present GVN government in the months to come.[4]

Kennedy was determined to get the Vietnam War on a better path within three months, and he wanted to learn more about the growing conflict.

One of his first tutors was Edward Lansdale, a brilliant and often reckless CIA agent and major general. He had enormous fame (and some infamy), especially once he became the model for CIA agents in several best-selling spy novels. Among those books were Graham Greene's *The Quiet American*, published in 1956, and William Lederer and Eugene Burdick's sensational 1958 novel, *The Ugly American*, which drew broad attention to what the authors considered the failure of American foreign policy. It eventually became the source of a popular movie.[5]

Within a week of his inauguration, Kennedy was reading Lansdale's captivating reports on the conflict in Vietnam. Among them was a story of a fishing village that had come under attack from the Viet Cong. The villagers had taught themselves some of the same guerrilla tactics that their Viet Cong enemies had used. Landsdale described them as people of great courage. "They were confident that they were going to beat the enemy," he wrote, "and that free men everywhere were going to win out eventually over Communism. Having an American present, their repeated question was to ask if the U.S. was going to stand firm in its policy in Asia." They were unafraid to die for their cause. "Next year," Lansdale quoted them, "you will see somebody else here. Two hundred of us will be dead then."[6] Lansdale understood Kennedy's love of courage, and this was a narrative that he hoped would impress the president with the commitment of the South Vietnamese.

Kennedy soon came to believe that the United States had not done enough to protect South Vietnam. He wanted his aides to learn more about counterinsurgency and guerrilla warfare (an effort mostly organized by Robert Kennedy), and he authorized $19 million (on top of the more than $200 million already authorized) for training in unconventional methods of warfare. It would allow American soldiers to fight the new kinds of battles that were developing in Vietnam, where the Green Berets were much in demand. He tentatively authorized a task force in June 1961 to address "the problem of informing the public about the reasons for a decision to use force."[7]

And he began worrying, just as his predecessors had, about the reliability of Diem and his government. The CIA warned that Diem had very little popular support among the South Vietnamese. Theodore H. White, the journalist and chronicler of Kennedy's 1960 campaign, returned from Vietnam with similar opinions. "The government of Ngo Dinh Diem," he wrote, "has been completely unable to mobilize the people of South-Viet-Nam for political or emotional resistance to the Communists . . . Any investment of our troops in the paddies of the delta will, I believe, be useless—or worse. The presence of white American troops will feed the race hate of the Viet-Namese."[8] Ambassador at Large Averell Harriman was also skeptical about the value of military efforts there.[9]

But Diem also had influential allies in the United States. There was the growing political clout of the American Friends of Vietnam. There was the unwavering support from the American ambassador, Frederick Nolting, and from General Paul D. Harkins, the first commander of the U.S. advisory mission, Military Assistance Command Vietnam (MACV). And there was public praise from eminent members of Congress, including Senator Stuart Symington, and from Vice President Lyndon Johnson, who returned from a visit to Vietnam calling Diem the "Winston Churchill of Southeast Asia."[10]

Kennedy was not fully confident in the American supporters of Vietnam. He turned, as he often did, to his military mentor, General

Maxwell Taylor. In November 1961, he sent Taylor and Walt Rostow to Saigon to evaluate the strength of the Vietnamese military. The Taylor Report, as it came to be called, bluntly stated that "South Vietnam is in serious trouble . . . but if the U.S. promptly and energetically takes up the challenge, a victory can be had without a U.S. takeover of the war." The report continued:

> Despite the intellectuals who sit on the side lines and complain . . . it cannot be emphasized too strongly . . . that time has nearly run out for converting these assets into the bases for victory. Diem himself—and all concerned with the fate of the country—are looking to American guidance and aid to achieve a turning point in Vietnam's affairs. From all quarters of Southeast Asia the message on Vietnam is the same: vigorous American action is needed to buy time for Vietnam to mobilize and organize its real assets.

The Taylor Report concluded that "it will be necessary to include some combat troops for the protection of logistical operations and the defense of the area occupied by U.S. forces"—up to six thousand to eight thousand. "Any troops coming to VN may expect to take casualties."[11]

Back in Washington, Undersecretary of State George Ball told Kennedy bluntly that "Taylor is wrong . . . Within five years, we'll have three hundred thousand men in the paddies and jungles and never find them again."[12] But Taylor and Rostow steadied Kennedy's wavering confidence in Diem and in the importance of the U.S. role in the war. "The fall of South Vietnam to Communism," Taylor insisted, "would lead to the fairly rapid extension of Communist control, or complete accommodation to Communism, in the rest of mainland Southeast Asia right down to Indonesia. The strategic implications worldwide would be extremely serious." Taylor was making the case that there was no choice but to support South Vietnam.[13]

By the end of 1961, Kennedy was clearly committed to supporting South Vietnam and was even ready to order military intervention if necessary. He agreed to the creation of "Operation Ranch Hand," whose purpose was to use chemical defoliants (including napalm) to destroy the Viet Cong's sanctuaries and their food supplies. He assured Diem that "the United States is determined to help Viet-Nam preserve its independence, protect its people against Communist assassins, and build a better life through economic growth." And he promised, "We shall promptly increase our assistance to our defense effort."[14]

. . .

On January 18, 1962, Kennedy signed a national security memorandum authorizing active combat activities by some American soldiers in Vietnam (although the soldiers were still described as "advisers"). They were called the "Special Group," the first significant U.S. troop presence in Vietnam. In the early months of the American military presence, many Americans in Washington and in Vietnam felt certain that the war would soon be won. U.S. soldiers manned helicopters and attacked Viet Cong guerrillas from above without any significant cost. "Roaring in the treetops, a terrifying sight to the superstitious Viet Cong peasant . . . they simply turned and ran . . . easy targets," Roger Hilsman, who worked for the State Department in Saigon, later wrote enthusiastically.[15] *Time* magazine's cover story on Vietnam in May was a beaming description of progress: "Trim, with grey hair, steely blue eyes and a strong nose and chin, General [Paul] Harkins looked 'every inch the professional soldier.'" Maxwell Taylor reported "favorable trends in all military activities."[16] Robert McNamara promised, "We are going to win in Viet Nam. We will remain until we do." There was already, *Time* said, a "remarkable U.S. military effort, mounted in the few short months since Washington decided last October to hold South Viet Nam at all costs."[17] Things looked so promising that planning began for a withdrawal of troops in July 1962, with a schedule that would remove all American forces by the spring of 1964.

The ebullient optimism of these first months of combat did not last long. The withdrawals were postponed again and again. Only a modest one thousand men were withdrawn, and not until December

1963 (during which time many more troops had arrived). The war was still at a relatively low level, but neither was there the "tremendous progress" that McNamara had claimed in July 1962.[18] Internal memos flew through the White House asking pointed questions of the officers in Vietnam: "Why were the Special Warfare units withdrawn from Vietnam in November 1960? Why are they not being sent back to work?" "Why are the capabilities of the helicopter not being fully exploited in the counter-guerrilla program of the Vietnamese?" The answers were almost always the absence of enough equipment and the poor training of the Vietnamese army.[19] George Ball dutifully explained in a 1962 speech why this relatively unpopular war had to be supported. "We cannot continue to lead the Free World unless we enjoy—and deserve—the confidence of those who think we do . . . We are increasing our effort in training, in logistics, in the transport of the Viet-Nam forces."[20]

Within the White House, pessimism was slowly growing. Even during the relatively low-level combat in 1962, the war was going badly. "I've been President for a year. How can things like this go on happening?" Kennedy asked testily following reports of a failed bombing effort.[21] One of the most celebrated efforts in 1962—the Strategic Hamlet Program—was a program that Kennedy, and many others, hoped would be a great success. The United States and the South Vietnamese government set out to protect the hamlets by providing physical security and political persuasion to support the anticommunist forces. But the program, which ran from late 1961 until late 1963—despite occasional successes—was unable to protect the hamlets effectively and was even less successful in changing what was called "hearts and minds." The South Vietnamese peasants were particularly vulnerable to the Viet Cong soldiers. And because of the tremendous pressure from them, many rural Vietnamese shifted their loyalties to the Viet Cong. John Hebel, a U.S. consul in Hue, reported that the countryside was "deteriorating," and that "the strategic hamlet program is mostly pure façade."[22] Its failure was a tremendous blow to the U.S. mission.

• • •

By late 1962, almost all Americans involved in the Vietnam War were rapidly losing confidence in President Diem. Kennedy continued to support him publicly, and he tried repeatedly to persuade Diem to increase the war effort and to cooperate with the American military more effectively. In an October letter, on the anniversary of South Vietnam's independence, Kennedy saluted "the valiant struggle of the past year, the sacrifices and sorrows of countless heroes and the introduction of new institutions such as the strategic hamlet to bring lasting social and economic benefits to the people . . . [and would] earn for Viet-Nam the world's admiration." But the compliments did not include any direct praise for Diem.[23]

As 1963 began, many officials in the Kennedy administration were struggling to find a way to get rid of Diem and his powerful family. American military leaders loyal to Diem accumulated glowing statistics, but lower-level officers told the press that the numbers were unreliable. The reporter Neil Sheehan came to believe that the Vietnamese soldiers did not want "to risk suffering heavy casualties in close-up fighting and possibly 'lose face.' "[24]

General Harkins continued to defend the war effort. "I believe," he said, "that anyone who criticizes the fighting qualities of the armed forces of the Republic of Viet Nam is doing a disservice to the thousands of gallant and courageous men who are fighting in the defense of their country."[25] He laid out a new program for making the South Vietnamese regime more effective. But it was already clear that Diem was not allowing the South Vietnamese army to do what Harkins needed—or almost anything else that the American government wanted.[26]

The beginning of the end of the Diem regime came not from anything the Americans or the Viet Cong did, but from what Diem himself began. For many months, Diem and his Catholic family had been worried about the power of the Buddhists in South Vietnam, who were the largest religious group in the country. The government was taking steps to weaken them by restricting their political and religious activities. In response, a group of Buddhists began a series of nonviolent protests in multiple cities. The conflict escalated dramatically on May 8, 1963, when government troops fired on

Buddhist protesters in Hue, killing nine Buddhists and wounding fourteen others. In the aftermath of the massacre, Buddhist leaders insisted on their right to fly Buddhist flags and to have religious equality with Catholicism (the religion of most of the government). Ambassador Nolting, who had almost always supported Diem, insisted on an end to attacks on the Buddhists and on compensation for the victims. But Diem ignored him. Instead, on June 8, Diem's powerful sister-in-law Madame Nhu intensified the conflict by accusing the Buddhists of collaborating with communists. Three days later, a Buddhist monk named Thich Quang Duc set himself on fire as a protest in a prominent intersection in Saigon.[27]

The suicide was broadcast around the world, and a photograph of the monk in flames was published on the front page of many newspapers. Kennedy was shocked. "No news picture in history has generated as much emotion around the world as that one has," he remarked glumly.[28] As the Buddhist crisis grew, American efforts to defuse it proved impotent. Madame Nhu contemptuously described the suicide as a "barbecue . . . with imported gasoline."[29] Diem's brother Ngo Dinh Nhu sent out raids to the Buddhist pagodas to round up monks, killing several of them in the process. Kennedy, while on a series of visits in Europe, recalled Ambassador Nolting and replaced him with Henry Cabot Lodge (his onetime Senate opponent in Massachusetts), who took office in September. Unlike Nolting, Lodge believed that no progress in the war was likely to occur without removing Diem.[30]

The questions posed to Kennedy in television interviews in early September revealed some of the growing skepticism about the war. "Have you had any reason to doubt this so-called 'domino theory,' that if South Viet-Nam falls, the rest of southeast Asia will go behind it?" the NBC News anchorman David Brinkley asked. "I believe it," Kennedy replied. "If South Viet-Nam went, it would . . . give the impression that the wave of the future in southeast Asia was China and the Communists." Chet Huntley, Brinkley's coanchor, asked, "Could it be that our Government tends occasionally to get locked into a policy . . . and finds it difficult to alter or shift that policy? . . . Are we likely now to reduce our aid to South Viet-Nam now?" Kennedy tersely said that he would continue to support Diem and that he would insist that the aid would continue.[31] Walter Cronkite of CBS News also asked, in another interview with the president, about the "difficulties" with the Diem regime. "I don't think that unless a greater effort is made by the government to win popular support that the war can be won out there," Kennedy responded, a veiled threat to the Diem regime. "With changes in policy and perhaps personnel I think it can. If it doesn't make . . . changes, I would think that the chances of winning it would not be very good."[32]

Kennedy's hints of "personnel" changes in his interview with Cronkite were not insignificant. His concerns about Diem became particularly intense after Lodge—in his first days in Saigon—expressed shock by the "fear which pervades Saigon, Hue, and Da Nang" as the Diem regime desperately tried to shut down dissidents. Lodge described the regime as a "police state atmosphere."[33] A coup to overthrow Diem had already been planned by disgruntled Vietnamese generals early in the fall. (Lodge did not oppose the plan but said they would "proceed at their own risk.")[34] In the end, the conspiracy unraveled before any steps were taken. Roger Hilsman wrote from Vietnam that "the Nhus stand for . . . the GVN policy of repression . . . The Nhus must therefore go . . . They must . . . be barred from return until the war is won." Hilsman noted that members of the Senate were now saying that they were "no longer willing" to support the Diem regime.[35] A top-secret memo of October 4 from the White House ordered the American embassy to "test and probe the effectiveness of any actions the GVN actually takes," with the unstated, but understood, determination that Diem would have to go if he continued to obstruct the progress of the war. Diem's regime, the memo noted, "has the trappings of democracy but in reality it has been evolving into an authoritarian government maintained by police terrorist methods."[36] But it was not so much the absence of "democracy" that was driving the changes. It was Diem's stubborn isolation.

· · ·

There was growing disagreement in the White House as Kennedy tried to decide whether (and how) he might remove Diem. A coup would be an awkward step—overthrowing a sitting president from what the United States insisted was a sovereign state. Kennedy was still uncertain. He sent a military officer (General Victor Krulak) and a foreign service officer (Joseph Mendenhall) to judge the viability of Diem. The general told Kennedy that he thought Diem should continue to be supported. Mendenhall reported that the Diem government was in chaos. Given the uncertainty, it was not surprising that the recommendations were at odds with each other. "The two of you did visit the same country, didn't you?" the president responded skeptically.[37]

Kennedy then sent Taylor and McNamara to do another assessment. They returned cautiously optimistic about the war, but they both agreed that Diem was an obstacle to success. "There are serious political tensions in Saigon," they concluded, "where the Diem–Nhu government is becoming increasingly unpopular . . . We should recognize we may have to decide in two to four months to move to more drastic action."[38] Kennedy then wrote to Diem, threatening "to cut off our aid programs" unless there were "important changes and improvements in the relations" between the Diem regime and the United States.[39]

Rumors were growing in both Washington and Saigon that Ngo Dinh Nhu was negotiating with Hanoi. Communications were deteriorating between the White House and the Diem government. The Vietnamese generals who had participated in the earlier, aborted coup in August now approached Lodge in October to propose another coup against Diem. The official response was that the U.S. government did not want to support a coup but would not obstruct one. With that, General Duong Van Minh, one of the most powerful Vietnamese officers (known as "Big Minh"), began mobilizing for a strike against Diem.[40] Kennedy continued to waver while the coup was organizing. Right until the end, he was still asking questions of his aides. Would new leaders be any better than Diem? He called for a meeting on the morning of November 2 to "review position and urgently ask your recommendations." But time had run out.[41]

On October 29, with the generals gathering for their coup, the nervous Diem asked Lodge what the United States would do to protect him. "I do not feel well enough informed to tell you," Lodge replied cryptically. "It is 4:30 a.m. in Washington and the U.S. government cannot possibly have a view." He added, "I am worried about your physical safety," and offered to help Diem leave the country.[42] But even that level of support soon evaporated when the State Department warned that helping Diem flee would make the coup seem to be "American-inspired and manipulated."[43]

On November 1, without consulting Washington or the American embassy, the Vietnamese generals launched their coup. Diem and his brother Nhu fled to a private home in Saigon, from which they asked for an American plane to take them out of the country. CIA agents in Saigon refused, worried again that it would suggest American participation in the coup. The brothers then sought refuge in a Catholic church. Some of the generals had already concluded that leaving the brothers alive would be a threat to their authority. "To kill weeds, you must pull them up at the roots," one general said.[44] Diem and Nhu were escorted to an army vehicle, ostensibly to take them to safety. Instead, the van pulled aside, and an officer shot and killed them both. When asked by another general why they had been assassinated, Big Minh—now in control—replied, "And what does it matter if they are dead."[45]

Kennedy learned of the deaths of Diem and Nhu early on November 2. The *New York Times*, in a calm editorial the next morning, wrote that "the only surprising thing about the military revolt in Saigon is that it did not come sooner."[46] But Kennedy was not so hardhearted. According to Schlesinger, he was "somber and shaken." He said, "I had not seen [Kennedy] so depressed since the Bay of Pigs."[47] Maxwell Taylor recalled that he "leaped to his feet [at the news] and rushed from the room with a look of shock and dismay on his face which I had never seen before."[48] Kennedy's feeling of guilt was palpable, evidenced by a taped statement that he left for future scholars.

I feel that we must bear a good deal of responsibility for it, beginning with our cable of early August in which we suggested the coup . . . I was shocked by the death of Diem and Nhu . . . The way he was killed made it particularly abhorrent. The question now is whether the generals can stay together and build a stable government.[49]

For the next several years, the new government in Saigon would prove little better than the old one.

. . .

Would Kennedy have brought the Vietnam War to an end had he lived? On the one hand, he made clear through most of his presidency that he considered the survival of South Vietnam a linchpin of the free world. Only weeks before he died, he confirmed that belief, arguing that should Vietnam fall, all of Southeast Asia would follow, with devastating results for American prestige and power. He also spoke often of how politically damaging to him the fall of Vietnam would be—both domestically and internationally—especially in the aftermath of the failed Cuban invasion in 1961 and what many critics considered his timid role in trying to stabilize Laos. In his last press conference, on November 14, 1963, he responded sharply to a question about congressional efforts to reduce foreign aid: "I can't believe that the Congress of the United States is going to be so unwise . . . Are we going to give up Vietnam?"[50]

At the same time, however, he often spoke hopefully of recalling some American soldiers as early as 1962 and all of them by 1964 or 1965. He frequently rejected the military's request for more troops, and he resisted escalating the war. Like almost everyone who was drawn into the Vietnam War, Kennedy had doubts and reservations. At every step he hoped that each plateau would be the last, only to find that there were more, higher plateaus to come. There was no easy path to victory in Vietnam—and all the many presidents who were engaged in this process knew it.

But it would be a mistake to argue that all presidents would have acted the same way had they faced the rapidly changing war. McGeorge Bundy, the national security adviser to both Kennedy and Johnson, said years later that "Kennedy didn't want to be dumb . . . Johnson didn't want to be a coward."[51] In fact, Kennedy wavered back and forth on the war. When McNamara and Taylor returned from their October 1962 review of the Vietnam War, they assured Kennedy that the war could be completed by 1965. But, McNamara said, "if it extends beyond that period we believe we can train the Vietnamese to take over the essential functions and withdraw the bulk of our forces."[52] Neither McNamara nor Bundy were willing to suggest that the Vietnamese might not be able to defend themselves. Kennedy continued the same argument through November 1963, when he told reporters that a conference scheduled for Honolulu was "to attempt to assess the situation: what American policy should be . . . how can we intensify the struggle, how we can bring Americans out of there. Now, that is our object, to bring Americans home, permit the South Vietnamese to maintain themselves as a free and independent country."[53]

Nothing in this statement suggested what would happen if this scenario failed. In late 1963, the future of the war was still uncertain. American troops in Vietnam were few; American casualties were relatively small. There was still time to move in many different directions. "I have never thought it wise to speculate in public as to what John Kennedy would have done about Vietnam had he lived," Bundy said in 1978. "The public record shows him constantly asserting two propositions that could not have coexisted in later years: that we must not quit there and that in the end the Vietnamese must do the job for themselves."[54]

At times, Kennedy spoke of withdrawing even if it meant the defeat of South Vietnam. But more often, he talked about how he might transfer the burden to the South Vietnamese military. In the few weeks between the coup in Saigon and his death—however distraught Kennedy was about the assassinations of the Nhu brothers—he never said anything to suggest that the coup was likely to change his view of the future. On the contrary, he spoke at times in late 1963 of how he would withdraw from Vietnam after 1965, after his election, however the chips might fall. Arthur Schlesinger wrote later that "Kennedy had no intention of dispatching American ground troops to save South Vietnam."[55] Bundy agreed. At the same time,

however, Kennedy continued to speak forcefully about the importance of the survival of South Vietnam.

With hindsight, it would seem an easy decision to avoid the
quagmire of Vietnam. But as late as early 1967, the vast majority of
Americans continued to support the Vietnam War, even though an
antiwar movement was already rapidly growing. No one can say for
sure what Kennedy might have done. He was certainly more skit-
tish about escalating the war than Johnson later became, but he
consistently, if slowly, escalated it until his death.

In the end, the most important question remains: would Kennedy ever have accepted the fall of Vietnam? "How does a President
explain a 'defeat' without a commitment of U.S. ground troops?"
Bundy asked in retrospect. "We have to admit (a) that it is very hard
and (b) no one can be sure JFK would have done it."[56] At the time of
his death, Kennedy left this question unanswered.

• • •

The Vietnam War was not Kennedy's only problem in October
1963. Almost everyone in the White House was still troubled by
the president's seeming inability to pass significant legislation. Part
of the problem was still the narrow Democratic majorities in Congress and the large number of conservative southern Democrats in
both houses. But another part of the problem was Kennedy himself,
who was not adept at political "horse trading" and did not feel comfortable bargaining and persuading aggressively.

The tax cut, which he had first proposed in 1961, was a good
example of his problem. When the bill came up in the Senate Finance
Committee in October 1963, Kennedy's own secretary of the treasury, Douglas Dillon, proposed over five hundred "reforms" in
response to pressure from corporate interests. "Those robbing
bastards!" Kennedy said, convinced that the changes would destroy
the purpose of the tax cut, which was to create more purchasing
power for consumers. But even after the "reforms" were removed,
the president made little progress with the bill. He met with Wilbur
Mills, the powerful chairman of the House Ways and Means Com-

mittee, to ask for advice on how to improve the bill's chances. "I'm satisfied 100% of people in my district would welcome tax reduction," Mills told Kennedy. "But when they talk about reducing taxes, they get back to this old . . . concept that they've grown up with: If you're gonna cut taxes . . . you better cut your spending."[57]

The civil rights bill was also stalled by Congress. In the aftermath of the president's powerful television speech in June proposing the bill, African American leaders—once skeptical of Kennedy's commitment—now saw the president as an ally. But Kennedy was frank about how hard it would be to get two-thirds of the Senate to support it. Roy Wilkins, a leader of the NAACP, thought that if the House passed the bill, it would put pressure on the Senate. Others were more skeptical. A. Philip Randolph, the leader of the Brotherhood of Sleeping Car Porters and a civil rights activist, said, "It's obvious that it's going to take nothing less than a crusade to win approval for these civil rights measures." And he told Kennedy, "Nobody can lead this crusade but you."[58] The president balked. He was comfortable giving speeches on behalf of civil rights, but he was reluctant to throw himself into the battle, worried—probably correctly—that to do so would jeopardize other legislation. Kennedy resisted strong measures, such as a proposal by the Civil Rights Commission to cut off federal funding in Mississippi until the state took steps against racial discrimination. "We always felt that maybe this was going to be his political swansong," Robert Kennedy later said. "He would ask me every four days, 'Do you think we did the right thing by sending the legislation up? Look at the trouble it got us in.'" He once said that "this issue could cost me the election." But he also said, "We're not turning back."[59] It was clear, however, that the bill would not go to the floor until 1964.

Congress was unhappy with almost all of Kennedy's domestic legislation. His proposal for health insurance for elderly Americans (which led to Medicare in later years) was defeated in 1963. He was unable to stop cuts in the foreign aid program, something Kennedy considered of great importance. He was also unable to pass federal aid to education. His longtime effort to create a department of urban affairs foundered. The idea of what would later become a "war on poverty" was emerging from the White House, but it too made no progress in 1963.[60]

Kennedy believed that winning a second term would strengthen his hand with Congress once he had a mandate greater than his slim victory in 1960. Whether that would have happened—second terms are rarely as successful as first ones—is, of course, unknown.[61]

• • •

His legislative failures, however, did not weaken him politically. In November 1963, his approval rating was 59 percent. That number was down significantly from the beginning of the year, mostly because of the civil rights bill, which alienated many white southerners. But polls continued to show that he was ahead of all of his potential opponents—and well ahead of Senator Barry Goldwater of Arizona, his most likely Republican rival. He looked forward to the campaign, and a year before the election he was already ridiculing Goldwater. At his October 31 press conference, a reporter asked the president about Goldwater's charge that he was "mismanaging the news . . . to perpetuate [him]self in office." Kennedy enjoyed press conferences (he held sixty-four of them), and he was at his witty best in his response. He said of Goldwater:

> I am confident that he will be making many charges even more serious than this one in the coming months. And, in addition, he himself has had a busy week selling TVA and giving permission to or suggesting that military commanders overseas be permitted to use nuclear weapons, and attacking the President of Bolivia while he was here in the United States, and involving himself in the Greek election. So I thought it really would not be fair for me this week to reply to him.[62]

By early November, he was already campaigning. "He was doing the thing he liked even better than being President," Kenny O'Donnell later wrote, "getting away from Washington . . . where he was sure he could win over the people even though many of the bosses and most of the big money were against him."[63] He made four speeches in Florida on November 18, and three days later he began a schedule of events in Texas. He spoke at a dedication of a medical center in San Antonio, made remarks to groups in Houston, and gave a speech in Fort Worth much like those he had made at the beginning of his presidency. He focused mostly on international issues and on the dangerous world Americans confronted, and reminded them again of the sacrifices they would have to make.

> No one expects that our life will be easy, certainly not in this decade, and perhaps not in this century. But we should realize what a burden and responsibility the people of the United States have borne for so many years . . . So this country, which desires only to be secure . . . has borne more than its share of the burden, has stood watch for more than its number of years. I don't think we are fatigued or tired. We would like to live as we once lived. But history will not permit it.[64]

It was his last speech.

From Fort Worth, he took a short flight to Dallas on Friday, November 22, and began a long, slow motorcade snaking through the crowded city. The newspapers there were peppered that morning with harsh anticommunist advertisements bordered in black attacking the president. "We're heading into nut country today," Kennedy said to his wife as they drove into Dallas. "But Jackie, if somebody wants to shoot me from a window with a rifle, nobody can stop him so why worry about it?"[65] A few hours later, shots were fired in Dealey Plaza. Two bullets struck the president. His death was announced at 1 p.m.

—————

# 9

# The Afterlife of John F. Kennedy

The Sunday *New York Times* of November 24, 1963—the day before John Kennedy's funeral—was filled with reverential stories of the president's death, as were almost all other newspapers, magazines, and radio and television broadcasts. When one Kennedy colleague commented, "Life goes on, but brightness has fallen from the air," he was expressing sentiments that were already the common coin of public discourse.[1]

But also in that Sunday paper was a largely unnoticed item with a very different meaning. Sitting at the top of the weekly nonfiction best-seller list of the *New York Times Book Review*, as it had sat for several months before, was a book published by the conservative political writer Victor Lasky. It was *J.F.K.: The Man and the Myth*, a harsh (some believed scurrilous) attack designed to convince the public that the president's alluring image rested on a series of lies and deceptions. It claimed nothing less than that John Kennedy was a fraud, unfit for the presidency—by character, temperament, and intellect.[2] Lasky's book was the third best-selling nonfiction title of the year, according to *Publishers Weekly*.[3]

In the days after the assassination, Lasky's book fell rapidly off the best-seller list. Some bookstores removed it from their shelves. But the author's dark image of the president, as much as the reverent one that prevailed in the November 24 issue of the *Times*, suggested something about the complex way John Kennedy had already entered the American imagination.

• • •

On the one hand, Kennedy seemed then, and to many seems still, an embodiment of America's loftiest ideals and boldest hopes—a gallant warrior whose death marked the end of an age of confidence and optimism and the beginning of an era of conflict and disenchantment. His memory became an inspiration to countless younger men and women to devote their lives to public service (among them the future president Bill Clinton). On the other hand, Kennedy was then, and remains still, a symbol of the underside of our political life. He won the presidency in part through his father's money and power. His administration used the CIA and other agents (including members of the Mafia) to undermine the Castro regime and to attempt to kill Fidel Castro. Kennedy was a man whose private life was riddled with personal scandals and hidden health problems. These two conflicting images have managed to coexist with extraordinary duration.

It is hardly surprising that the sudden, violent death of a young and appealing president would create an exaggerated portrait of his life. The creation of that image began within minutes of his death, when the three television networks canceled all regular programming (including advertisements) and instead devoted almost four entire days to the coverage of his death and funeral. At about the same time, *Life* magazine published two issues on the assassination that sold millions of copies each. It was followed by a "special memorial edition" that combined the two earlier issues and sold another 3 million copies. The image grew further with dozens of books about his life and death published within months, and many more in later years. Among them was Arthur Schlesinger's emotional account of Kennedy's presidency, *A Thousand Days* (1965). He wrote in the aftermath of Kennedy's death:

> It was all gone now—the life-affirming, life-enhancing zest, the brilliance, the wit, the cool commitment, the steady purpose . . . One remembered Stephen Spender's poem:
> *I think continually of those who were truly great . . .*
> *The names of those who in their lives fought for life,*

*Who wore at their hearts the fire's center.*
*Born of the sun they traveled a short while towards the sun,*
*And left the vivid air signed with their honour.*[4]

·  ·  ·

John Kennedy served in office for fewer than three years. His tangible accomplishments during his foreshortened term were relatively modest. By most of the normal standards by which historians assess presidents, Kennedy seems in many ways to be a relatively minor president. A survey of historians ranking the presidents in 1982 placed Kennedy thirteenth. A 1996 poll by the *New York Times* placed him twelfth, moving him up only one notch in fourteen years. The historical Kennedy, as opposed to the Kennedy of legend, was a cautious, practical, often skillful politician driven by political reality much more than by lofty ideals. Members of his administration boasted that, unlike some of the militant cold warriors of the 1950s, they were pragmatists, not ideologues. It is one of the many ironies of Kennedy's posthumous image that a man who himself was so uncomfortable with passionate commitment would inspire so much of it in others.[5]

It was not just intimates who created the Kennedy legend. It was a public eager to believe in it. Even while he lived, he was becoming a national obsession: a man who had been elected to the presidency by one of the narrowest margins in history, but who by the middle of 1963 had already become so magnetic a figure that 58 percent of the public claimed they had voted for him, even though he actually received only 49.7 percent of the votes in 1960. After his death, this imaginary landslide grew to 65 percent.[6]

The power of the Kennedy legend did nothing but grow. The *New York Times* columnist James Reston noted after his death, "Deprived of the place he sought in history, he has been given in compensation a place in legend."[7] Two decades later, the journalist Theodore White wrote in his memoir:

> I still have difficulty seeing John F. Kennedy clear.
> The image of him that comes back to me, as to most who

knew him, is so clean and graceful—almost as if I can still see him skip up the steps of his airplane in that half lope, and then turn, flinging out his arm in farewell to the crowd, before disappearing inside. It was a ballet movement. The remembered pleasures of travel with him clutter the outline of history.[8]

• • •

The darker image of Kennedy was slower to emerge. But beginning in the late 1960s, and accelerating rapidly thereafter, it moved out of the shadows of Victor Lasky and into full public view. As time went on, the conservative attacks on Kennedy gradually withered, replaced by harsh attacks on him from the left. Some of the reassessment came from historians and other scholars who saw in Kennedy's policies an intensification, not a reduction, of a destructive Cold War militancy, and they argued that he had contributed to the escalation of the Vietnam War. Some veterans of the civil rights movement became disillusioned as they discovered that Kennedy had at times worked to contain the movement and had done little to block J. Edgar Hoover's efforts to discredit its leaders. (Robert Kennedy approved Hoover's wiretapping of King.) Others were alarmed by the sordid and illegal covert efforts in Cuba.[9]

This counterlegend also included a disillusionment with the man himself. In an age increasingly preoccupied with the personal behavior of public figures, Kennedy's now well-known private life has disillusioned many Americans. They have seen in him a recklessness and even a moral emptiness. A string of books appeared that created a picture of a much shallower and less accomplished figure than most Americans remembered. "The Kennedy rhetoric sounds flashy now," Garry Wills wrote in *The Kennedy Imprisonment*. "This is not simply a matter of passing time and changing fashions . . . Kennedy did not liberate the intellectuals who praised him; he subverted them. He played to all that was weakest and worst in them."[10] The journalist Ben Bradlee, Kennedy's onetime close friend, wrote in his memoir of his dismay at discovering the president's reckless womanizing and frequent vulgarity.[11] Malcolm Muggeridge, an acerbic English writer, wrote in the 1970s, "John F. Kennedy, it is now coming to be realized, was a nothing man—an expensively programmed wax-work, a camera-microphone-public relations creation whose career on examination turns into a strip cartoon rather than history."[12] I. F. Stone wrote in 1973, "By now he is simply an optical illusion."[13] Even some of his friends and acquaintances felt much the same way many years later. Historians, journalists, and other skeptical writers also challenged the dominant image of Kennedy—among them Herbert Parmet, Henry Fairlie, Peter Collier and David Horowitz, Richard Walton, Thomas Reeves, and even such friends and col-leagues as Harris Wofford.[14]

Some critics went even further and offered an image that wavered between malevolence and pettiness—a man described variously as driven by "an obsessive-compulsive need for power and recogni-tion," or as the "very embodiment of middlebrow culture climbing," or as a leader utterly lacking in "depth and seriousness."[15] In *The Dark Side of Camelot*, Seymour Hersh wrote of Kennedy as "a man whose personal weaknesses limited his ability to carry out his duties as president . . . Otherwise strong and self-reliant men and women were awed and seduced by Kennedy's magnetism and . . . competed with one another to please the most charismatic leader in our nation's history. Many are still blinded today."[16]

· · ·

And into this stew of conflicting images emerged a plethora of con-troversies about his assassination. It is not surprising that many Americans raised doubts about the Warren Commission, which Lyndon Johnson created a week after Kennedy's death. It was heavy with powerful, influential men who rushed through the process and failed to investigate some of the most controversial elements of the case. They worked in the shadow of a new president who pres-sured the commission to move quickly and to dig lightly in some areas. They concluded that the death of John Kennedy was the work of a single, lonely gunman.

But the Warren Commission was not alone. In 1968, Attorney General Ramsey Clark organized a group of physicians to examine the shooting, and they concluded that the forensic results were consistent with the commission's finding. In the 1970s, with conspiracy theories still growing, Vice President Nelson Rockefeller chaired a commission at the request of President Gerald Ford to investigate the assassination again and also supported the Warren Commission. (Ford himself had been a member of the original Warren Commission.) Gerald Posner, a respected writer, published a six-hundred-page book, *Case Closed*, in 1993 that concluded:

> Chasing shadows on the grassy knoll will never substitute for real history. Lee Harvey Oswald, driven by his own twisted and impenetrable furies, was the only assassin at Dealey Plaza on November 22, 1963. To say otherwise, in light of overwhelming evidence, is to absolve a man with blood on his hands, and to mock the President he killed.[17]

And the well-known prosecutor Vincent Bugliosi published a 1,648-page book in 2007, *Reclaiming History: The Assassination of John F. Kennedy*, that also debunked the conspiracy theorists and insisted that Oswald acted alone:

> Refusing to accept the plain truth and dedicating their existence for over forty years to convincing the American public of the truth of their own charges, the critics have journeyed to the outer margins of their imaginations.[18]

But the challenges to the Warren Commission have continued to overwhelm the official explanation. Mark Lane's 1966 book *Rush to Judgment*, which has sold more than a million copies, was one of the first books to cast doubt on the Warren Commission.[19] Articles in *Life*, the *New York Review of Books*, and other reputable magazines joined the growing number of skeptics.[20] Jim Garrison, the district attorney in New Orleans, organized his own highly publicized investigation of the assassination—convinced that a shadowy group of misfits and mercenaries had joined the conspiracy. The House of Representatives Committee on Assassinations concluded in 1979 that more than one assassin had shot at Kennedy. Public opinion polls, beginning in the late 1960s, showed a consistent growth of belief in conspiracy. In a Gallup poll in 2004, 64 percent of those participating believed that there had been a conspiracy to kill Kennedy. A year later, an ABC poll showed that the belief reached 70 percent.[21]

More than a thousand books have been published about the Kennedy assassination, the vast majority of them debunking the belief that Oswald acted alone. But it was not just obscure theorists who thought the assassination might have been a conspiracy. Within hours of his brother's death, Robert Kennedy himself gravitated briefly into the conspiracy world. He began looking into a shadowy nexus of forces that he believed were at odds with the policies of his brother's administration. Was it the CIA, he asked John McCone, the director of the agency? Was the assassination the work of anti-Castro Cubans? Was it the American Mafia? Was it Lyndon Johnson, as some conspiracies claimed? Or was it—since there were hidden but important connections among all these groups—a combined effort by them all? Before he had ever heard the name Lee Harvey Oswald, Robert Kennedy was considering, for a short while, scenarios that were little different from some of the myriad theories of conspiracy that have haunted the American imagination for half a century.[22]

The enormous interest in the assassination, and the persistence of conspiracy theories behind it, is yet more evidence of the power of Kennedy's posthumous life. "There was a heroic grandeur to John F. Kennedy's administration that had nothing to do with the mists of Camelot," argued David Talbot, the editor of *Salon* magazine and the author of one of the more serious books on the conspiracy theories. "It was a presidency that clashed with its own times, and in the end found some measure of greatness."[23]

Indeed, Talbot and others argue that it was the courage and vision of Kennedy—and the dangers he posed to entrenched interests in and out of government—that many people believe was the reason for his death. Kennedy had angered the CIA by refusing adequately to support the Bay of Pigs invasion, declining subsequent efforts to overthrow Castro, and considering a rapprochement with communist Cuba and the Soviet Union. He had infuriated some of the hard-core anti-Castro émigrés for the same reason. Together, the Kennedy brothers had antagonized Jimmy Hoffa and the Mafia through the Justice Department's relentless efforts to break their power. At the same time, the president had made bitter enemies of conservative white southerners because of his bold embrace of the civil rights movement. He had invited the contempt of much of the military by his cautious response to the Cuban missile crisis, and he had alarmed much of the foreign policy establishment with a supposed plan to end the Vietnam War.

John Kennedy, according to many conspiracy theorists, had challenged virtually all the premises that were at the heart of the Cold War. He had offered an alternative path, one that rejected reckless military action and sought instead to find common ground for peace, justice, and conciliation. There was little wonder, conspiracy theorists suggest, that so many powerful forces were eager to see him dead. To those who believed in conspiracy, there were no petty motives behind the killing of the Kennedys. The future of the world was at stake. "History cracked open" that day in Dallas, in the words of the playwright Tony Kushner.[24] And the sense of loss that still haunts American life survives in part because so many people believe in what Kennedy might have done to transform the nation and the world. Solving the mystery of Kennedy's world-changing death, conspiracy theorists insist, is essential to any hope of putting history back on track.

In reality, Kennedy did not live up to this "heroic grandeur." Few historians or politicians would describe his presidency as a radical challenge to the status quo. What made Kennedy's image so powerful and so enduring was not the product of his own achievements; it was that so many people have imagined what might have happened had he lived. In his life and in his death Kennedy was part of a transformative moment in American history. His identification with a moment of unusual public activism explains much of his appeal to many Americans of the 1960s, and even to many Americans born after his death. They look back nostalgically to an era that seemed to be a time of national confidence and purpose.

Kennedy reminds many Americans of an age when it was possible to believe that politics could be harnessed to America's highest aspirations, that it could be rooted in a sense of national community, that it could speak to the country's moral yearnings. And perhaps most of all, Kennedy reminds Americans of a time when the nation's capacities seemed limitless, when its future seemed unbounded, when it was possible to believe that the United States could solve social problems and accomplish great deeds.

In the conclusion to *A Thousand Days*, Arthur Schlesinger wrote of Kennedy's brief time in office:

> He had accomplished so much . . . Lifting us up beyond our capacities, he gave his country back to its best self, wiping away the world's impression of an old nation of old men, weary, played out, fearful of ideas, change and the future; he taught mankind that the process of discovering America was not over. He re-established the republic as the first generation of our leaders saw it—young, brave, civilized, rational, gay, tough, questing, exultant in the excitement and potentiality of history.[25]

To the many Americans who yearn for a new age of public activism and commitment, the image of a heroic John Fitzgerald Kennedy has endured as a bright and beckoning symbol of the world that many people believe they have lost. And that is why he remains, deserved or not, such an important figure in our national imagination.

# Notes

These notes use the following abbreviations:

*FRUS*: *Foreign Relations of the United States, 1961–1963* (edited by David S. Patterson)
JFK: John F. Kennedy
JFKL: John F. Kennedy Library
JPK: Joseph P. Kennedy Sr.
*PPP-JFK*: *Public Papers of the Presidents of the United States: John F. Kennedy, 1961–1963*

## INTRODUCTION

1. Arthur M. Schlesinger Jr., *A Thousand Days: John F. Kennedy in the White House* (Boston: Houghton Mifflin, 1965), p. 206.
2. Robert G. Athearn, ed., *An Illustrated History of the United States* (New York: Choice, 1988), vol. 16, p. 1432; *Daytona Beach Morning Journal*, November 22, 1963.
3. Schlesinger, *A Thousand Days*, p. 1027.

## 1: THE IRISH PRINCE

1. Doris Kearns Goodwin, *The Fitzgeralds and the Kennedys: An American Saga* (New York: Simon and Schuster, 1987), pp. 21–129.
2. Ibid.
3. Robert Dallek, *An Unfinished Life: John F. Kennedy, 1917–1963* (New York: Little, Brown, 2003), pp. 6–7.
4. Goodwin, *The Fitzgeralds and the Kennedys*, pp. 226–33.
5. Nigel Hamilton, *JFK: Life and Death of an American President*, vol. 1, *Reckless Youth* (London: Random House UK, 1992), pp. 5–23; Goodwin, *The Fitzgeralds and the Kennedys*, pp. 256–59, 262–63; Rose Kennedy,

with Robert Coughlan, *Times to Remember* (New York: Doubleday, 1974), pp. 15, 67, 72–78.

6. Goodwin, *The Fitzgeralds and the Kennedys*, pp. 235–36.

7. Ibid., p. 290.

8. Hamilton, *JFK*, pp. 51–57; Goodwin, *The Fitzgeralds and the Kennedys*, pp. 278–88.

9. David Heyman, *A Woman Named Jackie* (New York: Lyle Stuart, 1989), pp. 140–41; Peter Collier and David Horowitz, *The Kennedys: An American Drama* (New York: Simon and Schuster, 1984), pp. 39–45; Gloria Swanson, *Swanson on Swanson* (New York: Random House, 1980), pp. 209, 328–70.

10. Goodwin, *The Fitzgeralds and the Kennedys*, p. 309.

11. Rose Kennedy, *Times to Remember*, pp. 126, 174, 192; John Ney, *Palm Beach* (Boston: Little, Brown, 1966), p. 18; Hamilton, *JFK*, pp. 42, 87–88, 91–93, 101–5, 288, 301–17, 349–52.

12. JFK to JPK, December 9, 1931, Young Kennedy File, JFKL; JFK to JPK, n.d., Young Kennedy File, JFKL.

13. Riverdale Country School, report on JFK, February 25, 1930, Young Kennedy File, JFKL; Record of JFK, November 1 to December 6, 1930, Canterbury School, Young Kennedy File, JFKL; Ralph G. Martin, *Seeds of Destruction: Joe Kennedy and His Sons* (New York: G. P. Putnam, 1995), p. 32.

14. Report of JFK, Choate School, 4th Quarter, n.d., Young Kennedy File, JFKL.

15. Ibid.

16. Ibid.

17. Hamilton, *JFK*, pp. 88–101.

18. Ibid.

19. Herbert Parmet, *Jack: The Struggles of John F. Kennedy* (New York: Dial Press, 1980), p. 37.

20. JFK to JPK, n.d., 1933, JFKL. See also Hamilton, *JFK*, p. 110; Dallek, *An Unfinished Life*, pp. 77–78, 80.

21. Goodwin, *The Fitzgeralds and the Kennedys*, pp. 456–65, 486–89; Hamilton, *JFK*, pp. 112–13, 118–35.

22. Hamilton, *JFK*, pp. 122–33.

23. Ibid., pp. 143–45.

24. JFK to Billings, n.d., 1935, JFKL; Edward E. Moore to Richard M. Gummere, May 11, 1935, JFKL.

25. Application for Admission, Harvard College, May 8, 1935, JFKL.

26. "General Estimate," Harvard Admissions Application, April 30, 1935, JFKL.

27. JPK to Delmar Leighton, August 28, 1936, JFKL.

28. JPK to JFK, December 1, 1937, JFKL; multiple letters, JFK to JPK, n.d., 1939, JFKL. See also Goodwin, *The Fitzgeralds and the Kennedys*, pp. 505–6, 581–82; Hamilton, *JFK*, pp. 159–70, 176–77.

29. Multiple letters, JFK to JPK, n.d., 1939, JFKL.
30. Hamilton, *JFK*, p.192.
31. JFK to JPK, Vienna, n.d., 1939, JFKL.
32. Hamilton, *JFK*, pp. 185, 194, 199.
33. "Extra Curricular Activities," 1937–1938, "Extra Curricular Activities," 1939–1940, JFKL; Hamilton, *JFK*, pp. 208–10.
34. JFK to JPK, n.d., 1939, JFKL.
35. Ibid.
36. Ibid.
37. Ibid.
38. "Report on Thesis for Distinction," n.d., 1940, JFKL; Dallek, *An Unfinished Life*, p. 63.
39. JFK to JPK, n.d., March, April, 1940, JFKL.
40. JFK to JPK, spring 1940, n.d., 1940, JFKL; John F. Kennedy, *Why England Slept* (New York: Wilfred Funk, 1962, original edition 1940), p. 17.
41. Dallek, *An Unfinished Life*, p. 64.
42. Alan Brinkley, *The Publisher: Henry Luce and His American Century* (New York: Alfred A. Knopf, 2010), pp. 422, 425.
43. Hamilton, *JFK*, p. 331; Kennedy, *Why England Slept*, pp. 13–14.
44. Kennedy, *Why England Slept*, p. 217.
45. Ibid. p. 218.
46. Ibid., p. 185.
47. Edward M. Daugherty to JPK, November 1, 1940, JFKL; JFK to JPK, n.d., 1940, JFKL.
48. Goodwin, *The Fitzgeralds and the Kennedys*, pp. 632–35.
49. JPK to Stephen Galatti, February 2, 1942, JFKL; Max Beaverbrook to JPK, February 9, 1942, JFKL; Dallek, *An Unfinished Life*, pp. 87–95.
50. John Hersey, "Survival," *New Yorker*, June 17, 1944, pp. 31–44.
51. Ibid.
52. HQ 3rd Bombardment Division, APO 559, Subject: "Aphrodite," April 8, 1944, JFKL; HQ 8th Air Force Outgoing Message, August 12, 1944, JFKL; Goodwin, *The Fitzgeralds and the Kennedys*, pp. 688–89.
53. Hamilton, *JFK*, p. 659.
54. John F. Kennedy, ed., *As We Remember Joe* (Cambridge, Mass.: University Press, privately printed, 1945).
55. *New York Journal-American*, May 2, 3, 5, 7, 16, 21, 23, June 23, 1945; *Chicago Herald-American*, May 18, 1945.
56. John F. Kennedy, *Prelude to Leadership: The European Diary of John F. Kennedy* (Washington, D.C.: Regnery, 1995), p. 5.
57. Ibid., pp. 5, 9–10.
58. Ibid., p. 46.
59. Ibid., p. 69.
60. Dallek, *An Unfinished Life*, p. 119.
61. Hamilton, *JFK*, p. 673.
62. Dallek, *An Unfinished Life*, pp. 116–27.

63. Michael O'Brien, *John F. Kennedy: A Biography* (New York: St. Martin's Press, 2005), p. 19.

2: THE UNCERTAIN POLITICIAN

1. David Michaelis, *Best of Friends* (New York: William Morrow, 1983), p. 165; Ralph G. Martin and Ed Plaut, *Front Runners* (New York: Doubleday, 1960), p. 114.

2. Goodwin, *The Fitzgeralds and the Kennedys*, p. 712.

3. Hamilton, *JFK*, p. 753; Goodwin, *The Fitzgeralds and the Kennedys*, p. 713; John H. Davis, *The Kennedys: Dynasty and Disaster, 1848–1984* (New York: McGraw-Hill, 1984), p. 125.

4. Eric Freedman and Edward Hoffman, *John F. Kennedy in His Own Words* (New York: Citadel Press, 2005), p. 190.

5. S. Alexander Haslam, Stephen D. Reicher, and Michael J. Platow, *The New Psychology of Leadership: Identity, Influence, and Power* (New York: Psychology Press, 2011), p. 151.

6. Dallek, *An Unfinished Life*, p. 132.

7. Philip Abbott, *Strong Presidents: A Theory of Leadership* (Knoxville: University of Tennessee Press, 1996), p. 165; Dallek, *An Unfinished Life*, pp. 142–44.

8. Robert E. Gilbert, "JFK and Addison's Disease," JFKL; Robert E. Gilbert, *The Mortal Presidency: Illness and Anguish in the White House* (New York: Basic Books, 1992); Kenneth P. Crispell and Carlos F. Gomez, *Hidden Illness in the White House* (Durham, N.C.: Duke University Press, 1988), p. 186; O'Brien, *John F. Kennedy*, p. 225.

9. "Kathleen Kennedy," n.d., JFKL; *New York Times*, May 14, 1948.

10. Jonathan Bell, *The Liberal State on Trial: The Cold War in the Truman Years* (New York: Columbia University Press, 2004), p. 185.

11. Gary Donaldson, *The First Modern Campaign: Kennedy, Nixon, and the Election of 1960* (Lanham, Md.: Rowman & Littlefield, 2007), p. 38.

12. John F. Kennedy, "Our Foreign Policy in Connection with China," *Congressional Record*, January 29, 1949, p. 41; Dallek, *An Unfinished Life*, pp. 160, 162.

13. Thomas Whalen, *Kennedy versus Lodge* (Boston: Northeastern University Press, 2000), pp. 127–83.

14. "Rose Kennedy Speaks at a Tea, 1952," n.d., JFKL.

15. Goodwin, *The Fitzgeralds and the Kennedys*, p. 768.

16. Hamilton, *JFK*, p. 780.

17. John H. Davis, *Jacqueline Bouvier: An Intimate Memoir* (New York: John Wiley and Sons, 1996), pp. 157–95; Donald Spoto, *Jacqueline Bouvier Onassis: A Life* (New York: St. Martin's Press, 2010), pp. 105–206.

18. "The Gay Young Bachelor," *Saturday Evening Post*, June 13, 1953.

19. Collier and Horowitz, *The Kennedys*, p. 197.

20. Thomas C. Reeves, *A Question of Character* (New York: Arrow, 1992), p. 116.
21. Collier and Horowitz, *The Kennedys*, p. 780.
22. Ibid., p. 354.
23. Theodore Sorensen, *Counselor: A Life at the Edge of History* (New York: Harper, 2009), pp. 98–115; Collier and Horowitz, *The Kennedys*, p. 198.
24. John F. Kennedy, *Profiles in Courage* (New York: Harper and Brothers, 1956).
25. Sorensen, *Counselor*, pp. 144–55.
26. Remarks by Senator John F. Kennedy at the Democratic National Convention, Chicago, Ill., on August 16, 1956, Senate Speech File, JFKL.
27. Arthur M. Schlesinger Jr., *Journals, 1952–2000* (New York: Penguin Press, 2007), pp. 43–44.
28. "Stevenson, Truman and Kennedy," *Saturday Evening Post*, March 8, 1958, pp. 32–33.
29. Dallek, *An Unfinished Life*, pp. 782–86.
30. Paul Blanshard, *American Freedom and Catholic Power* (Boston: Beacon Press, 1949).
31. Goodwin, *The Fitzgeralds and the Kennedys*, pp. 791–92; Harold Martin, "The Amazing Kennedys," *Saturday Evening Post*, September 7, 1957, p. 49.
32. Nellie Bly, *The Kennedy Men* (New York: Kensington, 1996), p. 98. See also David Pietrusza, *1960: LBJ vs. JFK vs. Nixon* (New York: Sterling, 2006), pp. 15–18.

### 3: THE GREAT AMBITION

1. Donaldson, *The First Modern Campaign*.
2. Theodore H. White, *The Making of the President, 1960* (New York: Atheneum, 1961), pp. 3–4.
3. *New York Times*, August 23, 1959; Abraham Ribicoff to JFK, August 31, 1959, December 16, 1959, JFKL.
4. *New York Times*, August 25, 1959; Orville Freeman to Robert F. Kennedy, August 4, 1960, JFKL.
5. Benjamin C. Bradlee, *Conversations with Kennedy* (New York: W. W. Norton, 1975), p. 16.
6. Eleanor Roosevelt to JFK, June 2, 1958, JFKL.
7. JFK to Eleanor Roosevelt, June 29, 1958, JFKL.
8. JFK to Eleanor Roosevelt, December 11, 18, 1958; JFK to Eleanor Roosevelt, January 10, 1959, JFKL.
9. "Ben" to JFK, May 12, 1959, JFKL; Eleanor Roosevelt to Mary Lasker, August 15, 1960, Roosevelt, Eleanor file, June 1958–November 1960, JFKL.
10. Arthur M. Schlesinger Jr. to JFK, April 26, 1960, JFKL.
11. Sorensen, *Counselor*, pp. 158–63.

12. JFK, Address to the Greater Houston Ministerial Association, September 12, 1960, political campaign, 1960, JFKL.

13. JFK to Editor, *Denver Post*, August 25, 1959, JFKL; campaign memo on religion, n.d., 1959, JFKL; William Rivkin to Sargent Shriver, August 4, 1960, JFKL; "Remarks of Senator John F. Kennedy," American Society of Newspaper Editors, Washington, D.C., April 21, 1960, JFKL.

14. *New York Times*, August 25, 1959; "Agenda for Senator Kennedy," May 13, 1959, JFKL.

15. JFK to Newton N. Minow, January 13, 1960, JFKL; Robert Drew, *Primary*, a documentary film, 1960.

16. White, *Making of the President, 1960*, p. 99.

17. Ibid., pp. 95–105.

18. Ibid., pp. 107–8.

19. William McCormick Blair Jr. to JFK, August 12, 1960, JFKL.

20. Arthur M. Schlesinger Jr. to JFK, January 25, 1960, June 6, 1960, JFKL; Jean Baker, *The Stevensons: A Biography of an American Family* (New York: W. W. Norton, 1996), pp. 399–400.

21. Adlai Stevenson to JFK, May 11, 1960, JFKL

22. JFK to Adlai Stevenson, January 5, 1960, JFKL; Arthur M. Schlesinger Jr. to Adlai Stevenson, May 16, 1960, JFKL.

23. JFK to Adlai Stevenson, January 5, 1960, JFKL; Stevenson to JFK, January 5, 1960, JFKL

24. *Sacramento Bee*, July 29, 1960; Arthur M. Schlesinger Jr. to JFK, May 25, 1960, JFKL; William McCormick Blair Jr. to JFK, August 12, 1960, JFKL; John Bartlow Martin, *Adlai Stevenson and the World* (Garden City, N.Y.: Doubleday, 1977), pp. 521–25.

25. Martin, *Adlai Stevenson and the World*, p. 449. See also JFK to Adlai Stevenson, January 5, 1960, JFKL; Stevenson to JFK, January n.d., 1960, JFKL.

26. Schlesinger, *Journals*, pp. 64–66. See also Schlesinger to JFK, June 6, 1960, JFKL.

27. Schlesinger, *Journals*, pp. 67–69.

28. Ibid., pp. 69–70.

29. White, *Making of the President, 1960*, pp. 163–64.

30. *New York Times*, July 14, 1960. See also Baker, *The Stevensons*, pp. 401–5.

31. *Time*, July 18, 1960.

32. White, *Making of the President, 1960*, pp. 131–35.

33. *Time*, July 11, 1960; White, *Making of the President, 1960*, p. 155.

34. *New York Times*, July 14, 15, 1960; White, *Making of the President, 1960*, pp. 163–67.

35. Milton Gwertzman, "Counterattack Sourcebook," August 10, 1960, JFKL.

36. *Time*, July 25, 1960; Donaldson, *The First Modern Campaign*, pp. 78–81.

37. *New York Times*, July 16, 1960.
38. John F. Kennedy, "The New Frontier," July 15, 1960, JFKL.
39. "The Election of John F. Kennedy, President of the United States," film, n.d., 1961, JFKL.
40. White, *The Making of the President, 1960*, pp. 309–10; Richard M. Nixon, *RN: The Memoirs of Richard Nixon* (New York: Grosset and Dunlap, 1978), pp. 218–19.
41. Schlesinger, *Journals*, p. 85; Richard M. Nixon, *Six Crises* (New York: Doubleday, 1962), p. 323.
42. Donaldson, *The First Modern Campaign*, pp. 110–13, 119.
43. Sidney Kraus, ed., *The Great Debates* (Bloomington: Indiana University Press, 1962), pp. 348–50.
44. Ibid., pp. 350–52.
45. Garry Wills, *Nixon Agonistes: The Crisis of the Self-Made Man* (Boston: Houghton Mifflin, 1969), p. 409.
46. White, *The Making of the President, 1960*, pp. 286–87; Sorensen, *Counselor*, p. 190.
47. Dallek, *An Unfinished Life*, pp. 292–94.
48. "Remarks of Senator John F. Kennedy at Howard University," Washington, D.C., October 7, 1960, JFKL.
49. Nixon, *RN*, pp. 216–17.
50. JFK, Armory speech, Hyannis, Mass., November 9, 1960, JFKL.

## 4: THE PERILS OF THE NEW FRONTIER

1. Richard Reeves, *President Kennedy: Profile of Power* (New York: Simon and Schuster, 1993), p. 25.
2. Ibid., p. 44.
3. Dallek, *An Unfinished Life*, p. 300; *New York Times*, November 10, 1960, January 11, 17, 1961.
4. Sorensen, *Counselor*, pp. 201–3; Andrew Preston, *The War Council: McGeorge Bundy, the NSC, and Vietnam* (Cambridge, Mass.: Harvard University Press, 2006), pp. 38–45.
5. Schlesinger, *Journals*, pp. 93–96.
6. Bradlee, *Conversations with Kennedy*, pp. 142–43.
7. Arthur M. Schlesinger Jr., *Robert Kennedy and His Times* (Boston: Houghton Mifflin, 1978), p. 230.
8. Ibid.
9. Schlesinger, *Robert Kennedy and His Times*, p. 232.
10. Dallek, *An Unfinished Life*, pp. 316–17; Schlesinger, *Robert Kennedy and His Times*, pp. 228–29, 232–33; Evan Thomas, *Robert Kennedy: His Life* (New York: Simon and Schuster, 2000), pp. 109–13.
11. Schlesinger, *Journals*, pp. 95–96.
12. Ibid.

13. Ibid., pp. 102–3.
14. Reeves, *President Kennedy*, pp. 31–33.
15. Ibid., pp. 33–34. See also John F. Kennedy, "Areas of Trial," n.d., 1954, pp. 63–69, JFKL.
16. Garry Wills, *The Kennedy Imprisonment: A Meditation on Power* (Boston: Little, Brown, 1982), p. 112.
17. John F. Kennedy, "Inaugural Address," January 20, 1961, *PPP-JFK*, 1961, pp. 1–3.
18. *Washington Post*, January 21, 1961.
19. Schlesinger, *A Thousand Days*, p. 126.
20. Theodore Sorensen, *Kennedy* (New York: Harper and Row, 1965), pp. 281–85.
21. Reeves, *President Kennedy*, p. 88.
22. Wills, *The Kennedy Imprisonment*, p. 191.
23. Memorandum from the President's Special Assistant for National Security Affairs (Bundy) to President Kennedy, May 16, 1961.
24. "White House Organization," in David S. Patterson, ed., *Foreign Relations of the United States, 1961–1963* (Washington, D.C.: U.S. Government Printing Office, 2001), pp. 29–31.
25. Schlesinger, *A Thousand Days*, pp. 206–7.
26. Benjamin Bradlee, *That Special Grace* (New York: Lippincott, 1964).
27. Schlesinger, *A Thousand Days*, pp. 355–56.
28. Reeves, *President Kennedy*, p. 154; Bradlee, *Conversations with Kennedy*, pp. 118–19.
29. Schlesinger, *Journals*, p. 122.
30. Press conference transcript, January 18, 1961, President John F. Kennedy's news conference, January 25, 1961, Evelyn Lincoln to Kermit Gordon, October 31, 1963, "What If Peace Breaks Out?"—memo for press conference, October 31, 1963, Press Conferences, 1961–1963, JFKL.
31. "Annual Message to the Congress on the State of the Union, January 30, 1961," *PPP-JFK*, 1961, pp. 19–28.
32. Sorensen, *Kennedy*, pp. 339–43.
33. Reeves, *President Kennedy*, pp. 55–56; Nick Bryant, *The Bystander: John F. Kennedy and the Struggle for Black Equality* (New York: Basic Books, 2006), pp. 221–41.
34. Robert Dallek, *Nixon and Kissinger: Partners in Power* (New York: HarperCollins, 2007), p. 21.
35. "Special Message to the Congress on the Peace Corps," March 1, 1961, "Address at a White House Reception for Members of Congress and for the Diplomatic Corps of the Latin American Republic," March 13, 1961, *PPP-JFK*, 1961, pp. 143–46, 170–75.
36. Dallek, *An Unfinished Life*, p. 370; Schlesinger, *A Thousand Days*, pp. 187–205.
37. Reeves, *President Kennedy*, p. 32.

38. *New York Times*, October 20, 1960.
39. "Plan for Cuba," n.d., 1961, JFKL.
40. "Evaluation of Proposed Supplementary Phase," March 10, 1961, JFKL; "Discussion—TOP SECRET," n.d., JFKL.
41. Peter Wyden, *The Bay of Pigs: The Untold Story* (New York: Simon and Schuster, 1962), p. 95.
42. Ibid., p. 94.
43. Arthur M. Schlesinger Jr. to JFK, February 11, 1961, March 10, 1961, JFKL; Adlai Stevenson to JFK, April 27, 1961, JFKL.
44. Schlesinger, *Journals*, pp. 109–12. See also Schlesinger, *A Thousand Days*, pp. 245–49.
45. James W. Hilty, *Robert Kennedy: Brother Protector* (Philadelphia: Temple University Press, 1997), p. 277.
46. "Details of Proposed Supplementary Phase to the CIA Para-Military Plan, Cuba," March 10, 1961, JFKL; McGeorge Bundy to JFK, February 8, 1961, JFKL; W. W. Rostow to JFK, February 6, 1961, JFKL; untitled CIA memo, n.d., 1961, NLK-79-185, JFKL.
47. "Discussion—TOP SECRET," April n.d., 1961, JFKL; "Facts on the Problem—TOP SECRET," n.d., 1961, JFKL.
48. Dallek, *An Unfinished Life*, p. 371.
49. Reeves, *President Kennedy*, pp. 82–83.
50. *New York Times*, April 14, 1961.
51. Wyden, *Bay of Pigs*, p. 269.
52. Ibid., p. 294.
53. "Cuban Freedom Brigade," April 25, 1961, JFKL.
54. Haynes Johnson, *The Bay of Pigs* (New York: W. W. Norton, 1964), pp. 177–80.
55. Schlesinger, *A Thousand Days*, p. 289.
56. Wyden, *Bay of Pigs*, pp. 305, 315. See also Schlesinger, *Journals*, pp. 120–21.
57. Thomas Fensch, ed., *The Kennedy-Khrushchev Letters* (Woodlands, Tex.: New Century Books, 2001), pp. 13–16.
58. Ibid., p. 18. See also Frederick Kempe, *Berlin 1961: Kennedy, Khrushchev, and the Most Dangerous Place on Earth* (New York: G. P. Putnam, 2011), pp. 8–10.
59. Jacqueline Kennedy, *Historic Conversations on Life with John Kennedy* (New York: Hyperion, 2011), pp. 185–86.
60. Albert Gore Sr., interview, n.d., JFKL.
61. Reeves, *President Kennedy*, pp. 95, 677. See also Kenneth P. O'Donnell and David F. Powers, *Johnny, We Hardly Knew Ye* (Boston: Little, Brown, 1972), pp. 316–17; Hugh Sidey, *John F. Kennedy: President* (New York: Atheneum, 1964), p. 129.
62. Schlesinger, *A Thousand Days*, p. 278.
63. Stanley Meisler, *The United Nations: The First Fifty Years* (New York: Grove Atlantic, 1995), p. 140.

64. Martin, *Adlai Stevenson and the World*, pp. 624–25; Baker, *The Stevensons*, pp. 415–17.
65. Reeves, *President Kennedy*, p. 140.
66. Ibid., p. 105.
67. "Statement by the President on the Tractors-for-Freedom Movement," May 24, 1961, *PPP-JFK*, 1962, p. 201.
68. Schlesinger, *Journals*, p. 121.
69. *Time*, May 5, 1961; *New York Times*, June 3, 1961.
70. Reeves, *President Kennedy*, p. 99.
71. Ibid., p. 294. See also "Statement by Attorney General Robert F. Kennedy," April 24, 1961, JFKL.

## 5: "FLEXIBLE RESPONSE"

1. "Special Message to the Congress on Urgent National Needs," May 25, 1961, *PPP-JFK*, 1961, pp. 396–406.
2. Marks Williamson, *Spacecraft Technology: The Early Years* (London: Institute of Engineering and Technology, 2006), p. 263.
3. "Remarks at a Meeting with the Headquarters Staff of the Peace Corps," June 14, 1962, *PPP-JFK*, 1962, p. 485.
4. Reeves, *President Kennedy*, pp. 286–88; Dallek, *An Unfinished Life*, pp. 651–53.
5. John Foster Dulles, "How Dulles Averted War," *Life*, January 16, 1956, p. 78.
6. John Lewis Gaddis, *Strategies of Containment: A Critical Appraisal of Postwar American National Security Policy* (New York: Oxford University Press, 1982), pp. 127–97.
7. Ibid., pp. 198–236; Wills, *The Kennedy Imprisonment*, pp. 249–52; L. W. Nordheim, "Tests of Nuclear Weapons," *Bulletin of the Atomic Scientists*, September 1955, pp. 253–55, 272–73; Dorothy Zinberg, "The Public and Nuclear Waste Management," *Bulletin of the Atomic Scientists*, January 1979, pp. 34–39.
8. Robert Dallek, *John F. Kennedy* (New York: Oxford University Press, 2011), p. 35.
9. Kempe, *Berlin 1961*, p. 209.
10. *New York Times*, June 1, 1961.
11. *Washington Post*, June 2, 1961.
12. Kempe, *Berlin 1961*, p. 217.
13. Charles Kenney, *John F. Kennedy: The Presidential Portfolio* (New York: PublicAffairs, 2000), p. 72.
14. Richard Rovere, *New Yorker*, June 17, 1961, p. 96.
15. Dallek, *John F. Kennedy*, p. 35.
16. "Memo of Correspondence Between N. S. Khrushchev and Robert F. Kennedy," May n.d., 1961, JFKL.
17. Michael R. Beschloss, *The Crisis Years: Kennedy and Khrushchev, 1960–*

*1963* (New York: HarperCollins, 1991), pp. 164–65; Dallek, *John F. Kennedy*, p. 35; "Memo of Correspondence Between N. S. Khrushchev and Robert F. Kennedy," May n.d., 1961, JFKL.

18. William Taubman, *Khrushchev: The Man and His Era* (New York: W. W. Norton, 2003), pp. 490–91.

19. "Memos of Conversation," Vienna meeting, June 3, 1961, JFKL.

20. O'Donnell and Powers, *Johnny, We Hardly Knew Ye*, p. 342.

21. Kempe, *Berlin 1961*, pp. 234–36.

22. "Memos of Conversation," June 3, 1961, JFKL; "Joint United States–Soviet Communique," Gettysburg, Pa., n.d., 1959, JFKL; "Memoranda of Conversation," September 15, 26, 1959, JFKL; Dallek, *John F. Kennedy*, p. 36.

23. "President's Meeting with Khrushchev, Laos—Talking Points," June 3–4, 1961, JFKL; "Memoranda of Conversation," June 3–4, 1961, JFKL.

24. "Memos of Conversation," June 4, 1961, JFKL.

25. "Berlin: Questions That Might Be Raised," n.d., 1961, JFKL.

26. "Memos of Conversation," June 4, 1961, JFKL; Taubman, *Khrushchev*, p. 500.

27. John F. Stacks, *Scotty: James B. Reston and the Rise and Fall of American Journalism* (Boston: Little, Brown, 2003), p. 199; *New York Times*, June 6, 1961. See also Kempe, *Berlin 1961*, pp. 256–57.

28. Reeves, *President Kennedy*, p. 176.

29. Preston, *The War Council*, p. 56.

30. Reeves, *President Kennedy*, pp. 179–81.

31. Ibid., p. 180.

32. *Saturday Review*, August 5, 1961, p. 3.

33. Spencer R. Weart, *Nuclear Fear: A History of Images* (Cambridge, Mass.: Harvard University Press, 1988), pp. 254–55.

34. Schlesinger, *A Thousand Days*, p. 394.

35. R. Gerald Hughes, *Britain, Germany, and the Cold War: The Search for a European Detente, 1949–1967* (Oxford: Routledge, 2007), p. 197. See also "The President's News Conference of July 19, 1961," "Radio and Television Report to the American People on the Berlin Crisis, July 25, 1961," *PPP-JFK*, 1961, pp. 513–14, 533–34, 538; *Time*, July 14, 1961.

36. Reeves, *President Kennedy*, p. 212. See also Frederick Taylor, *The Berlin Wall: A World Divided, 1961–1989* (New York: HarperCollins, 2007), p. 146; Schlesinger, *A Thousand Days*, p. 394.

37. *New York Times*, October 21, 1961.

38. Reeves, *President Kennedy*, pp. 246–47.

39. *New York Times*, October 28, 1961.

40. Kennedy, "Address in Los Angeles at a Dinner of the Democratic Party of California, November 18, 1961," *PPP-JFK*, 1961, pp. 733–36. See also David Talbot, *Brothers: The Hidden Story of the Kennedy Years* (New York: Free Press, 2007), p. 75.

41. Jeff Shesol, *Mutual Contempt: Lyndon Johnson, Robert Kennedy, and the Feud that Defined a Decade* (New York: W. W. Norton, 1997), p. 127.

42. Chester Bowles, *Promises to Keep: My Years in Public Life, 1941–1969* (New York: Harper and Row, 1971), p. 343.

43. Thomas, *Robert Kennedy*, pp. 147, 157.

44. Mark J. White, *The Kennedys and Khrushchev: The Declassified Documentary History* (New York: Ivan R. Dee, 2001), p. 78.

45. Schlesinger, *Robert Kennedy and His Times*, p. 492.

46. Reeves, *President Kennedy*, p. 337.

47. *FRUS, Cuba 1961–1962*, p. 606. See also Tim Weiner, *Legacy of Ashes: The History of the CIA* (New York: Doubleday, 2007), p. 210; Reeves, *President Kennedy*, pp. 335–37.

48. "Vienna Meeting: Memos of Conversation," June 4, 1961, JFKL; "Vienna Meeting: Background Documents," n.d., 1961, JFKL; David R. Inglis, "Ban H-Bomb Tests and Favor the Defense," *Bulletin of the Atomic Scientists*, November 1954, pp. 353–56.

49. Richard A. Falk, Samuel S. Kim, and Saul H. Mendrovitz, eds., *Disarmament and Economic Development* (Washington, D.C.: World Law Fund, 1966), p. 46.

50. Beschloss, *The Crisis Years*, pp. 213–14.

51. J. P. Weisner and H. E. York, "National Security and the Nuclear Test Ban," *Scientific American*, October 1964; Shane J. Maddock, "Defending the American Way and Containing the Atom: Ideology and U.S. Nuclear Proliferation Since 1945," in Rosemary B. Mariner and G. Kurt Piehler, eds., *The Atomic Bomb and American Society: New Perspectives* (Knoxville: University of Tennessee Press, 2009), pp. 121–52.

52. William Rust, *Perpetual Crisis: The American Experience in Laos, 1954–1961* (Lexington: University of Kentucky Press, 2012).

53. "The President's News Conference of March 23, 1961," *PPP-JFK*, 1961, pp. 213–15.

54. *Time*, May 5, 1961.

55. Reeves, *President Kennedy*, pp. 112, 689.

56. Charles de Gaulle, *Memoirs of Hope: Renewal and Endeavor* (New York: Simon and Schuster, 1971), p. 256.

57. Reeves, *President Kennedy*, p. 112.

58. Sorensen, *Kennedy*, pp. 396–99, 591.

59. "Memos of Conversation," June 4, 1961, Vienna, JFKL; "President's Meeting with Khrushchev, Vienna, June 3–4, 1961, Laos: Talking Points," Briefing Book, JFKL.

60. Fensch, *The Kennedy-Khrushchev Letters*, pp. 244–45. See also Roger Hilsman, *To Move a Nation: The Politics of Foreign Policy in the Administration of John F. Kennedy* (New York: Doubleday, 1967), p. 134; Lawrence Freedman, *Kennedy's Wars: Berlin, Cuba, and Laos* (New York:

Oxford University Press, 2000), p. 475n; "Memos of Conversation," June 4, 1961, Vienna, JFKL; "President's Meeting with Khrushchev, Vienna, June 3–4, 1961, Laos: Talking Points," Briefing Book, JFKL; A. J. Langguth, *Our Vietnam: The War, 1954–1975* (New York: Simon and Schuster, 2000), p. 132.

61. Rust, *Perpetual Crisis*, pp. 18–56, 342–45.
62. Beschloss, *The Crisis Years*, p. 349.
63. "Telegram from the Department of State to the Embassy in the Soviet Union, December 30, 1961," in Fensch, *The Kennedy-Khrushchev Letters*, p. 146. See also Beschloss, *The Crisis Years*, p. 352.
64. *Time*, January 5, 1962.

6: FREEDOM

1. "Annual Message to the Congress on the State of the Union, January 11, 1962," *PPP-JFK*, 1962, pp. 5–6.
2. Ibid.
3. Ibid.; *Wall Street Journal*, February 27, 1961.
4. Schlesinger, *Robert Kennedy and His Times*, pp. 404–5.
5. *New York Times*, April 12, 1962; Walter Heller to Lloyd Ulman, "Reuther's Letter to the President," April 12, 1962, Council of Economic Advisers, JFKL; "The President's News Conference of April 11, 1962," *PPP-JFK*, 1962, pp. 315–16.
6. *Time*, April 20, 1962; *Business Week*, April 21, 1962.
7. Reeves, *President Kennedy*, p. 296.
8. Reeves, *A Question of Character*, p. 332; Jim Bellows, *The Last Editor* (Kansas City, Mo.: Andrews McMeel, 2002), p. 88.
9. Benjamin A. Javits to JFK, June 11, 1962, JFKL; Roy Harrod to Seymour Harris, May 9, 1962, Council of Economic Advisers, JFKL; Bradlee, *Conversations with Kennedy*, p. 77; Reeves, *President Kennedy*, pp. 296–302.
10. "Why the Market Fell," May 29, 1962, Council of Economic Advisers, JFKL.
11. *New York Times*, May 29, 1962; "The Present Decline in Perspective," "Why the Market Fell," "Possible Government Action," May 29, 1962, Council of Economic Advisers, JFKL; Walter Heller to JFK, May 31, 1962, Council of Economic Advisers, JFKL.
12. "Annual Message to the Congress on the State of the Union, January 14, 1963," *PPP-JFK*, 1963, pp. 11–13.
13. *Economist*, May 19, 1962; Walter Heller to JFK, December 16, 1962, Council of Economic Advisers, JFKL; Schlesinger, *A Thousand Days*, pp. 630–31.
14. Dallek, *An Unfinished Life*, pp. 375–76, 475–80.
15. William Chafe, *Private Lives/Public Consequences: Personality and*

*Politics in Modern America* (Cambridge, Mass.: Harvard University Press, 2005), pp. 122–23.

16. Ibid.

17. Reeves, *President Kennedy*, pp. 288–89; Athan Theoharis, *From the Secret Files of J. Edgar Hoover* (New York: I. R. Dee, 1991), pp. 40–41; Seymour M. Hersh, *The Dark Side of Camelot* (Boston: Little, Brown, 1997), pp. 298–325.

18. O'Brien, *John F. Kennedy*, p. 763; David Reynolds, *Summits: Six Meetings that Shaped the Twentieth Century* (New York: Basic Books, 2007), pp. 201–2.

19. Alistair Horne, *Harold Macmillan, 1959–1986*, vol. 2 (New York: Viking, 1989), p. 512; Reeves, *President Kennedy*, pp. 242–43.

20. Reeves, *President Kennedy*, p. 43.

21. Dallek, *An Unfinished Life*, p. 705.

22. "First Debate, September 26, 1960," in Kraus, *The Great Debates*, pp. 349–50.

23. "Inaugural Address, January 20, 1961," *PPP-JFK*, 1961, p. 1.

24. "Annual Message to the Congress on the State of the Union," January 30, 1961, *PPP-JFK*, 1961, p. 22.

25. Reeves, *President Kennedy*, p. 169.

26. Franklin H. Williams, "The Shifting Negro Vote," *Frontier*, January 1961, pp. 4, 13–14.

27. Hyman H. Bookbinder, "Appointment of Qualified Negro to Business Advisory Council," April 14, 1961, JFKL; Carl Brauer, *John F. Kennedy and the Second Reconstruction* (New York: Columbia University Press, 1977), pp. 75–76.

28. Harris Wofford notes, "MLK," n.d., JFKL. See also Reeves, *President Kennedy*, pp. 100–101.

29. Frank J. Munger and Richard F. Fenno, *National Politics and Federal Aid to Education* (Syracuse, N.Y.: Syracuse University Press, 1962) p. 132.

30. Harris Wofford to Kenneth O'Donnell, October 4, October 9, 1961, JFKL; Robert A. Wallace to Harris Wofford, November 22, 1961, JFKL.

31. Executive Order 10590, January 19, 1955, 20 Federal Record, 409; Executive Order 10925, March 6, 1961, 26 Federal Record 1977.

32. John L. Moore to Heads of Federal Agencies, "Nondiscrimination in Employment," March 29, 1961, JFKL; JFK to A. Philip Randolph, February 17, 1961, JFKL; Carlisle P. Runge, Assistant Secretary of Defense, to Frederick G. Dutton, April 10, 1961, JFKL; Robert A. Wallace, Assistant Secretary to the Secretary of the Treasury, to Fred Dutton, April 7, 1961, JFKL; L. D. Battle to Frederick G. Dutton, April 11, 1961, JFKL.

33. Helen Fuller, *Year of Trial: Kennedy's Crucial Decisions* (New York: Harcourt, Brace, 1962), p. 29.

34. "Report of the Attorney General to the President on the Department of Justice's Activities in the Field of Civil Rights," December 29, 1961, JFKL. See also Franklin D. Reeves to Clarence T. R. Nelson, March 20, 1961, JFKL; "Summary Memorandum of Executive Action on Civil Rights," n.d., 1961, JFKL; U.S. Commission on Civil Rights press release, September 9, 1961, JFKL.
35. "Summary Memorandum of Executive Action on Civil Rights," n.d., 1962; "Executive Order: Equal Opportunity in Housing," November 20, 1962, 27 Federal Record, 11527; JFK to Roy Wilkins, November 27, 1962, JFKL; JFK to Robert Weaver, November 27, 1962, JFKL; JFK to Whitney Young, November 27, 1962, JFKL; Jack Conway, "Draft Reply to Correspondence from Mayor C. Ben Holleman, West Palm Beach, Florida," JFKL; Brauer, *John F. Kennedy and the Second Reconstruction*, pp. 131–35.
36. *Progressive*, vol. 2, no. 49, p. 16.
37. "Summary of Civil Rights Progress, January 20 through October 1961," n.d., 1961, JFKL; Lee C. White, "Civil Rights Achievements Since January 1962," December 13, 1962, JFKL; Brauer, *John F. Kennedy and the Second Reconstruction*, pp. 63, 127.
38. Taylor Branch, *Parting the Waters: America in the King Years, 1954–1963* (New York: Simon and Schuster, 1988), pp. 143–205, 271–73; William Chafe, *Civilities and Civil Rights: Greensboro, North Carolina, and the Black Struggle for Freedom* (New York: Oxford University Press, 1981), pp. 111–18.
39. *Time*, June 2, 1961; Raymond Arsenault, *Freedom Rides 1961 and the Struggle for Racial Justice* (New York: Oxford University Press, 2006), pp. 11–54, 90–182.
40. *New York Times*, May 15, 1961; *Time*, May 26, 1961.
41. Schlesinger, *Robert Kennedy and His Times*, p. 288.
42. *New York Times*, May 24, 30, 1961; *Time*, June 2, 1961; Arsenault, *Freedom Rides 1961*, pp. 140–85.
43. Thomas, *Robert Kennedy*, p. 129.
44. Arsenault, *Freedom Rides 1961*, p. 194. See also Bryant, *The Bystander*, p. 278.
45. "Statement by the President Concerning Interference with the 'Freedom Riders' in Alabama," May 20, 1961, *PPP-JFK*, 1961, p. 391.
46. Bryant, *The Bystander*, pp. 270, 275.
47. "Special Message to the Congress on Urgent National Needs," May 25, 1961, *PPP-JFK*, 1961, pp. 396–406.
48. "Statement by the President Upon Signing the Plans for Progress," Washington, D.C., July 12, 1961, JFKL.
49. "Improvement in Non-White Industrial Employment—During 'Plans for Progress' Program, May 15, 1961–December 15, 1961, December 15, 1961–June 15, 1962," JFKL.

50. "Results of 'Plans for Progress' Program—(A) One Year Results and (B) Six Months Results," JFKL.

51. "Remarks of the President Before Participants in Signing of Plans for Progress in the East Room," June 22, 1962, JFKL.

52. Robert Troutman Jr. to JFK, June 30, 1962, JFKL; JFK to Robert Troutman Jr., August 22, 1962, JFKL.

53. Brauer, *John F. Kennedy and the Second Reconstruction*, pp. 147–51, 214–16.

54. Martin Luther King Jr., "Letter from a Birmingham Jail," in *Why We Can't Wait* (New York: Signet, 1964), pp. 64–84.

55. Branch, *Parting the Waters*, pp. 647–68.

56. "Radio and Television Report to the Nation on the Situation at the University of Mississippi," September 30, 1962, *PPP-JFK*, 1962, pp. 726–27.

57. Aaron Henry to JFK, n.d., 1962, JFKL; "Executive Order 11053: Providing Assistance for the Removal of Obstructions of Justice in the State of Mississippi," September 30, 1962, JFKL; Jack Rosenthal, "Some Possible Ideas for the President's Remarks to the United States Attorneys," October 9, 1962, JFKL; JFK to C. B. Powell, October 11, 1962, JFKL; *Amsterdam News*, October 6, 1962; Brauer, *John F. Kennedy and the Second Reconstruction*, pp. 180–203.

58. Branch, *Parting the Waters*, pp. 782–85. See also Dallek, *An Unfinished Life*, p. 595.

59. King, "Letter from a Birmingham Jail," pp. 64–84.

60. Bryant, *The Bystander*, p. 381.

61. Ibid., p. 4. See also Thomas, *Robert Kennedy*, p. 243.

62. Diane McWhorter, *Carry Me Home: Birmingham, Alabama—The Climactic Battle of the Civil Rights Revolution* (New York: Simon and Schuster, 2001), p. 463.

63. Bryant, *The Bystander*, p. 394.

64. McWhorter, *Carry Me Home*, pp. 463–64; Bryant, *The Bystander*, p. 394.

65. *Washington Post*, February 13, 1963; Reeves, *President Kennedy*, pp. 464–65.

66. Schlesinger, *A Thousand Days*, p. 959.

67. Ibid., pp. 959–66; Brauer, *John F. Kennedy and the Second Reconstruction*, p. 240.

68. "Radio and Television Report to the American People on Civil Rights," June 11, 1963, *PPP-JFK*, 1963, pp. 468–71.

69. Brauer, *John F. Kennedy and the Second Reconstruction*, p. 264.

70. Reeves, *President Kennedy*, p. 520. .

71. Schlesinger, *Robert Kennedy and His Times*, pp. 346–49. See also Brauer, *John F. Kennedy and the Second Reconstruction*, p. 247.

72. "Civil Rights—Public Accommodations, Hearings of the Committee on Commerce," U.S. Senate, S 1732 (July 1, 1963), p. 25.

73. *Washington Post*, August 29, 30, 1963.

74. *New York Times*, August 29, 1963; *Time*, August 30, 1963.

75. William F. Theford to JFK, September 18, 1963, JFKL.

76. Harold Chase and Allen H. Lerman, eds., *Kennedy and the Press: The News Conferences* (New York: Crowell, 1965), p. 518; Lee C. White to Burke Marshall, September 18, 1963, JFKL; Lee C. White to Charles C. Diggs Jr., September 24, 1963, JFKL; Brauer, *John F. Kennedy and the Second Reconstrution*, p. 310.

77. John Richard Snyder, *John F. Kennedy: Personality, Policy, Presidency* (New York: SR Books, 1988), p. 62. See also Brauer, *John F. Kennedy and the Second Reconstruction*, p. 310. A similar argument emerged in 2006, from the British journalist Nick Bryant, author of *The Bystander*, p. 11. Bryant, like Dirksen, harshly criticized Kennedy for his delay in joining the battle and for squandering his best opportunity. "Kennedy was partly responsible for the crisis in race relations," he wrote. "Handed an historic opportunity at the beginning of the 1960s to map out a trajectory for the country that could have carried millions of black Americans closer to freedom, he decided to adopt a policy of inaction."

## 7: THE EVOLVING COLD WAR

1. Schlesinger, *Robert Kennedy and His Times*, p. 649. See also Gus Russo and Stephen Molton, *Brothers in Arms: The Kennedys, the Castros, and the Politics of Murder* (New York: Bloomsbury, 2008), pp. 157–58, 168–71.

2. Reeves, *President Kennedy*, p. 341.

3. Ernest R. May and Philip D. Zelikow, eds., *The Kennedy Tapes: Inside the White House During the Cuban Missile Crisis* (New York: W. W. Norton, 2002), p. 10.

4. Michael H. Hunt, *Crises in U.S. Foreign Policy* (New Haven: Yale University Press, 1996), p. 255.

5. Robert Dallek, *Flawed Giant: Lyndon Johnson and His Times, 1961–1973* (New York: Oxford University Press, 1998), p. 53; Abram Chayes to McGeorge Bundy, "International Law Problems of Blockade," September 10, 1962, JFKL; "Briefing Paper for President's Press Conference—Subject: NATO Shipping and Cuban Trade," September 13, 1962, JFKL; May and Zelikow, *The Kennedy Tapes*, p. 10; "The President's News Conference," September 13, 1962, *PPP–JFK*, 1962, pp. 674–75; Elie Abel, *The Missile Crisis* (New York: J. B. Lippincott, 1966), pp. 6–80.

6. May and Zelikow, *The Kennedy Tapes*, p. 13.

7. Ibid., pp. 12–15.

8. Graham Allison, *Essence of Decision: Explaining the Cuban Missile Crisis* (Boston: Little, Brown, 1971), p. 57. See also Dallek, *An Unfinished Life*, p. 544; Abel, *The Missile Crisis*, p. 20; Sorensen, *Kennedy*, p. 675.

9. Hunt, *Crises in U.S. Foreign Policy*, pp. 257–58.

10. The meetings of ExComm were taped and later published. Only the president knew of the taping, which he alone controlled.

11. May and Zelikow, *The Kennedy Tapes*, p. 36.

12. Ibid., p. 44.

13. Ibid., p. 115; Abel, *The Missile Crisis*, pp. 48–51.

14. May and Zelikow, *The Kennedy Tapes*, pp. 123–25.

15. Ibid., p. 122.

16. Ibid., p. 124.

17. Ibid.

18. Allison, *Essence of Decision*, p. 61; Abel, *The Missile Crisis*, pp. 84–85.

19. *Washington Post*, October 21, 1962.

20. "Radio and Television Report to the American People on the Soviet Arms Buildup in Cuba," October 22, 1962, *PPP-JFK*, 1962, pp. 806–9.

21. "Proclamation 3504: Interdiction of the Delivery of Offensive Weapons to Cuba," October 23, 1962, pp. 809–10, JFKL.

22. Reeves, *President Kennedy*, p. 397.

23. *Washington Post*, October 23, 24, 1962; *New York Times*, October 23–28, 1962; *Time*, November 2, 1962; Aleksandr Fursenko and Timothy Naftali, *"One Hell of a Gamble": Khrushchev, Castro, and Kennedy, 1958–1964* (New York: W. W. Norton, 1997), pp. 237–39; transcript, Gilpatric-JFK phone conversation, October 23, 1962, JFKL.

24. May and Zelikow, *The Kennedy Tapes*, p. 189.

25. Khrushchev to JFK, October 23, 1962, JFKL.

26. JFK to Khrushchev, October 23, 1962, JFKL.

27. May and Zelikow, *The Kennedy Tapes*, p. 213.

28. Ibid., pp. 213–14.

29. Ibid., p. 153.

30. Ibid., pp. 218–20, 229; "Overseas Reactions to President Kennedy's Cuban Announcement," October 23, 1962, JFKL; "News Conference," Pierre Salinger, October 23, 1962, JFKL.

31. Timothy Naftali, Philip D. Zelikow, and Ernest R. May, eds., *The Presidential Recordings: John F. Kennedy*, vols 1–3, *The Great Crises* (Charlottesville, Va.: Miller Center, 2001), vol. 3, p. 213.

32. Abel, *The Missile Crisis*, p. 126.

33. Khrushchev to JFK, October 24, 1962, JFKL; JFK to Khrushchev, October 25, 1962, JFKL; May and Zelikow, *The Kennedy Tapes*, pp. 242–43, 257.

34. May and Zelikow, *The Kennedy Tapes*, p. 292.

35. Ibid., p. 297.

36. Khrushchev to JFK, October 26, 1962, JFKL; Khrushchev to Secretary of State, October 26, 1962, JFKL.

37. Taubman, *Khrushchev*, p. 531.

38. May and Zelikow, *The Kennedy Tapes*, p. 230.

39. Ibid., p. 383.

40. Abel, *The Missile Crisis*, pp. 161–64, 180–81.

41. Betty Goetz Lall, "NATO—Warsaw Détente?" *Bulletin of the Atomic Scientists*, vol. 20, no. 9 (November 1964), pp. 37–39.

42. Khrushchev to JFK, October 28, 1962, JFKL.

43. May and Zelikow, *The Kennedy Tapes*, p. 489.

44. "Message in Reply to a Broadcast by Chairman Khrushchev on the Cuban Crisis," October 28, 1962, *PPP-JFK*, 1962, pp. 814–15. See also "Memorandum for the Secretary of State from the Attorney General," October 30, 1962, JFKL.

45. "The President's News Conference of November 20, 1962," *PPP-JFK*, 1962, pp. 830–32; Khrushchev to JFK, November 12, 1962, JFKL; Khrushchev to JFK, December 11, 1962, JFKL.

46. Schlesinger, *A Thousand Days*, p. 830; *Life*, November 12, 1965.

47. Jim Heath, *Decade of Disillusionment: The Kennedy-Johnson Years* (Bloomington: Indiana University Press, 1975), p. 131.

48. Schlesinger, *Robert Kennedy and His Times*, p. 525.

49. Abel, *The Missile Crisis*, p. 193.

50. Reeves, *President Kennedy*, p. 351.

51. Ibid.; Wills, *The Kennedy Imprisonment*, pp. 262–63; Richard J. Walton, *Cold War and Counterrevolution: The Foreign Policy of John F. Kennedy* (Baltimore: Penguin Books, 1972), pp. 10, 116, 224; Robert Weisbrot, *Maximum Danger: Kennedy, the Missiles, and the Crisis of American Confidence* (Chicago: Ivan R. Dee, 2001), pp. 199–202.

52. Glen T. Seaborg, *Kennedy, Khrushchev, and the Test Ban* (Berkeley: University of California Press, 1981), pp. 51–60.

53. "ACDA Special Report No. 15: Consideration of Test Ban During Recess of Geneva Disarmament Conference," September 11, 1962, JFKL.

54. *Bulletin of the Atomic Scientists*, March 1963, pp. 32–37.

55. Fensch, *The Kennedy-Khrushchev Letters*, pp. 476–77.

56. Dallek, *An Unfinished Life*, p. 619.

57. Sorensen, *Counselor*, pp. 325–28; Schlesinger, *Journals*, p. 194.

58. "Commencement Address at American University in Washington," June 10, 1963, *PPP-JFK*, 1963, pp. 459–64.

59. G. Calvin MacKenzie and Robert Weisbrot, *The Liberal Hour: Washington and the Politics of Change in the 1960s* (New York: Penguin Books, 2008), pp. 278–79.

60. Seaborg, *Kennedy, Khrushchev, and the Test Ban*, pp. 216–18.

61. *Time*, August 30, 1963.

62. Ibid.; Reeves, *President Kennedy*, p. 555.

63. "Statement by the President Following the Senate Vote on the Nuclear Test Ban Treaty," September 24, 1963, *PPP-JFK*, 1963, p. 704. See also "Remarks at the Signing of the Nuclear Test Ban Treaty," October 7, 1963, *PPP-JFK*, 1963, p. 765–66.

64. Benjamin S. Loeb, "The Limited Test Ban Treaty," in Michael Kredon and Dan Caldwell, eds., *The Politics of Arms Control of Treaty Ratification*

(New York: St. Martin's Press, 1991), p. 169; Seaborg, *Kennedy, Khrushchev, and the Test Ban*, pp. 226–31, 235–82.

65. Dallek, *An Unfinished Life*, pp. 624–25; Kempe, *Berlin 1961*, pp. 498–500.

66. "Remarks in the Rudolph Wilde Platz, Berlin," June 26, 1963, *PPP-JFK*, 1963, pp. 524–25.

67. Reeves, *President Kennedy*, p. 537.

68. *New York Times*, June 27, 1963; Sorensen, *Counselor*, p. 325; Reeves, *President Kennedy*, p. 537; "Address at the Free University of Berlin," June 26, 1963, *PPP-JFK*, 1963, pp. 525–29.

69. Schlesinger, *A Thousand Days*, p. 888.

## 8: QUAGMIRE

1. John F. Kennedy, "Partial Remarks Before the Executives Club of Chicago," May 28, 1954, JFKL.

2. John F. Kennedy, "America's Stake in Vietnam," *Vital Speeches of the Day*, August 1, 1956, pp. 617–19, JFKL.

3. Reeves, *President Kennedy*, p. 46.

4. *FRUS*, vol. I, Vietnam 1961, p. 15, note 6.

5. William J. Lederer and Eugene Burdick, *The Ugly American* (New York: W. W. Norton, 1958). A similar, although less polemical, novel about the American CIA in Vietnam is Graham Greene, *The Quiet American* (New York: Viking Press, 1956).

6. Edward G. Lansdale, "Binh Hung: A Counter-Guerilla Case Study," February 1, 1961, JFKL.

7. JFK to General Lemnitzer, February 5, 1961, JFKL; Oliver E. Clubb Jr., "The Struggle in South Vietnam," March 1961, JFKL, pp. 18–20.

8. Theodore H. White to JFK, October 11, 1961, JFKL.

9. Averell Harriman to Arthur M. Schlesinger Jr., October 17, 1961, JFKL.

10. Stuart Symington to JFK, October 21, 1961, JFKL; Robert D. Schulzinger, *A Time for War: The United States and Viet Nam, 1941–1975* (New York: Oxford University Press, 1996), pp. 102–6.

11. "The Taylor Report," November 3, 1961, *The Pentagon Papers: The Defense Department History of United States Decisionmaking on Vietnam* (Boston: Beacon Press, 1971), vol. 2, pp. 88, 92–98; "A Threat to the Peace: North Viet-Nam's Effort to Conquer South Viet-Nam," Department of State, 1961, JFKL, pp. 18–37; Walt Rostow to JFK, November 7, 1961, JFKL. See also Preston, *The War Council*, pp. 88–100.

12. Reeves, *President Kennedy*, p. 257.

13. David Kaiser, *American Tragedy: Kennedy, Johnson, and the Origins of the Vietnam War* (Cambridge, Mass.: Harvard University Press, 2000), pp. 109–10.

14. JFK to Diem, October 23, 1961, JFKL; Diem to JFK, December 12, 14, 1961, JFKL; JFK to Diem, December 15, 1961, JFKL; "Internal

Warfare and the Security of the Underdeveloped States," November 20, 1961, Department of State, JFKL.

15. Hilsman, *To Move a Nation*, p. 444; Roger Hilsman to JFK, January 13, 1962, JFKL.

16. Maxwell Taylor to JFK, "Summary of Military Operations in Vietnam," n.d., 1962, JFKL.

17. *Time*, May 11, 1962.

18. *Pentagon Papers*, vol. 2, pp. 162–63, 165.

19. "Questions Concerning Guerrilla Programs," July 7, 1962, JFKL.

20. George W. Ball, "Viet-Nam—Free World Challenge in Southeast Asia," Detroit, April 30, 1962, JFKL; McGeorge Bundy to JFK, May 1, 1962, JFKL.

21. Hilsman, *To Move a Nation*, p. 428.

22. "The Strategic Hamlet Program, 1961–1963," *Pentagon Papers*, vol. 2, pp. 128–59; Schulzinger, *A Time for War*, p. 115.

23. JFK to Diem, October 24, 1962, JFKL.

24. *Washington Post*, March 19, 1963; Kaiser, *American Tragedy*, pp. 194–95.

25. Associated Press, January 10, 1963, JFKL.

26. "Draft telegram to Saigon," n.d., 1963, JFKL.

27. *Pentagon Papers*, vol. 2, pp. 202–4; Thomas L. Hughes to the Acting Secretary, "Diem Versus the Buddhists: The Issue Joined," August 21, 1963, JFKL; Preston, *The War Council*, pp. 120–23.

28. Schulzinger, *A Time for War*, p. 120.

29. David Reynolds, *One World Indivisible: A Global History Since 1945* (New York: W. W. Norton, 2000), p. 276.

30. Henry Cabot Lodge to McGeorge Bundy, August 27, 1963, JFKL.

31. "Transcript of Broadcast on NBC's 'Huntley-Brinkley' Report," September 6, 1963, *PPP-JFK*, 1963, pp. 658–59.

32. "Transcript of Broadcast with Walter Cronkite Inaugurating a CBS Television News Program," September 2, 1963, *PPP-JFK*, 1963, pp. 650–51.

33. Henry Cabot Lodge to Dean Rusk, September 9, 1963, JFKL.

34. "Eyes Only for Ambassador," August 28, 1963, JFKL; Henry Cabot Lodge to Dean Rusk, August 26, 1963.

35. Hilsman memo, September 11, 1963, JFKL; "Visit to Vietnam," September 6–10, 1963, JFKL; Roger Hilsman to Henry Cabot Lodge, September 5, 1963, JFKL.

36. "Report to the Executive Committee," October 4, 1963, JFKL.

37. Kaiser, *American Tragedy*, p. 251.

38. Robert S. McNamara, *In Retrospect: The Tragedy and Lessons of Vietnam* (New York: Times Books, 1995), pp. 78–79.

39. *Pentagon Papers*, vol. 2, p. 205; Reeves, *President Kennedy*, p. 609.

40. CIA Memorandum, "The Coup in South Vietnam," November 1, 1963, JFKL.

41. Schulzinger, *A Time for War*, pp. 199–222; Kaiser, *American Tragedy*, pp. 266–69; Reeves, *President Kennedy*, p. 648.

42. Reeves, *President Kennedy*, p. 646.
43. Schlesinger, *A Thousand Days*, p. 997.
44. Ellen J. Hammer, *A Death in November: America in Vietnam, 1963* (New York: Dutton, 1987), p. 297.
45. CIA memorandum, "The Coup in South Vietnam," November 1, 1963, JFKL; CIA memorandum, "The Situation in Vietnam," November 2, 1963, JFKL; Hammer, *A Death in November*, pp. 296–98.
46. *New York Times*, November 3, 1963.
47. Schlesinger, *A Thousand Days*, p. 997.
48. Maxwell Taylor, *Swords and Plowshares* (New York: W. W. Norton, 1972), p. 301. See also Sorensen, *Counselor*, pp. 354–55; Dallek, *An Unfinished Life*, p. 683.
49. Kaiser, *An American Tragedy*, p. 278; Preston, *The War Council*, pp. 126–28.
50. "The President's News Conference of November 14, 1963," *PPP-JFK*, 1963, p. 848.
51. Gordon M. Goldstein, *Lessons in Disaster: McGeorge Bundy and the Path to War in Vietnam* (New York: Times Books, 2008), pp. 2–3.
52. Ibid., pp. 82–83.
53. "The President's News Conference of November 14, 1963," *PPP-JFK*, 1963, pp. 846–48.
54. McGeorge Bundy, "The History-Maker," *Proceedings of the Massachusetts Historical Society* (1978), p. 84.
55. Schlesinger, *Robert Kennedy and His Times*, p. 764. See also Kai Bird and William Pfaff, "Would JFK Have Left Vietnam: An Exchange," *New York Review of Books*, June 10, 2010; Preston, *The War Council*, pp. 97–106.
56. Goldstein, *Lessons in Disaster*, p. 233. See also Preston, *The War Council*, pp. 125–28.
57. Reeves, *President Kennedy*, pp. 622–24. See also "Annual Message to the Congress on the State of the Union," January 14, 1963, *PPP-JFK*, 1963, pp. 14–15; Schlesinger, *Robert Kennedy and His Times*, p. 348.
58. Reeves, *President Kennedy*, p. 585.
59. Schlesinger, *Robert Kennedy and His Times*, p. 348; Thomas, *Robert Kennedy*, p. 249.
60. Schlesinger, *A Thousand Days*, pp. 1010–11; Reeves, *President Kennedy*, pp. 622–24.
61. Sorensen, *Counselor*, pp. 350–51.
62. "The President's News Conference of October 31, 1963," *PPP-JFK*, 1963, p. 828.
63. Dallek, *An Unfinished Life*, p. 692.
64. "Remarks at the Breakfast of the Fort Worth Chamber of Commerce," November 22, 1963, *PPP-JFK*, 1963, pp. 889–90.
65. Talbot, *Brothers*, p. 242.

## 9: THE AFTERLIFE OF JOHN F. KENNEDY

1. Pierre Salinger and Sander Vanocur, eds., *A Tribute to John F. Kennedy* (Chicago: Encyclopedia Britannica, 1964), p. 14.
2. *New York Times Book Review*, November 24, 1963; Victor Lasky, *J.F.K.: The Man and the Myth* (New Rochelle, N.Y.: Arlington House, 1963).
3. Alice Payne Hackett and James Henry Burke, *80 Years of Bestsellers, 1895–1975* (New York and London: R. R. Bowker, 1977), pp. 189–91.
4. Schlesinger, *A Thousand Days*, p. 1030.
5. *Time*, November 14, 1983; Arthur M. Schlesinger Jr., "The Ultimate Approval Rating," *New York Times Magazine*, December 15, 1996, pp. 46–47; Norman Mailer, "Enter Prince Jack," *Esquire*, June 1983, pp. 204–8.
6. Christopher Lasch, "The Life of Kennedy's Death," *Harper's*, October 1983, pp. 32–36; Godfrey Hodgson, *America in Our Time* (New York: Doubleday, 1976), p. 5.
7. James Reston, *Sketches in the Sand* (New York: Alfred A. Knopf, 1969), p. 470.
8. Theodore H. White, *In Search of History: A Personal Adventure* (New York: Harper and Row, 1978), p. 457.
9. David J. Garrow, "The FBI and Martin Luther King," *Atlantic*, July/August 2002.
10. Wills, *The Kennedy Imprisonment*, p. 148.
11. Benjamin Bradlee, *A Good Life: Newspapering and Other Adventures* (New York: Simon and Schuster, 1995), pp. 238–40.
12. Robert G. Athearn, *American Heritage Illustrated History of the United States* (New York: Choice, 1988), vol. 12, pp. 1429–32.
13. William E. Leuchtenburg, "John F. Kennedy: Twenty Years Later," *American Heritage*, December 1983, p. 53.
14. Collier and Horowitz, *The Kennedys*; Parmet, *Jack*; Wills, *The Kennedy Imprisonment*; Henry Fairlie, *The Kennedy Promise: The Politics of Expectation* (Garden City, N.Y.: Doubleday, 1973); Lewis J. Paper, *The Promise and the Performance: The Leadership of John F. Kennedy* (New York: Crown, 1975); Reeves, *A Question of Character*; Hersh, *The Dark Side of Camelot*; David Halberstam, *The Best and the Brightest* (New York: Random House, 1972); Walton, *Cold War and Counterrevolution*.
15. Irving Shulman, *Jackie! The Exploitation of a First Lady* (New York: Trident Press, 1970), p. 143.
16. Hersh, *The Dark Side of Camelot*, pp. ix–xx.
17. Gerald Posner, *Case Closed: Lee Harvey Oswald and the Assassination of JFK* (New York: Random House, 1993), pp. 471–72.
18. Vincent Bugliosi, *Reclaiming History: The Assassination of President John F. Kennedy* (New York: W. W. Norton, 2007), p. xxvi.

19. Mark Lane, *Rush to Judgment* (New York: Holt, Rinehart and Winston, 1966).
20. Richard H. Popkin, "The Second Oswald: The Case for a Conspiracy Theory," *New York Review of Books*, July 28, 1966; *Life*, November 25, 1966.
21. Thomas Brown, *JFK: History of an Image* (Bloomington: Indiana University Press, 1988), p. 129.
22. Talbot, *Brothers*, pp. 1–12.
23. Ibid., p. 406.
24. James Fisher, *The Theater of Tony Kushner: Living Past Hope* (New York: Routledge, 2002), p. 75.
25. Schlesinger, *A Thousand Days*, pp. 1030–31.

# Milestones

1917     Born in Brookline, Massachusetts, May 29

1935     Graduates from the Choate School in Wallingford, Connecticut

Enrolls at Princeton University and withdraws after six weeks because of health problems

1936     Enrolls at Harvard College

1938     Joseph P. Kennedy becomes U.S. ambassador to Great Britain

John Kennedy takes time off from Harvard to join him

1939     Tours Europe in preparation for his Harvard senior thesis

1940     Completes his senior thesis, "Appeasement at Munich"

Graduates from Harvard College cum laude in international affairs

Publishes his revised thesis, *Why England Slept*, a best seller

1941     Rejected from the navy because of chronic back problems

Joins the navy after his father persuades friends in the Office of Naval Intelligence

1943     Captains PT 109 in the Pacific and survives destruction of the ship by Japanese destroyer

Helps rescue survivors and becomes national celebrity

1944     Joseph P. Kennedy Jr. dies in combat

1946     Elected member of Congress from Massachusetts' Eleventh District

1952     Elected to the United States Senate from Massachusetts

1953     Marries Jacqueline Bouvier

1954–55   Undergoes serious back surgeries

1956     Publishes *Profiles in Courage* during convalescence

Pursues but fails to win nomination for vice president

| 1957 | Receives Pulitzer Prize for *Profiles in Courage* |
|------|--------------------------------------------------|
|      | First child, Caroline Kennedy, born November 27 |
| 1959 | Second Vietnam War begins |
| 1960 | Announces candidacy for president, January 2 |
|      | Nominated for president at Democratic convention, July 14 |
|      | Participates in first televised presidential debates, September–October |
|      | Elected president, November 8, with 49.75 percent of popular vote |
|      | John F. Kennedy Jr. born November 25 |
| 1961 | Inaugurated president, January 20 |
|      | Begins effort to neutralize Laos |
|      | Peace Corps created, March 1 |
|      | Orders invasion of Cuba at Bay of Pigs, to begin April 17; invasion fails several days later |
|      | Alan Shepard becomes first American to fly into space, May 5 |
|      | Addresses Congress and vows to send a man to the moon |
|      | Summit meeting with Nikita Khrushchev, Vienna, June 3–4 |
|      | Alliance for Progress in Latin America, August |
|      | Berlin Wall divides city, August 13 |
|      | Revived effort to end Castro regime, November |
| 1962 | John Glenn becomes first American to orbit the earth, February 20 |
|      | Pressures steel executives to rescind price raises |
|      | Cuban missile crisis, October 16–28 |
|      | Midterm elections strengthen Democratic Congress |
|      | Signs executive order banning housing discrimination, November 20 |
| 1963 | Gives speech at American University, June 10 |
|      | Calls civil rights for African Americans a "moral crisis," June 11 |
|      | Gives speech at Berlin Wall, June 26 |
|      | Visits Ireland, June 26–29 |
|      | Proposes civil rights legislation to Congress, July 1 |
|      | Patrick Bouvier Kennedy born, August 5; dies two days after birth |
|      | Limited Nuclear Test Ban Treaty, October 7 |
|      | Begins campaign trip to Texas, November 21 |
|      | Assassinated in Dallas, November 22 |

# Selected Bibliography

This book relies heavily on the papers of John F. Kennedy in the Kennedy Library in Boston, in particular the digital archive that the library recently opened. It also relies on *Public Papers of the Presidents of the United States: John F. Kennedy, 1961–1963* (Washington, D.C.: U.S. Government Printing Office, 1962–64). Other primary sources come from the *New York Times*, the *Washington Post*, the *Wall Street Journal*, *Time* magazine, and many other periodicals and newspapers.

## BOOKS

Abbott, Philip. *Strong Presidents: A Theory of Leadership*. Knoxville: University of Tennessee Press, 1996.

Abel, Elie. *The Missile Crisis*. New York: J. B. Lippincott, 1966.

Allison, Graham. *Essence of Decision: Explaining the Cuban Missile Crisis*. Boston: Little, Brown, 1971.

Arsenault, Raymond. *Freedom Rides 1961 and the Struggle for Racial Justice*. New York: Oxford University Press, 2006.

Athearn, Robert G. *American Heritage Illustrated History of the United States*. Vol. 12. New York: Choice, 1988.

Baker, Jean. *The Stevensons: A Biography of an American Family*. New York: W. W. Norton, 1996.

Bellows, Jim. *The Last Editor*. Kansas City, Mo.: Andrews McMeel, 2002.

Beschloss, Michael R. *The Crisis Years: Kennedy and Khrushchev, 1960–1963*. New York: HarperCollins, 1991.

Blanshard, Paul. *American Freedom and Catholic Power*. Boston: Beacon Press, 1949.

Bly, Nellie. *The Kennedy Men*. New York: Kensington, 1996.

Bowles, Chester. *Promises to Keep: My Years in Public Life, 1941–1969*. New York: Harper and Row, 1971.

Bradlee, Benjamin C. *Conversations with Kennedy*. New York: W. W. Norton, 1975.

——. *That Special Grace*. New York: Lippincott, 1964.

Branch, Taylor. *Parting the Waters: America in the King Years, 1954–1963*. New York: Simon and Schuster, 1988.

Brauer, Carl. *John F. Kennedy and the Second Reconstruction*. New York: Columbia University Press, 1977.

Brinkley, Alan. *The Publisher: Henry Luce and His American Century*. New York: Alfred A. Knopf, 2010.

Bryant, Nick. *The Bystander: John F. Kennedy and the Struggle for Black Equality*. New York: Basic Books, 2006.

Bugliosi, Vincent. *Reclaiming History: The Assassination of President John F. Kennedy*. New York: W. W. Norton, 2007.

Chafe, William. *Civilities and Civil Rights: Greensboro, North Carolina, and the Black Struggle for Freedom*. New York: Oxford University Press, 1981.

——. *Private Lives/Public Consequences: Personality and Politics in Modern America*. Cambridge, Mass.: Harvard University Press, 2005.

Chase, Harold, and Allen H. Lerman, eds. *Kennedy and the Press: The News Conferences*. New York: Crowell, 1965.

Collier, Peter, and David Horowitz. *The Kennedys: An American Drama*. New York: Simon and Schuster, 1984.

Crispell, Kenneth P., and Carlos F. Gomez. *Hidden Illness in the White House*. Durham, N.C.: Duke University Press, 1988.

Dallek, Robert. *Flawed Giant: Lyndon Johnson and His Times, 1961–1973*. New York: Oxford University Press, 1998.

——. *John F. Kennedy*. New York: Oxford University Press, 2011.

——. *An Unfinished Life: John F. Kennedy, 1917–1963*. New York: Little, Brown, 2003.

Davis, John H. *Jacqueline Bouvier: An Intimate Memoir*. New York: John Wiley and Sons, 1996.

——. *The Kennedys: Dynasty and Disaster, 1848–1984*. New York: McGraw-Hill, 1984.

de Gaulle, Charles. *Memoirs of Hope: Renewal and Endeavor*. New York: Simon and Schuster, 1971.

Divine, Robert A. *The Cuban Missile Crisis*. New York: Markus Weiner, 1988.

Donaldson, Gary A. *The First Modern Campaign: Kennedy, Nixon, and the Election of 1960*. Lanham, Md.: Rowman and Littlefield, 2007.

Fairlie, Henry. *The Kennedy Promise: The Politics of Expectation*. Garden City, N.Y.: Doubleday, 1973.

Fensch, Thomas, ed. *The Kennedy-Khrushchev Letters*. Woodlands, Tex.: New Century Books, 2001.

Fisher, James. *The Theater of Tony Kushner: Living Past Hope*. New York: Routledge, 2002.

Freedman, Lawrence. *Kennedy Wars: Berlin, Cuba, and Laos.* New York: Oxford University Press, 2000.

Friedman, Milton. *Capitalism and Freedom.* Chicago: University of Chicago Press, 1962.

Fuller, Helen. *Year of Trial: Kennedy's Crucial Decisions.* New York: Harcourt, Brace, 1962.

Fursenko, Aleksandr, and Timothy Naftali. *"One Hell of a Gamble": Khrushchev, Castro, and Kennedy, 1958–1964.* New York: W. W. Norton, 1997.

Gaddis, John Lewis. *Strategies of Containment: A Critical Appraisal of Postwar American National Security Policy.* New York: Oxford University Press, 1982.

Gilbert, Robert E. *The Mortal Presidency: Illness and Anguish in the White House.* New York: Basic Books, 1992.

Goldstein, Gordon M. *Lessons in Disaster: McGeorge Bundy and the Path to War in Vietnam.* New York: Times Books, 2008.

Goodwin, Doris Kearns. *The Fitzgeralds and the Kennedys: An American Saga.* New York: Simon and Schuster, 1987.

Greene, Graham. *The Quiet American.* New York: Viking Press, 1956.

Hackett, Alice Payne, and James Henry Burke. *80 Years of Bestsellers, 1895–1975.* New York and London: R. R. Bowker, 1977.

Halberstam, David. *The Best and the Brightest.* New York: Random House, 1972.

Hamilton, Nigel. *JFK: Life and Death of an American President.* Vol. 1, *Reckless Youth.* London: Random House UK, 1992.

Hammer, Ellen J. *A Death in November: America in Vietnam, 1963.* New York: Dutton, 1987.

Haslam, S. Alexander, Stephen D. Reicher, and Michael J. Platow. *The New Psychology of Leadership: Identity, Influence, and Power.* New York: Psychology Press, 2011.

Heath, Jim. *Decade of Disillusionment: The Kennedy-Johnson Years.* Bloomington: Indiana University Press, 1975.

Hersh, Seymour M. *The Dark Side of Camelot.* Boston: Little, Brown, 1997.

Heyman, David. *A Woman Named Jackie.* New York: Lyle Stuart, 1989.

Hilsman, Roger. *To Move a Nation: The Politics of Foreign Policy in the Administration of John F. Kennedy.* New York: Doubleday, 1967.

Hodgson, Godfrey. *America in Our Time.* New York: Doubleday, 1976.

Horne, Alistair. *Harold Macmillan.* 2 vols. New York: Viking, 1989, 1991.

Hunt, Michael H. *Crises in U.S. Foreign Policy.* New Haven: Yale University Press, 1996.

Johnson, Haynes. *The Bay of Pigs.* New York: W. W. Norton, 1964.

Kaiser, David. *American Tragedy: Kennedy, Johnson, and the Origins of the Vietnam War.* Cambridge, Mass.: Harvard University Press, 2000.

Kempe, Frederick. *Berlin 1961: Kennedy, Khrushchev, and the Most Dangerous Place on Earth.* New York: G. P. Putnam, 2011.

Kennedy, John F. *Prelude to Leadership: The European Diary of John F. Kennedy.* Washington, D.C.: Regnery, 1995.

———. *Profiles in Courage.* New York: Harper and Brothers, 1956.

———. *Why England Slept.* New York: Wilfred Funk, 1940.

Kennedy, Rose, with Robert Coughlan. *Times to Remember.* New York: Doubleday, 1974.

Kenney, Charles. *John F. Kennedy: The Presidential Portfolio.* New York: PublicAffairs, 2000.

King, Martin Luther, Jr. *Why We Can't Wait.* New York: Signet, 1964.

Kraus, Sidney, ed. *The Great Debates.* Bloomington: Indiana University Press, 1962.

Kredon, Michael, and Dan Caldwell, eds. *The Politics of Arms Control of Treaty Ratification.* New York: St. Martin's Press, 1991.

Lane, Mark. *Rush to Judgment.* New York: Holt, Rinehart and Winston, 1966.

Langguth, A. J. *Our Vietnam: The War, 1954–1975.* New York: Simon and Schuster, 2000.

Lasky, Victor. *J.F.K.: The Man and the Myth.* New Rochelle, N.Y.: Arlington House, 1963.

Lederer, William J., and Eugene Burdick. *The Ugly American.* New York: W. W. Norton, 1958.

MacKenzie, G. Calvin, and Robert Weisbrot. *The Liberal Hour: Washington and the Politics of Change in the 1960s.* New York: Penguin Books, 2008.

Mariner, Rosemary B., and G. Kurt Piehler, eds. *The Atomic Bomb and American Society: New Perspectives.* Knoxville: University of Tennessee Press, 2009.

Martin, John Bartlow. *Adlai Stevenson and the World.* Garden City, N.Y.: Doubleday, 1977.

Martin, Ralph G. *Seeds of Destruction: Joe Kennedy and His Sons.* New York: G.P. Putnam, 1995.

Martin, Ralph G., and Ed Plaut. *Front Runners.* New York: Doubleday, 1960.

May, Ernest R., and Philip D. Zelikow, eds. *The Kennedy Tapes: Inside the White House During the Cuban Missile Crisis.* New York: W. W. Norton, 2002.

McNamara, Robert S. *In Retrospect: The Tragedy and Lessons of Vietnam.* New York: Times Books, 1995.

McWhorter, Diane. *Carry Me Home: Birmingham, Alabama—The Climactic Battle of the Civil Rights Revolution.* New York: Simon and Schuster, 2001.

Michaelis, David. *Best of Friends.* New York: William Morrow, 1983.

Neustadt, Richard. *Presidential Power: The Politics of Leadership.* New York: Wiley, 1960.

Nixon, Richard M. *RN: The Memoirs of Richard Nixon.* New York: Grosset and Dunlap, 1978.

———. *Six Crises*. New York: Doubleday, 1962.

O'Brien, Michael. *John F. Kennedy: A Biography*. New York: St. Martin's Press, 2005.

O'Donnell, Kenneth P., and David F. Powers. *Johnny, We Hardly Knew Ye*. Boston: Little, Brown, 1972.

Paper, Lewis J. *The Promise and the Performance: The Leadership of John F. Kennedy*. New York: Crown, 1975.

Parmet, Herbert. *Jack: The Struggles of John F. Kennedy*. New York: Dial Press, 1980.

Patterson, David S., ed. *Foreign Relations of the United States, 1961–1963*. Washington, D.C.: U.S. Government Printing Office, 2001.

*The Pentagon Papers: The Defense Department History of United States Decisionmaking on Vietnam*. Vol. 2. Boston: Beacon Press, 1971.

Pietrusza, David. *1960: LBJ vs. JFK vs. Nixon*. New York: Sterling, 2006.

Posner, Gerald. *Case Closed: Lee Harvey Oswald and the Assassination of JFK*. New York: Random House, 1993.

Preston, Andrew. *The War Council: McGeorge Bundy, the NSC, and Vietnam*. Cambridge, Mass.: Harvard University Press, 2006.

*Public Papers of the Presidents of the United States: John F. Kennedy, 1961–1963*. Washington, D.C.: U.S. Government Printing Office, 1962–64.

Reeves, Richard. *President Kennedy: Profile of Power*. New York: Simon and Schuster, 1993.

Reeves, Thomas C. *A Question of Character*. New York: Arrow, 1992.

Reston, James. *Sketches in the Sand*. New York: Alfred A. Knopf, 1969.

Reynolds, David. *One World Indivisible: A Global History Since 1945*. New York: W. W. Norton, 2000.

———. *Summits: Six Meetings that Shaped the Twentieth Century*. New York: Basic Books, 2007.

Russo, Gus, and Stephen Molton. *Brothers in Arms: The Kennedys, the Castros, and the Politics of Murder*. New York: Bloomsbury, 2008.

Rust, William. *Perpetual Crisis: The American Experience in Laos, 1954–1961*. Lexington: University of Kentucky Press, 2012.

Salinger, Pierre, and Sander Vanocur, eds. *A Tribute to John F. Kennedy*. Chicago: Encyclopedia Britannica, 1964.

Schlesinger, Arthur M., Jr. *Journals, 1952–2000*. New York: Penguin Press, 2007.

———. *Robert Kennedy and His Times*. Boston: Houghton Mifflin, 1978.

———. *A Thousand Days: John F. Kennedy in the White House*. Boston: Houghton Mifflin, 1965.

Schulzinger, Robert D. *A Time for War: The United States and Viet Nam, 1941–1975*. New York: Oxford University Press, 1996.

Seaborg, Glen T. *Kennedy, Khrushchev, and the Test Ban*. Berkeley: University of California Press, 1981.

Shesol, Jeff. *Mutual Contempt: Lyndon Johnson, Robert Kennedy, and the Feud that Defined a Decade*. New York: W. W. Norton, 1997.

Shulman, Irving. *Jackie! The Exploitation of a First Lady*. New York: Trident Press, 1970.

Sidey, Hugh. *John F. Kennedy: President*. New York: Atheneum, 1964.

Snyder, John Richard. *John F. Kennedy: Personality, Policy, Presidency*. New York: SR Books, 1988.

Sorensen, Theodore. *Counselor: A Life at the Edge of History*. New York: Harper, 2009.

———. *Kennedy*. New York: Harper and Row, 1965.

Spoto, Donald. *Jacqueline Bouvier Onassis: A Life*. New York: St. Martin's Press, 2010.

Stacks, John F. *Scotty: James B. Reston and the Rise and Fall of American Journalism*. Boston: Little, Brown, 2003.

Swanson, Gloria. *Swanson on Swanson*. New York: Random House, 1980.

Talbot, David. *Brothers: The Hidden Story of the Kennedy Years*. New York: Free Press, 2007.

Taubman, William. *Khrushchev: The Man and His Era*. New York: W. W. Norton, 2003.

Taylor, Frederick. *The Berlin Wall: A World Divided, 1961–1989*. New York: HarperCollins, 2007.

Theoharis, Athan. *From the Secret Files of J. Edgar Hoover*. New York: I. R. Dee, 1991.

Thomas, Evan. *Robert Kennedy: His Life*. New York: Simon and Schuster, 2000.

Walton, Richard J. *Cold War and Counterrevolution: The Foreign Policy of John F. Kennedy*. Baltimore: Penguin Books, 1972.

Weart, Spencer R. *Nuclear Fear: A History of Images*. Cambridge, Mass.: Harvard University Press, 1988.

Weiner, Tim. *Legacy of Ashes: The History of the CIA*. New York: Doubleday, 2007.

Weisbrot, Robert. *Maximum Danger: Kennedy, the Missiles, and the Crisis of American Confidence*. Chicago: Ivan R. Dee, 2001.

Whalen, Thomas. *Kennedy versus Lodge*. Boston: Northeastern University Press, 2000.

White, Theodore H. *The Making of the President, 1960*. New York: Atheneum, 1961.

———. *In Search of History: A Personal Adventure*. New York: Harper and Row, 1978.

Wills, Garry. *The Kennedy Imprisonment: A Meditation on Power*. Boston: Little, Brown, 1982.

———. *Nixon Agonistes: The Crisis of the Self-Made Man*. Boston: Houghton Mifflin, 1969.

Wyden, Peter. *The Bay of Pigs: The Untold Story*. New York: Simon and Schuster, 1962.

# Acknowledgments

I am particularly grateful to Arthur Schlesinger, who persuaded me to write a book about John Kennedy in his distinguished series of presidential biographies. I wish he were here to see it. I also thank the friends and colleagues who have read some or all of this book and have offered comments. Among them are Ellen Fitzpatrick, David Nasaw, Andrew Preston, Frank Rich, Marc Selverstone, and Sean Wilentz, who succeeded Schlesinger as editor of the series. And I am, as always, grateful to my wife, Evangeline Morphos, whose comments and editing have been, as always, invaluable.

I am indebted to the John F. Kennedy Library in Boston and to the digital archive that it has recently created. I have also relied on and am grateful for the vast body of previous scholarship on John Kennedy that has been of great value to all who have worked and continue to work on the Kennedy years.

Finally, I wish to acknowledge the people at Times Books and Henry Holt and Company for their generous help with this book: Paul Golob, Christopher O'Connell, Emi Ikkanda, Ruth Fecych, and Francesca Giacco.

# Index

# ABOUT THE AUTHOR

ALAN BRINKLEY is the author most recently of *The Publisher: Henry Luce and His American Century*, which was a Pulitzer Prize finalist. He is also the author of *Voices of Protest: Huey Long, Father Coughlin, and the Great Depression*, which won the National Book Award, *The End of Reform: New Deal Liberalism in Recession and War*, and *Liberalism and its Discontents*. He is the Allan Nevins Professor of History and Provost Emeritus at Columbia University. He has also taught at Harvard, Oxford, and Cambridge. He lives in New York City.